ADDITIONAL PRAISE FOR *SISTERH*

"Someone should make a t-shirt for Deborah Siegel that says, 'This is what a feminist historian looks like.' Moving decidedly away from the 'catfight' model of feminist history towards a more fair and useful collaborative vision, Siegel traces the persistent questions and conflicts within the contemporary women's movement in her thorough and engaging narrative."

—Merri Lisa Johnson, Director of the Center for
Women's and Gender Studies, USC Upstate

"Siegel has her finger on the pulse of one of the main issues concerning women today: generational infighting around the unfinished business of feminism. It's an issue that concerns everyone—whether or not they use the f-word."

—Catherine Orenstein, author of
Red Riding Hood Uncloaked

"Read *Sisterhood, Interrupted* and you will have an inside look at a movement born out of earnestness and hope—one filled with the intrigues of strategizing, contesting, connecting, and questioning. Siegel's well written and researched book draws you into the passions, continuing relevance, and persistent inequalities that drive twenty-first century feminism. You won't look at the feminist movement in the same way again."

—Linda Basch, President, National Council
for Research on Women

"*Sisterhood, Interrupted* is a smart, thorough, and extremely readable history of contemporary feminism and its generational tensions. Deborah Siegel presents an evenhanded view of both second- and third-wave feminism, without losing sight of the complexity of either. A must-read for women of any generation who want to better understand feminism in the twenty-first century."

—Astrid Henry, author Not My Mother's Sister:
Generational Conflict and Third-Wave Feminism

"Effectively captures the passion and politics that have shaped contemporary feminism. Siegel shows us that the feminist movement is indeed alive and well, or it would not inspire so much fierce debate."

—*Allison Kimmich, Executive Director, National Women's Studies Association (NWSA)*

"*Sisterhood, Interrupted* is a crash course in feminist history. Deborah Siegel's refreshing and contemporary approach makes history relevant for our future progress. With wit and what reads like an insider's perspective, Siegel illuminates how past controversies will be future successes."

—*Amy Richards, co-author* Manifesta: Young Women, Feminism and the Future *and a founder of the Third Wave Foundation*

ACKNOWLEDGMENTS

This book would not have been written without the sisterhood—uninterrupted—of teachers, colleagues, and friends who have sustained me. I am immensely grateful for my teachers: Sherry Medwin, the one who sparked my interest in feminism in eleventh grade, and Susan Friedman, Susan David Bernstein, and the late Nellie Y. McKay, who deepened and gave texture to my intellectual questioning in graduate school. I thank the scholars and activists who paved the way *and* got it down, in particular: Susan Douglas, Rachel Blau DuPlessis, Alice Echols, Sara M. Evans, Ruth Rosen, Ann Snitow, and also Betty Friedan and Gloria Steinem. Their stories enabled my own. Deepest gratitude to historian Linda Gordon, both for her work and her thoughtful read. I thank my colleagues from the National Council for Research on Women, especially Linda Basch, Mary Ellen Capek, Mariam Chamberlain, Heather Johnston-Nicholson, and Cynthia Secor. Their commitment to women's research has allowed so many of us to thrive. I'm grateful to all my former interns, and to Council coworkers Tonni Brodber, Lybra Clemons, Sunny Daly, Andrea Greenblatt, Liz Horton, and Leslie Weber for tolerating the unusual schedule that enabled me to write this book.

Gratitude to my "third-wave" colleagues and peers, those I agree with and those whose work I take issue with in these pages, for they have kept the conversation alive. Special thanks to pioneers Leslie Heywood, for early encouragement and for giving us an encyclopedia; Amy Richards and Rebecca Walker, for initiative and bravery; Lisa Johnson, for honesty and eloquence; and Naomi Wolf, for walking the walk and for cofounding the Woodhull Institute for Ethical Leadership, training ground for future leaders. Profound gratitude to Jennifer Baumgardner, for her savvy, her wit, and her foreword.

I am grateful to the many friends—women, and more than a few good men—who have doubled as teachers and sounding boards along the way. Katie Orenstein, whose brilliance as a thinker and editor is surpassed only by the brightness of her spirit, helped enliven my prose. Robert Berson, Ken Cain, Deborah Carr, Jean Casella, Cora Fox, Susan Devenyi, Tamera Gugelmeyer, Heather Hewett, Wende Jager-Hyman Allison Kimmich, Rebecca London, Lia Macko, Jami Moss, Sam Nelson, Susan Nierenberg, Eileen O'Halloran, Catherine Prendergast, Virginia Rutter, Debra Schultz, John Seaman, Rebecca Segall, Ilana Trachtman, Daphne Uviller, and Jacki Zehner harbored me and this project in one way or another and helped shape my ideas. Michael Heller's deep encouragement and belief in me as a writer meant much to me. Annie Murphy Paul and Alissa Quart, who sensed that this business of writing is better navigated together, facilitated a network of unparalleled support known as the Invisible Institute. My thanks to each of its members. And to my agent, Tracy Brown, for helping realize dreams.

At Palgrave Macmillan, I thank Amanda Moon for coming to that panel at Barnard and finding me, for virtuoso editing, unfailing professionalism, enthusiasm, and all the work that goes on behind the scenes. Thanks to Emily Leithauser for her perspective and ideas. Dara Hochman, rising feminist media critic, provided impeccable research assistance and pop culture savvy. Gwendolyn Beetham provided the resource section, friendship, and inspiration. Special thanks to the librarians at Tamiment Library at New York University and the Schlesinger Library for helping me navigate the archives.

I thank my family for putting up with me during the long years during which this book consumed me: all my first cousins; Rita and Nick Lenn; Pearl Pearlman; Margaret Siegel; Renee Siegel, whose assistance went far beyond the duty of motherhood; and Allen Siegel. The next one, I'm writing from Wyoming. Raise the barn.

Finally, to Marco Acevedo, who sat across from me, laptop to laptop, for hours while I ate his scones and furrowed my brow. Thank *you* for finding me. And for reminding me. Libations, always, to Kate Chopin.

FOREWORD

It's funny. Just before writing this foreword, I got an extreme bikini wax in Los Angeles with my writing partner and fellow feminist Amy Richards at this place on Melrose called, simply, Wax. We had a few hours to kill before heading to the airport to come back to New York. Her three-month-old son was with us. She's still breast-feeding. My nineteen-month-old, Skuli, and her three-year-old son were back home with their dads, so it seemed like a good moment to do things we normally couldn't schedule. I also bought some makeup at Fred Segal, shopped around, and Amy got a pedicure.

Of course, we weren't in LA just to have our pubic hair removed by a Temple University graduate who makes more than $200,000 a year doing just that. We were there, working on my birthday no less, to address students at UCLA about how to change the world. These were students who directed the UCLA production of the *Vagina Monologues*, students who created the recycling programs in their dorm, and students who dealt with gay-bashing incidents. In other words, they were feminists and activists and we were feminist activists. I cite these details of our free-time endeavors because all of the above activities are seen, when young women are reported to be doing them, as the sum total of their relationship to feminism. So *retrograde!* In fact, the fear that the daughters of the second wave are squandering their legacy on masochistic grooming rather than selfless political organizing is rampant, and it is mentioned in the author's introduction to the book that you are about to read.

The intro also mentions, near the line about bikini waxes, that polls proclaim that 22 million unmarried women (many of them under the age of thirty) don't vote. Are you picturing that same girl who waxes or has a pole (not a poll, sadly) installed in her living room so she can do a cardio strip-tease? Or the women from *Sex in the City?* In fact, the single women under thirty who don't vote are much more likely to be unwed mothers on welfare or the recently incarcerated than the Carrie Bradshaw types associated with waxed bikini lines. I raise this because I think our sartorial choices are part of an old argument once very crucial to feminism, today almost archaic. Not voting is about social structures—is there child-care? voter registration that reaches out to moms in Section 8 housing?—more than it is about privileged gals who just don't have time to vote.

I started this foreword with a somewhat contentious stance, even though Deborah Siegel and I have much more in common than not and I learned from or agreed with her book more often than I took issue with it. Still, her book is about the stands and splits that characterize becoming a feminist and the feminist movement. This movement is constantly remaking itself, challenging orthodoxies, and creating new theories. Feminist theory and action draw most profoundly from the truth of personal experience, and thus women's liberation is one of the most diverse movements and one of the most contentious. I have learned about this fight-y vibrancy over the years, but I used to think feminism meant something else—essentially, that it meant all women agreed on what was sexist and what was worth fighting for. I thought my feminist foremothers had that unity and that was why they were sisters (Sisterhood is Powerful!) while we were girls (grrrls!).

Since you have picked up this book, I assume that you have more than a glancing interest in recent feminist history. Perhaps you, like me, think of Shulamith Firestone (author of *Dialectic of Sex*) as on par with J. D. Salinger and would be tongue-tied if you ran into *Black Macho and the Myth of the Superwoman* author Michele Wallace. You know that Michele Wallace is the daughter of the famous quilt artist Faith Ringgold and that Shulie quit the movement in 1971 and refuses interviews to this day but threatened to put a hex on third wave filmmaker Elisabeth Subrin when she remade the short *Shulie*. Rebecca Walker, Naomi Wolf, or (*gasp*) Katie Roiphe *are* celebrities. Okay, maybe Katie Roiphe no longer elicits a gasp, as she is no longer the bête noire of feminism, not even the Bette Midler of feminism, but rather a mid-list writer of reviews and books that didn't garner the insane fire of her first book (which you deplored and denounced, but were thrilled by, too). So you're the type who believes that Katie, Rebecca, Shulie, and the rest should be in *US Weekly,* right next to Jennifer Aniston and Jennifer Garner, or at least in *Ms.,* in the gossip column that doesn't, but *should,* exist. You already knew that feminists didn't burn their bras—they tried to, of course, but couldn't get a permit at the famous 1968 Miss America demo. You knew about WITCH and Redstockings and read *Daring to Be Bad* and *The Feminist Memoir Project* for gossip.

Or maybe you're not that reader. Even though this is a book that looks at the self-identified instigators of feminism, from the New York Radical Women to the riot grrrls, and their theories and contributions, maybe you are like most people who identify with feminism and in fact don't consider yourself an architect of the movement, don't go to meetings where you debate about whether your Mitchum deodorant constitutes a fragrance and is thus oppressive to others in the room. Maybe the existence of Katie Roiphe never titillated or incensed you. You identify with feminism's most broad principles—that all people *are* created equal *and* deserve respect and the freedom to pursue a happy, meaningful life of their own design. You believe in the movement for social, economic, and political equality of all people. You think work traditionally associated with women should be valued and that gender shouldn't designate what job you have, but rather your interests and talents.

This book gives a primer of the waves of feminism, the major arguments put forth by different theorists, the enormous disagreements that emerged, and the effects (both intended and unintended) of the movements. Deborah Siegel wonders whether feminism is a cultural movement or a political one, and if the former, if that's a problem. She has her own views of what is going on, too, and what needs to happen to save women from remaking the wheel every twenty years. Ultimately, to me, the book provokes the one real question about feminism; in short: What does feminism mean to *you?*

Seventy-something Gloria Steinem—who is, many would argue, the most famous living feminist—often meets women admirers who say, with great urgency, "Look, I think feminism might have failed—my daughter (or son) doesn't even know who you are!" Gloria's answer is warm but also philosophical. She says: "It doesn't matter if she knows who I am—does she know who she is?" At the end of the day, feminism is expressed in individual women and men unlearning pointless self-sacrifice, artifice, and self-suppression and believing that they, in fact, own feminism, too, and can contribute to social justice.

My hope is that after reading this book, regardless of your depilatory practices, you will have a deeper sense of many of the stories that make feminist history and philosophy, and you will use them to continue to figure out what feminism means to you. Sisterhood was never about everybody agreeing, and the interruption in this book's title doesn't need to convey paralysis or even getting knocked off course. Instead, imagine a room full of women passionately debating and learning, so excited to express another insight that they can't wait for the previous woman to totally finish. That view describes what an evening with my real sisters, as in the two Baumgardner girls with whom I was raised, sounds like—lots of laughter, rehashing of old stories, and planning the future. I say, *Long live our interrupting sisters!*

—*Jennifer Baumgardner*
New York City, June 2006

THE MOVEMENT THAT HAS NO NAME

On February 15, 1969, the day I was born, the newly formed women's liberation movement launched its national attack on domesticity. In New York City, members of the Women's International Terrorist Conspiracy from Hell—WITCH—stormed a Madison Square Garden bridal fair. They marched among the faux flowers, folded napkins, and lamé bridesmaid dresses and hexed the vendors (whom they dubbed "manipulator-exhibitors") as they advanced. "Always a Bride, Never a Person!" they chanted. "Here Comes the Slave, Off to Her Grave!" they sang. Meanwhile, their movement sisters in San Francisco picketed a bridal fair and passed out leaflets printed with similar warnings to stunned brides-to-be.[1]

That previous September, some one hundred young radicals protested the Miss America pageant in Atlantic City, throwing aprons, high heels, bras, and hair rollers into a "Freedom Trashcan." Pictures from that day show images of young women with long hair parted in the middle standing behind a poster of a naked woman whose body is labeled like meat: Rump. Rib. Chuck. Round. "Welcome to the Miss America Cattle Auction," banners proclaimed. "Atlantic City is a town with class—they raise your morals and they judge your ass!" Suddenly, just as the oldest members of the future Generation X were entering the world, all the commonplace assumptions about femininity, sexuality, and domesticity that a baby girl could expect to inherit were under siege. Everyday choices, like wearing stilettos or tying the knot, now had significant political implications. Family life, standards of beauty, and relations with men were no longer private matters of individual choice or social custom but issues of national import.

The personal became political.

It was an age of unprecedented action. During the late 1960s and early 1970s, a hundred women took over the offices of *Ladies' Home Journal* and suggested retitling the magazine's famous monthly column, "Can This Marriage Be Saved?" to "Can This Marriage." Women in Seattle created pamphlets on women's reproductive health with titles like "Have Intercourse without Getting Screwed." Women in Boston created a 138-page booklet that later became *Our Bodies, Ourselves.* Valerie Solanas, author of the man-hating tract known as the S.C.U.M. (Society for Cutting Up Men) Manifesto, shot Andy Warhol. The National Organization for Women celebrated Mother's Day by organizing demonstrations nationwide for "Rights, Not Roses" and dumping piles of aprons on the White House lawn—near the exact spot where a group of suffragists had chained themselves to a White House fence fifty years earlier—to symbolize their rejection of the 1950s housewife role. The National Black Feminist Organization organized black women nationwide. Mothers staged a mother-and-baby sit-in at the office of the Secretary of Heath, Education, and Welfare. Lesbian women formed a guerrilla group called "Lavender Menace" and staged "zap" actions (a combination of disruptive protest and street theater). Single women and others disrupted Senate hearings on the safety of the birth control pill, which was released less than a decade earlier. Women in New York disrupted a legislative hearing on abortion—then still illegal—overseen by a panel of so-called objective witnesses comprising fourteen men and one nun.

To women of the Baby Boomer generation, these opening salvos of a revolution are moments of canonical—and personal—feminist history. But to women born circa 1969, many of them raised by feminists, these momentous occasions that have shaped us forever are shrouded in a collective amnesia. Feminism is not yet dead, but our memory of its past is dying. Younger women run from the word "feminist" without quite knowing why, or what the word has stood for. The movement's architects are aging, some are dying, and the names of others are hardly known. In 2007, we hardly know the history that surrounded our births and gave us our identity. We are barely acquainted with the story of the movement that has shaped our lives.

This book unearths the battles that have shaped our modern conceptions (and misconceptions) of feminism and what it was supposed to be. It is about mothers and daughters, and promises both realized and unfulfilled. In particular, it explores the women's movement from the perspective of those who have fought hardest—and often with each other—to define it. And it argues that seemingly personal matters still do have political implications, in spite of contemporary messages that tell us they do not.

Women fighting for rights, power, and parity generally share some rudimentary goals, hopes, and dreams. But from its inception, the movement known as feminism has been one of the most internally fragmented and outwardly controversial—perhaps because so many have so much to gain. Today many of the conflicts that characterize public debates about the meaning and relevance of feminism are generational, with yesterday's flaming radicals and today's cool girl bloggers rarely recognizing each other as fellow travelers in the fight for social equality and personal satisfaction. "Where are the younger feminists?" cry founders of women's organizations, now approaching retirement, as they e-mail each other about their often unformulated succession plans. "Why don't older women get us?" ask younger women on social networking Web sites like MySpace—women who may know more about the life of Bettie Page than that of Betty Friedan.

With little awareness of a shared history, younger women seeking to rally their peers and continue the forward march toward advancement are stuck reinventing the wheel. At the same time, framers of the 1960s and 1970s women's movement (commonly known as the second wave) are proving increasingly blind to interpretations of empowerment that they didn't themselves initiate. Blocked by their own inability to see members of the next generation as sisters in a struggle that they themselves inherited from members of an earlier wave, second-wave movement mothers worry that they have failed younger women. Or that younger women, ungrateful daughters, have in turn failed them. Have they? Have we?

In spite of our differences, older and younger women concerned with women's continued progress have much more in common than we think. But a mounting generation gap—fueled by divergent understandings of power and empowerment—obscures the larger war. How can younger women relate to their movement mothers and narrow the chasm between their mothers' style of empowerment and their own? Instead of brushing aside generational differences in the name of an abstract concept once known fondly as sisterhood, women young and old must appreciate where the alienation is coming from and seek first, as the old adage implores us, to understand.

The age gap is not, of course, the only chasm preventing women concerned with equity and continued advancement from uniting in common cause. Today as in the past, lack of sensitivity to race and class, and other markers, often precludes any shot at solidarity. But against this already divisive landscape, age is fast becoming an unnecessary divider.

Why don't younger women call themselves feminists? Perhaps, in part, it is a matter of spin. Feminism the movement and feminist the identity have never been an easy sell. The question of how to "fix" feminism's meaning and sell revolution to a critical mass of American women has plagued popularizers and would-be popularizers of the movement for forty years. The current sales quandary—that of "selling" the movement to the young—is but the latest in a long line of attempts to mainstream a hotly contested cause. Across the generations and at the heart of the battle to articulate feminism as a movement with mass appeal has been that singular tagline: *The Personal Is Political.* These words more than any others link the far-flung battles of women fighting for equality—including the ones we are in the midst of today.

In 2007, veteran feminists accuse younger women of turning their backs on feminism's history and turning back the clock. For many women in their twenties and thirties, "politics" refers to elections or politicians—not necessarily the underlying currents that shape their personal lives. For them, the conditions shaping individual trajectories and private lives no longer seem political, at least not in the way they seemed to be for the Boomer women who preceded them.

But the disconnect between personal life and social context is not solely the fault of younger women. Individualism seems to have trumped collective action—not just among women, but throughout American culture more generally during the past thirty years. Recent decades have seen the decline of liberalism and a decline in social commitment to collective, progressive change more broadly, though the emergence of Internet activism around recent elections offers a propitious sign for the future of citizen movements. Still, from a historical perspective, civic participation in general has been on the wane.[2] Liberals have lost political power as conservatives have gained it, and the social movements that historically have dominated progressive politics—including those for women, labor, and civil rights—have less overall impact on politics today. Collective social movements decrease in political relevance when high finance trumps grassroots organizing, and this is exactly what we have seen happening of late. Political parties once dependent on the number of volunteers on the ground are now media-driven and depend less on foot soldiers than on massive television buys. For women, the fallout from these shifts is profound.

Although women's organizations and activism certainly still exist, younger women today do not always experience the direct support of a movement behind them. And without a movement behind them, the reasons women still can't have it all—fulfilling career, committed relationships, kids—seem, as in the days before Betty Friedan's *Feminine Mystique,* merely "personal." Many of women's social problems once again have no public names. The word "revolution" itself has lost its political edge. Google the words "women" and "revolution" and you are likely to dredge up stories about the "opt-out revolution"—a headline-making term for what happens when well-heeled, well-educated daughters of feminists drop out of their careers. This so-called trend, cavalierly dubbed so by prominent newspapers, is neither revolutionary nor counterrevolution, but rather the adjustment of a privileged few to a workplace that doesn't make room for mothers. Even though it is often framed as such, a well-off woman's choice to stay home is hardly the pinnacle of broad-scale empowerment. Elite women's sense that their only option is to opt out is a copout—but it is hardly the fault of the individual women who cannot find a way to make it all work. Rather, it signals our common failure to see the shared themes in women's personal struggles, across race and class and geography, as connected to larger structural issues or addressable by collective formulas for change. Instead of questioning what's wrong with "the system," a younger woman struggling today for "balance" (or, on the other end of the economic spectrum, to "get by") more typically asks herself: What's wrong with *me?* The result? A series of parallel individual meltdowns where instead a *real* revolution should be.

It is ironic, perhaps, that members of a generation raised on the Barbie slogan, "You Can Do Anything," and philosophies that emanated from hit albums like *Free to Be You and Me* today demonstrate scant awareness of women's collective power. Younger women, who are more likely to be single, are portrayed on television, in Hollywood, and in the news as being more concerned with dating than changing the world. Polls proclaimed that 22 million unmarried women did not vote in the 2000 presidential election.[3] Popular culture reinforces, by amplification, this assumed image of apathy. On shows like *Laguna Beach,* or as starlets-turned-role models like Paris Hilton and Jessica Simpson, younger women are portrayed as more obsessed with lip gloss, Manolo Blahniks, and "hotness" than liberation, critical mass, and social change. What has happened to us, the daughters of women's liberation? This is hardly the world the architects of a movement for women's social, political, and economic equality envisioned. It's no wonder the aging visionaries seem upset.

But it's not as if women of a younger generation are sitting on their duffs. They are coming of age in a world that has changed—though, as many of them recognize, not enough. Yes, women of Generations X and Y live in a different environment, but it is no less complex than the one Boomer women faced. The difference, and the problem, is that they often lack an awareness that many of their conflicts are shared. In a recent book on how the stakes have changed for a new generation, *Midlife Crisis at Thirty*, Gen X-ers Lia Macko and Kerry Rubin offer their personal anxiety attacks as evidence of a broader generational angst. That angst, they argue, is a response to the lingering social and economic contradictions that continue to affect women of all ages—or, as they put it, the gap between women's progress and old-school corporate structures and rigid social conventions. It's the gap between What Has Changed and What Has Stayed the Same. In this breach, confusion is born: We've come a long way . . . maybe.

So where do we go from here?

The trendy notion that we are living in a "postfeminist" era has lulled many young women into inertia. Younger women assume their equality and take it for granted, but they aren't the first to dismiss the movement prematurely. The word "postfeminist" was first uttered in 1919—just a few decades after the coining of the word "feminist"—by a group of female literary radicals in Greenwich Village who rejected the feminism of their mothers, one year before women won the right to vote.[4] To the generation that came of age in the 1920s—many of them dancing, bobbed-haired fun-seekers—feminism seemed unfashionable and obsolete. The word "postfeminist" was resurrected in the backlash 1980s to describe an era in which feminism was, once again, deemed unhip and unnecessary. In a *New York Times Magazine* article published in 1982, Susan Bolotin popularized the idea that women in their twenties were fast becoming "postfeminists."[5] The media ran with this term, as did conservative pundits, who were all too happy to dance gleefully once again on feminism's so-called grave.

If "postfeminist" is a word twice coined to describe an era that is past patriarchy, surely the word—though popular—is woefully premature. Without a doubt, second-wave feminists opened doors. Title IX. *Roe v. Wade*. Later, the Violence against Women Act. But today, two of these crowning and hard-won achievements are in danger of being yanked away. Having made tremendous inroads in politics, business, and law, in 2007, still only 16 of 100 U.S. senators and 71 of 435 representatives are women. Following the 2006 midterm elections, there are more women in Congress than ever before, but the percentage only went up from 15.4 to 16.4. The number of female Supreme Court justices has recently been reduced by 50 percent (from 2 to 1), and the only female president this country has seen is Geena Davis, the doe-eyed movie star who played President MacKenzie Allen on ABC's short-lived drama *Commander in Chief.* Despite the significantly high numbers of women receiving law degrees, PhDs, and MBAs—more, in some cases, than men—women are only 20 percent of full professors and 17 percent of partners at law firms. Thirteen years after feminists switched the voice boxes of Teen Talk Barbie doll ("Math is hard!") and Talking Duke G.I. Joe ("Eat lead, Cobra!"), we have Harvard's then-president, Lawrence Summers, telling us that women might be biologically inferior in science, and one of the world's leading advertising executives, Neil French, telling us that women creative directors are "crap."[6] Only 10 Fortune 500 CEOs are women, and, according to The White House Project, an organization that tracks women's political influence and authority, women make up only 14 percent of guests on the five Sunday morning talk shows.[7]

Equal pay for equal work is still a joke. For every dollar a man earns, a woman still earns only 77 cents—an increase from the 59 cents she earned when the second wave of feminism began, but still far from equal. Women own only 1 percent of the world's assets. We continue to make up the majority of the world's poor.[8] We are disproportionately victims of violent crime. We are still, forty years after Simone de Beauvoir coined the term, the "second sex."

In de Beauvoir's day, the question was not whether women were oppressed but who, and what, was to blame. Today, in spite of the evidence, women are arguing over the question of whether women are oppressed at all. And therein lies the rub: How do younger women reconcile the gap between the tremendous opportunities they've been given and the inequalities that persist? How do they continue the fight for equality when they are constantly told—by the media, by each other, and often by their leaders—how good they already have it? These are the ironies younger women inhabit today.

It's true: Younger women shy away from the "f-word," as Karen Rowe-Finkbeiner called it, in her book of that title. But they do so for a reason.

As Jennifer Baumgardner and Amy Richards write in *ManifestA: Young Women, Feminism, and the Future,* some younger women flee from the feminist label "because they don't want to be associated with spooky stereotypes about feminists and their freaky excesses, or because they resist being identified solely as feminists. You know this rap: *some feminists think all sex is rape, all men are evil, you have to be a lesbian to be a feminist, you can't wear girlie clothes or makeup, married women are lame, et cetera.*"[9] To the women who believe the rap, the specter they call Feminism is scary. And it's small wonder, as the capital "F" version of the cause has been scarily framed.

From its debut on the public stage of history, feminism has been blamed by opponents for going too far and by advocates for not going far enough. The women's movement has been lambasted by dreamers for failing to transform women's lives, damned by detractors for failing to make women happy, and blamed by everyone for failing to institutionalize enough profound and lasting change. In the 1990s, right-wing ideologue Pat Robertson charged feminists with encouraging women to leave their husbands, kill their children, practice witchcraft, become lesbians, and destroy capitalism, while conservative talk show host Rush Limbaugh coined that unflattering term, "feminazi."[10] The antifeminist fervor surrounding Hillary Clinton in her 2000 bid for the U.S. Senate makes the 1970s stereotype of a feminist as a hairy-lipped man-eater seem quaint. A line in *Bridget Jones's Diary* tells us "Nothing is more unattractive to a man than a feminist." Actress Jennifer Aniston, who directed a film for a series sponsored by *Glamour* magazine as part of a project to address the paucity of female directors working in Hollywood, anxiously reassured an interviewer that she wasn't, like, "a bleeding heart feminist," while twenty-six-year-old singer-songwriter Kelis recently told *Essence* not to call her one: "Whenever you say that word, people think of some crazy, hairy lesbian."[11] In television shows like *Desperate Housewives* and spooky Hollywood remakes like *Stepford Wives,* feminists are portrayed as wily or deviant examples of contemporary womanhood run amok. And in books with maudlin titles like *Women Who Make the World Worse and How Their Radical Feminist Assault Is Ruining Our Families, Military, Schools, and Sports* or *We've Gone the*

Wrong Way, Baby: Feminism's Proud Destruction of Mankind, feminists, as a species of liberal, continue to be blamed for every evil under the sun.

In 2007, it is not only conservatives or men who villianize the tenets of women's equality in public and in print. Progressive-leaning women—and members of the media, regardless of their political bent—do it, too. It's become almost a reflex. In a much-discussed article appearing in the *New York Times Magazine* in October 2005, op-ed columnist Maureen Dowd loudly blamed feminism for intensifying conflict between the sexes—and keeping her from getting a date. In the phantasmagoric publicity around economist Sylvia Ann Hewlett's book *Creating a Life: Professional Women and the Quest for Children,* published a few years earlier, newspapers and television shows focused on one element of Hewlett's argument—the limits of female fertility—and fanned the flames of a backlash hysteria. Hewlett had also made an extremely convincing case for changing the structure of our workplace to account for the nonlinear nature of many women's careers—but few seemed interested in listening to that plea. More often than not, the media misinterpret or spin "feminist" messages until they are hardly recognizable to those who've actually read the study or the book.

We are left, instead, with vacuous images that fuel and perpetuate misunderstandings. For instance, when the words "young women" and "feminism" appear yoked together in a sentence these days, it's increasingly in reference to Girls-Gone-Wild types who fight valiantly for their right to bare their breasts on camera and flash their thongs. If most brands of feminism are framed as taboo or outré, the one form that the media loves to play up as popular and even ultra-hip—"bimbo feminism"—is, in many ways, an anachronistic throwback to an earlier time. In her provocative book *Female Chauvinist Pigs: Women and Raunch Culture,* thirty-something *New York* magazine writer Ariel Levy describes how many young women have internalized the bad news about old feminism and end up projecting the old patriarchy instead. They are now "empowered" enough to get Brazilian bikini waxes and install stripping poles in their living rooms. Is this what our foremothers had in mind when they threw out their bras?

Levy is no doubt onto something, though mainstream portrayals of young female empowerment today—including, at times, Levy's—are as cartoonish as they are incomplete. Most younger women are neither the self-hating sexual throwbacks nor the postfeminists and antifeminists they are made out to be. Although they may be far less visible because they are not out there flashing for tv cameras, there are younger women who grapple intensely with issues of parity in their relationships and their workplaces, if not on Capitol Hill. Younger women volunteer in record numbers, throwing their creativity and, when possible, their wallets behind a range of causes. Younger women's membership in the National Organization for Women may be down because they consider the organization old-fashioned, but the number of younger women founding their own organizations is on the rise. In 2005, 130 women from 42 states attended a Meet-Up to found the Younger Women's Task Force, a grassroots movement that now boasts 11 chapters and a membership over 1,000. A 2005 poll by the Partnership for Public Service found that, following 9/11, many young people are turning causes into careers.[12] There are models for young activism within mainstream culture—consider Jehmu Greene (former president of Rock the Vote), Wendy Kopp (founder of Teach for America, whose program continues to receive record numbers of applications from recent college grads seeking to teach in urban and rural public schools), Zainab Salbi (whose Women for Women International helps women in wartorn regions rebuild their lives and who has appeared on *Oprah* seven times), or the Woodhull Institute for Ethical Leadership, a training ground for ethical, pro-woman leaders. There are many more. Young women are organizing and championing social causes in spirited and imaginative ways—like the women behind The Real Hot 100, a campaign to redefine "hotness" and counter the impossible beauty standards informing *Maxim* magazine's Hot 100 list (which ranks women for their sex appeal) by refiguring the criteria to honor women for their guts and not just their glam. Pro-woman activism scans younger and younger. In an action reminiscent of an earlier day, in 2005, twenty-four teenage girls from Allegheny waged a national "Girlcott" against Abercrombie & Fitch after the popular clothing company came out with a line of female T-shirts with sexist and racist messages like "Who needs brains when you have these?" Apparently, there *are* younger women who still wrestle with feminism, whether they call it by its name or not.

Contrary to the popular notion that younger women's greatest aspirations are to transform themselves into America's next top supermodel or be hot like The Pussycat Dolls, scores of younger women recognize a need for uplift that's more structural—and they're not talking about push-up bras. According to a March 2006 Lifetime Women's Pulse poll, 51 percent of Generation Y women believe that there are more advantages today to being a man. And in a 2003 report *Progress and Perils: New Agenda for Women* by the Center for the Advancement of Women, a majority of the 3,300 women surveyed believed more effort should be made to improve the status of women in the United States today. More than six in ten agreed that "the United States continues to need a strong women's movement to push for changes that benefit women." A poll conducted by the Peter Harris Research Group for *Ms.* magazine that same year found that 83 percent of all women queried said they approved of the movement to strengthen women's rights. Among eighteen-to-twenty-four-year-olds, a full 92 percent rated the women's movement favorably.[13] Younger women's support for social causes remains strong. They may be perceived as politically disengaged, but this caricature masks a more complicated reality. The low turnout among young female voters during the 2004 election doesn't mean that *all* women under thirty-five are apathetic but rather, perhaps, that many are turned off and disillusioned by politicians who fail to take on their issues. And their rejection of the "f-word" does not mean that feminism is dead.

So, then, the questions remain: Does it matter that droves of young women reject the f-word? What, for that matter, *is* "feminism"? Who decides? Does sisterhood have a future, or only a short-lived past? Is feminism today a culture, an identity, or a cause? The problem or the cure?

These very questions have plagued and stymied—but also propelled and shaped—the modern American women's movement from the start. Despite myriad attempts over the past four decades to fix feminism's meaning, despite media caricatures that younger generations continue to internalize and movement veterans continue to deplore, "a feminist" has never been a frozen or static classification. The very act of defining one has led to a fragmentation that has become as predictable as it is inevitable. Today, as soon as one woman says "sister," another woman turns away.

But conflict has long been feminism's lifeblood, and for a good number of reasons—many of which are covered in this book. Women invested in changing the status quo often encounter ruthless resistance not only from other women but from the establishment they wish to change. Perhaps this is one reason why feminism's most public warriors have held each other up to such intense scrutiny. Regardless of why, the fact remains that the fight for women's social, economic, and political equality remains one of the most dynamic movements—the most debated, negotiated, fought over and fought for, owned, disowned, blamed, and reclaimed—of the last forty years. Since the days when the Women's International Terrorist Conspiracy from Hell crashed the Madison Square Garden bridal fair and young radicals protested Miss America, raising eyebrows and tempers within their own nascent movement, internal battles over the nature of feminist politics, its tactics, the sources of women's oppression, and the paths for "true" and lasting change have engaged a broad swath of women in an ongoing conversation about what it means for women to be powerful and empowered. The deep tension between change as internal and change as institutional has animated most of these fights. These fights did not begin in 1969, nor have they ended with the emergence of a more individualistic generation. They rage on now with more intensity, and greater consequence, than ever before.

FIGHTING FOR FEMINISM

American culture is obsessed with the girlfight. Images of women fighting are sexualized, sensationalized, and manufactured to titillate—think of the cultural obsession with female mud wrestling. In recent years, women's fighting has become a cottage industry, with movies, studies, and books. In the early 1990s, female fighting became the subject of psychological inquiry, led by Harvard educational psychologist Carol Gilligan and Lyn

Mikel Brown.[14] Gilligan stressed the importance of relationships and social networks to girls' development, noting that our fighting is not martial but social, and more backchannel. The girlfight, Gilligan-style, was memorialized in the 1989 Hollywood spoof *Heathers* and explored dramatically in the more recent *Mean Girls*. Books on women's fighting abound. New ones about girls' physical animosity, like *See Jane Fight,* vie for shelf space with earlier explorations of grown women's mutual social aggression, such as Leora Tannenbaum's *Catfight* and Phyllis Chesler's *Woman's Inhumanity to Woman.* The spectacle of moms facing off about their choices in print and online is by now de rigueur. And now, as women slowly rise within the professional ranks, we are reading more and more about competition among women and female fighting at work.[15] But the most publicly celebrated fight remains the one among feminists. Hear us roar.

For those solely interested in a catfight, this book is bound to disappoint. Cattiness is not what interests me—though I do find it fascinating that feminist in-fighting ranks high among evergreen stories in both the mainstream and alternative press. When the editor-in-chief of *Ms.* magazine resigned in 2005 and there were rumors among feminist insiders about a conflict of visions, *The New York Observer* ran a front-page story complete with illustrations and the attention-grabbing headline *"Meow!* Feminist Fur Flies."[16] When the well-known blogger Ana Marie Cox (aka "Wonkette") slammed veteran journalist Katha Pollitt's new book in the *New York Times Book Review,* the smackdown—and Pollitt's witty counter-offense (an op-ed titled "Thank You for Hating My Book")—reverberated in the form of snarky headlines Internet-wide. When Jessica Valenti of the blog feministing.com was attacked by law blogger Ann Althouse for having her picture taken with former President Clinton, the male-dominated liberal blogosphere went wild with snide.

I mention these episodes less for the sake of recounting who did what to whom than to suggest that these well-publicized debacles are nothing new. Feminism has always been a fight, and a public one at that. As media critic Susan Douglas puts it, the American public—or rather, the media— loves a dirty catfight, *Dynasty*-style, where women slog it out in the mud. Yet as Douglas also writes, "The media referees insist on putting feminism in one corner and antifeminism in the other, as if feminism could never be in the middle, but what they fail to recognize is that feminism *is* this middle ground. It may be filled with ambivalence and compromise, tradition and rebellion, but the space between the two cats—the space where we, the girls, are—is what feminism is all about."[17]

A preliminary word on some terms: The word "feminism" came into being in late-nineteenth-century France. It was adopted by a segment of the U.S. movement for women's right to vote in the 1910s, women who sought cultural as well as legal change. While its meaning and enactment in more recent decades is the very subject of this book, I use the term in a general sense to refer to the philosophy powering a movement to eradicate sexism and better women's lives.

Feminist history is often explained through the metaphor of waves. In the oceanography of the U.S. and British women's movements, "first wave" usually refers to the surge of activism that began in the 1830s and culminated with women's suffrage in 1920 in the United States (1928 in the United Kingdom). To launch their movement, "first wavers" borrowed theories, tactics, and language from the abolitionist debates around them. At the Seneca Falls women's rights convention in 1848, for starters, activists demanded full participation in public and civic life for women, calling for higher education and professional opportunities, the right to divorce, own property, claim inheritance, win custody of children, and vote. In parallel, they worked to enact the Thirteenth Amendment, which abolished slavery in 1865. After 1920, the year the Nineteenth Amendment granted women the right to vote, the first wave is widely assumed to have ebbed. In the following years, the successful "suffragist" coalition scattered and its members joined other social justice and activist causes, including unionization, antipoverty, and antimilitarist campaigns. Daughters of first-wave feminists generally rejected the suffragists' feminism wholesale, and it wasn't until a few generations later that women collectively identified with an organized women's movement again.

The "second wave" describes the resurgence of women's organizing beginning in the mid-1960s and, in the United States, ending—or at least suffering major setbacks—with the defeat of the Equal Rights Amendment and the advent of the Reagan-Bush era. The term was first used by Martha Lear in a 1968 *New York Times* magazine article to connect the new women's movement to the past. Historians of that era tend to refer to two distinct branches of the second-wave movement, alternately characterized by generation ("older" or "younger"), vision ("women's rights" or "women's liberation"), attitude ("liberal/reformist" or "radical/revolutionary"), or mode of organization ("bureaucratic" or "collectivist").[18] Although these categories can be useful, they tend to oversimplify, and I generally avoid them. The "third wave," a term used frequently in the second half of this book, generally refers to the period beginning with the Clinton-Gore era in 1993 and continues, though the term is much debated, today.

My focus here is on the women who have sought or received the media spotlight and have been most involved and invested in public conversations about the movement's identity and direction during the second and third waves. My emphasis on feminism's self-identified instigators and visible spokeswomen may seem, to some, ironic, for early second-wave feminist theorists and activists abhorred the very idea of a leader. Yet leaders and spokeswomen inevitably emerged. In a culture increasingly obsessed with celebrity, where the mainstream media latches on to personae upon whom can be projected all sorts of hopes and dreams, to ignore the prominence and impact of feminism's most public voices on popular conceptions of feminism would be disingenuous.[19] Whether self-appointed or media anointed, like it or not, and regardless of its a priori inability to represent women in all their diversity, feminism—in its popular incarnations—has had its leaders.

The history of the women's movement that I present here is selective. I am aware of the historical omissions that a book about *popular* feminism entails. This book does not claim to be a history of feminism in its entirety. Because I am concerned with internal fights over how feminism has been popularly articulated and framed, I give special emphasis to the public speeches, activities, and writings by some of the movement's most vocal and public theorists and spokeswomen. They are largely white and middle class. In Part I, "Mothers," I focus on those with the most access to media: namely, the radical feminists who largely clustered in and around media-capital New York City (Kate Millet, Robin Morgan, and many of their less widely known comrades-in-arms), Gloria Steinem and others associated with *Ms.* magazine, and Betty Friedan. In revisiting this particular subset of the women's movement, I establish a context for understanding the responses of some of the later spokeswomen, rebels, and instigators. In Part II, "Daughters," I turn to a new generation of public spokeswomen—the Katie Roiphes, Naomi Wolfs, Rebecca Walkers, *BUST* and *Bitch* magazines—again, self-declared articulators visible in and through the mainstream press, and argue that conflicts in feminism are today being recycled, in part, perhaps, because many younger women are not in touch with even this most popular vision of feminism's past. But the debates remain alive also because many of the original problems feminism set out to fix are still with us.

The need for more histories on different aspects of the women's movement remains profound. This book is only one of what I hope and suspect will be many attempts by younger women to revisit our rich and complicated collective past. Here I limit the discussion solely to conversations about U.S. feminism, from the late 1960s through the present. The resource section at the end of the book offers readers a list of where to go, online, to learn more about current and past debates.

Although some of the most vibrant debates about feminism today are now taking place on a global scale, I am amazed at the paucity of histories written about the U.S. women's movement—first, second, or third wave. I am equally amazed at how much in the histories that *do* exist still seems to be news—as, for instance, the fact that sex-positive feminism was part and parcel of the early second wave and not an invention of today's younger generation, or the fact that the idea that women needed their own civil rights organization was first articulated by an African American woman. Gerda Lerner once said that the only constant in feminist history seems to be a constant forgetting of our past. I remain both intrigued and disheartened by the way that past battles over rhetoric and theory (in particular, the question of "What is feminism?") are uncannily reenacted by my own generation—reluctant heiresses of a vision as yet only partially fulfilled.

Sisterhood, Interrupted is a bridge and a call to action. It is neither a manifesto nor a comprehensive history but a fresh reading of the old and new battles that have shaped modern conceptions of feminism across a generation of mothers and daughters, both figurative and real.

Feminism itself has a layered and remarkably cyclical past. From WITCH to *Bitch*—a popular third-wave magazine critiquing a still-sexist culture—much has changed in the world of feminism, its rhetorics, and its fights. But far more has stayed the same. The personal remains political. Women young and old sometimes lose sight of how and why, or fail to see each other as engaged in the same larger battle. Instead, we are left fighting ourselves.

But there is too much at stake to let such fights continue to derail women's continued social, political, and economic evolution. Although women who care about women's collective future may never stop fighting over the means and the methods of change, we can learn to fight with a deeper awareness of shared goals, a greater appreciation of our history, and a greater respect for new ways of doing things. This book combines the stories of feminisms past and present, with one eye on the future. It is for all those interested in better understanding the strains of dissent within modern feminism and in building bridges across the waves.[20]

Part I

Mothers

CHAPTER 1

A SLOGAN IS BORN

Let it all hang out. Let it seem bitchy, catty, dykey, frustrated, crazy, nutty, frigid, ridiculous, bitter, embarrassing, man-hating, libelous, pure, unfair, envious, intuitive, low-down, stupid, petty, liberating. We are the women that men have warned us about.

—Robin Morgan, *"Goodbye to All That"*

In 1963, a young reporter from East Toledo graced with long legs and good looks went undercover as a waitress at Hugh Hefner's new Playboy Club in New York City. It was an upscale gentleman's club with tasteful furnishings, good alcohol, and a girl-next-door preference in waitresses. The young reporter fit right in. In photos taken of her at the time, she is an hourglass beauty, dressed in a satin bustier bunny outfit and upswept hair, like the pin-up girls of the 1940s—with a tail. But at age twenty-nine, the tenacious journalist was anything but a timid bunny. She was there to do an exposé for *Show* magazine. As it turned out, the story she stumbled onto would reach far beyond the club itself. And though she may not have known it at the time, it was a story in which she would ultimately play a pivotal role. Her name was Gloria Steinem.[1]

Within a few short years, Steinem became a columnist at the newly founded *New York* magazine, where she covered a variety of topics then holding the attention of informed New York City readers—the Nixon campaign, Jackie O, Paul Newman, and, of course, the emerging phenomenon of "women's liberation." Her column, "The City Politic," captured an emergent awareness of feminism's explosive potential. It was going to be big, Steinem opined about the women's movement in her column of April 7, 1969, "the next big thing in revolutions."[2]

Steinem's words resonated. Before long, she was a media-anointed spokeswoman for that movement, already well under way. Her writing and speech-making talents were well suited for the times—it was an age of persuasion, superlatives, and slogans. Some Steinem famously supplied; others she amplified in her columns and other journalistic offerings. Mostly, however, Steinem chronicled the explosion of words and ideas that spread with organic momentum and extraordinary speed among ordinary women—"not so much by organization as contagion."[3]

Thumbing through memoirs from the time, a younger woman who doesn't currently feel the support of a women's movement behind her may be struck by second-wave women's growing awareness of the movement's importance, for themselves and for the nation. Dana Densmore, a tiny but tough MIT computer scientist and draft resistance counselor who would later become a founding editor of the radical feminist journal *No More Fun and Games,* recalls in *The Feminist Memoir Project,* "I knew that once I had embarked on this path, there would be no stopping short." She remembers the excitement of her mother, Donna Allen, who phoned her up in January 1968 to say "Women's liberation! It has begun!"[4]

Other women whose memoirs are collected in *The Feminist Memoir Project* recall the same contagious, organic momentum. It was as if a new way of thinking, seeing, and speaking had spontaneously come into being. "Each time we talked, we generated new insights," remembers Amy Kesselman, a Chicago high school teacher for whom the world was coming "dramatically and miraculously" into focus.[5] Poised on the "trembling edge of a transformation," women felt energized by a force both feminine and fertile. Some described the onset of "women's lib" (as male newscasters jokingly called it) as a quasi-religious experience. It was "as though light and music were bursting across the top of my skull," recalls Vivian Gornick, who was sent by *The Village Voice* in November 1970 to investigate "those women's libbers" without knowing who, or what, they were and, a week later, became a convert. To Steinem, who articulated these sentiments most publicly, the movement was almost apocalyptic. The language she invoked to describe it was mythic: "the ideas of this great sea-change in women's view of ourselves are contagious and irresistible. They hit women like a revelation, as if we had left a dark room and walked into the sun."[6]

A young woman reading these lines now might scoff at such breathless sentiment. For the I'm-not-a-feminist-but generation, an unqualified embrace of women's liberation may seem difficult to comprehend. Twenty-something international pop singer Shakira's reluctance to call herself "feminist" today is far more common: "I'm not a feminist, no. At least I wouldn't like to hang that sign around my neck."[7]

But feminism wasn't always the "f-word." Feminism was once associated with the words "young," "right on," and "strong." And feminist conversion back in those days was as swift as it was sweeping. In 1962, few women in America showed any interest in feminism, according to a *Harper's* magazine survey issued that year. But by May 1971, only nine years later, a full 62 percent of women polled believed that they had to "speak up" in order to accomplish anything.[8]

Feminism, once, was less like a dirty word and more like a big bang. Emerging leaders referred to the rapid spread of the new women's movement as "the Wonderful Explosion." Words and action converged. Reflecting back on those early heady days, Betty Friedan, who founded the National Organization for Women (NOW) in 1966, invoked an atomic metaphor: "We came together as crucial molecules, finally reaching a critical mass—catalyzing each other into the actions that became a chain reaction, until the movement of women exploded through all the strata of American society."[9]

The right words at the right time can change history: Black Is Beautiful. Think Global, Act Local. Remember the Alamo. Some slogans have launched wars and salvaged peace. Others have swung elections. In the late 1960s and early 1970s, slogans abounded, as sharp and stimulating as drum beats: "Sisterhood Is Powerful!" claimed radical women seeking to raise the consciousness of their antiwar sisters during a peace demonstration at the opening of Congress in January 1968. "Nobody Should

Legislate My Rights to My Body!" claimed protestors at a demonstration for abortion law repeal in February that same year. And soon: "Equality NOW!" "Equal Pay for Equal Work!" "Make Policy Not Coffee!" Steinem herself popularized one of the most sublimely absurd: "A Woman without a Man Is Like a Fish without a Bicycle!"

Some slogans provoked anger; others, laughter. The one about fish and bicycles has since graced a thousand T-shirts, but it was not the most important of the day, nor of the movement. That distinction goes to another, as enigmatic as it was powerful: *The Personal Is Political.* In the latter half of the twentieth century, few words have been more important to women's equality and women's empowerment than these.

ORIGIN STORIES

First issued on an underground mimeograph, "The Personal Is Political" was the title of an article about a theory written in 1969 by Carol Hanisch, a native Iowan who had quit her job as a United Press International reporter in 1965 to join the civil rights struggle in Mississippi before converting to women's liberation in Gainesville, Florida. After circulating widely underground, Hanisch's article was reprinted in a collection of influential writings from that year, published together in 1970.[10] But the words—"personal" and "political"—had taken on particular meaning within the culture at large before the women's movement ever appeared on the scene. Like all slogans that stick, the one that propelled the women's movement resonated beyond immediate circumstances. Part of the reason the slogan would strike a chord for so many American women was that it captured, in shorthand, aspects of a broader cultural orientation already under way.[11]

A massive shift had already changed the course of history. Intimations that personal life was in some way "political" first permeated the American ethos by way of various radical movements of the 1960s. In a concerted reaction against suburban uniformity, Gray Suit culture, Levittown, and other manifestations of 1950s conformism, the youthful American counterculture of the 1960s embraced personal (or private) experience and expression as new realms in which to stage public rebellion. These were the days of sit-ins, teach-ins, be-ins, love-ins, happenings, civil rights protests, boycotts, massive antiwar demonstrations—and Woodstock. During a rainy weekend in August 1969, over 400,000 people came together to hear The Who, Jefferson Airplane, Jimi Hendrix, the Band, and Janis Joplin at the rock festival held on a 600-acre dairy farm in Bethel, New York. Celebrating antiauthoritarianism and advocating a philosophy of "Do Your Own Thing," flower children of the 1960s signaled defiance in the way they dressed, the music they played, the drugs they took, the art they made, and the poetry they wrote. Many of the radical movements that rocked the decade, including Black Power and the Berkeley Free Speech movement, as well as the alternative cultures surrounding Timothy O'Leary, folkies, and the Beats, were putting a new spin on the "revolutionary" promise of individual expression. "Let It All Hang Out," "Don't Trust Anyone over 30," and "Make Love, Not War" were slogans that carried the day.

Today, twenty-somethings of the MTV generation may share these once countercultural sentiments but generally feel far less part of a movement working together for change. Back then, there was a sense that individuals rebelling together could, in effect, transform the world. It was an era of tremendous hope and promise, turned abruptly, in many realms, to confusion and despair. The civil disobedience tactics of the civil rights movement advocated by Dr. Martin Luther King Jr. had led to profound and historic change. Then, in 1968, both King and Robert Kennedy were assassinated, leaving the movement—and the nation—bereft. As the 1960s came to a close, the United States sent more troops to Vietnam. In August 1968, antiwar protesters clashed with police at the Democratic National Convention in Chicago while the rest of the nation watched the televised violence. All of this, combined with the massive failures of government and business to stabilize the economic order and the belief that major social problems remained forever insoluble, left many Americans feeling lost and hopeless.

Within branches of the New Left (an intellectually driven movement that attempted to correct the perceived errors of Old Left parties in the post–World War II era), activists disillusioned with politics-as-usual were beginning to question the meaning of the word "politics" and searching for new ways to integrate personal with political change. Fueled by the outrage of many American students toward the government's dishonesty and the brutal, unilateral war in Vietnam, the New Left had mushroomed into a mass movement that aggressively challenged the legitimacy of America's political institutions and pushed for peace. In November 1969, 250,000 people marched in the largest antiwar demonstration in the history of Washington, D.C. Another 200,000 gathered in Golden Gate Park in San Francisco. When the anti-war movement proved ineffective in instigating a U.S. withdrawal from Vietnam, however, many New Left activists grew cynical about the unattainable vision of "participatory democracy"—an ideal they had held sacred.

Instead of overtly challenging institutions, activists channeled their disillusionment in different directions. Turning their backs on what were perceived as "establishment" groups, large segments of the New Left abandoned forms of activism directed toward working within the framework of institutions, such as protests, petitions, and demonstrations. Some radicals turned to militancy. Voices from the radical fringe proposed socially untenable solutions to the nation's woes.[12] Following the Black Panthers' rise to prominence in 1966, The Weathermen, a small sect that formed in 1969 out of the breakup of Students for a Democratic Society (SDS), embraced a paramilitary style and destroyed property belonging to those it deemed to be colluding in the war. Individual radicals became violent as well. Before she shot Andy Warhol as they entered his downtown Manhattan studio, Valerie Solanas wrote her infamous S.C.U.M. Manifesto, which articulated bald female rage: "Life in this society being, at best, an utter bore and no aspect of society being at all relevant to women, there remains to civic-minded, responsible, thrill-seeking females only to overthrow the government, eliminate the money system, institute complete automation, and destroy the male sex."[13] Although the stances taken by the likes of Solanas and The Weathermen were extreme, their search for alternatives to the organizing strategies and tactics originally advocated by the New Left and the civil rights movement reflected a more general disaffection with nonviolent protest in America overall.

Things got worse. In contrast to the chipper portrayal of the era on *That '70s Show*, to many, the problems facing the nation around 1970 seemed insurmountable, and breakdown unavoidable. When President Nixon went on national television and stunned the nation by announcing that U.S. troops were being sent into Cambodia on April 30, 1970, student protests escalated. And when, on May 4, National Guardsmen opened fire on students demonstrating at Kent State University in Ohio, chaos intensified further. On May 14–15, black students demonstrating against the war and for civil rights at Jackson State in Mississippi suffered a similar fate. Following rumors of the murder of Charles Evers, older brother of civil rights martyr Medgar Evers, a mini-riot fueled by an atmosphere of racism resulted in tragedy when police and National Guardsmen opened fire, killing two students and injuring twelve. Although the Presidential Commission on Campus Unrest investigated the event, there were no arrests, and the incident received scant publicity. Meanwhile, students were striking on campuses nationwide. In New York City, antiwar protesters occupied major thoroughfares, bringing traffic to a halt.

Many Americans, having lost their faith in conventional political instruments and institutions, began to look elsewhere for solutions to social and political disrepair. New trends in religion, psychotherapy, and fitness held out attractive alternatives, each offering a more personal solution to problems potentially rooted in experiences of social dislocation. Millions of Americans became interested in transcendental meditation, yoga, charismatic religion, mysticism, Asian religions, and religious movements and cults. For many, the increased focus on personal life these alternatives held out often accompanied a decreased interest in the political life of the nation. Changing one's consciousness became an immediate way to effect change—in the world inside one's head.

New Left groups, too, had turned inward, redefining activism as a "lifestyle revolution"—a way to work, personally, for peace. If one could not effectively change the world, one could at the very least, in the lingo of the day, "change one's head." And with the lifestyle revolution came a redefinition of terms. For New Left activists, "revolution" was something an individual could undertake. Whereas the Old Leftists of the 1930s had emphasized class-based economic oppression, members of the New Left focused increasingly on elements of personal life and individual decisions—in addition, of course, to peace. Revolution became something one could live on a daily basis; "Liberation in Our Lifetime!" they declared.

The lifestyle revolution brought with it a new understanding of power. New Leftists emphasized the ways late capitalist society dominated individuals and groups, both psychologically and culturally. They looked to Herbert Marcuse, the theorist who brought subjectivity and irrationality into social analysis, rather than to Karl Marx. To New Leftists, anyone who felt oppressed was a potential revolutionary. Included as recruits for rebellion were ethnic minorities, the dispossessed, and the unemployed, as well as the alienated white middle class.[14] Fighting the mechanisms of oppression in one's own life by dealing with one's personal "hang ups" became an act of political engagement. It was this kind of thinking that transformed personal decisions into political statements.

Politics, then, became how you lived and not just who you voted for, as Youth International Party (Yippie) leader Jerry Rubin put it. This definition went hand in hand with the more general interest in "the personal" as a locus for change. The idea that politics were "how you lived" reflected a breakdown of the traditional separation between public and private life. Why was this breakdown so significant? Liberal political philosophy, beginning with the seventeenth-century English philosopher John Locke, divides public and private life into separate categories. According to political theorists, the operation of classical capitalist societies depends on this separation. When New Leftists expanded the definition of politics to include so-called private behaviors between people, they fundamentally challenged the binary opposition between "public" and "private." Rather than that which required a legislative act, politics became something that transpired in interactions between individuals, one on one.

The idea of "politics" as rooted in individual behavior found its earliest articulation in the civil rights movement. Members of the Student Nonviolent Coordinating Committee (SNCC), an organization defined, in part, by its aspiration to realize a vision of the "beloved community" here on earth, had paid heightened attention to how people treated one other within their movement community. SNCC's attempts to force whites out of the organization and the movement had been, in part, due to an understanding of everyday forms of racism and patronizing attitudes toward nonwhites as fundamentally "political." The theoretical insights around interpersonal politics and power developed within SNCC and other organizations would profoundly influence radical women, many of whom received their training in political theory in both the civil rights movement and the New Left.[15] Ironically, it was the sexist politics of both movements that eventually led a number of women to drop out and form a movement of their own.

RADICAL FEMINISM: A PRIMER

Dana Densmore, the antiwar activist who remembered her mother's remarkable telephone call ("Women's Liberation! It has begun!"), was one such woman who became a feminist by dropping out. During a time when the government had instituted a mandatory draft, Densmore had been counseling men who were anxious about the prospect of being sent to Vietnam. Some were conscientious objectors. Others opposed the war, and still others whom she helped were undecided or confused. Densmore helped them understand their options. A pro at navigating draft boards and the Selective Service, Densmore was a member of a group known as The Resistance, a loose support group of men who had already refused or were about to refuse induction and women who also opposed the war. Women in the group were mentally preparing themselves to go to Canada or Sweden with husbands or lovers who chose exile. They were planning to put off childbearing or, if they already had children, to raise them without the support of their partners, who were preparing to spend time in jail.

During weekly dinner meetings, Densmore and other women cooked and cleaned up while the men bonded, strategized, and postured in a separate room—a division that Densmore found infuriating. "Though of equal intelligence and thoughtfulness, and equal commitment, we had no legitimacy as part of the struggle," she recalls. "They were laying their balls on the line, and we were . . . what? The girls enjoined to say yes to the boys who said no?"[16] Eventually, Densmore left "The Resistance" and joined one of her own.

Densmore was far from alone. In many New Left groups and organizations, women did political housekeeping and grunt work for the male "heavies," as they were called, who occupied the leadership positions. Women poured the coffee and licked the stamps. They were also frequently expected to be sexually available to the men who led the movements. Male national leaders of SDS would breeze in and out of cities, cavalierly making passes at the SDS women they met. But these men would show complete indifference to their women's committee.[17] When women activists refused the heavies' advances, they were labeled "selfish" and lambasted as not authentically down with the cause. "What is now called sexual harassment was then called 'prove you believe in civil rights,'" explains Jo Freeman, author of the famed "BITCH Manifesto" of 1969.[18] If a white woman rejected advances from black men, she was then not only considered prudish, but "racist" as well.

Much like the young women who would, in the early 1990s, form all-girl bands after being tired of playing sexual side dish to the drummer, in the late 1960s, as women gradually began to look to their own oppression within the liberationist networks of which they were a part, they balked at the way they were valued for their bodies and their typing skills, but not their minds.[19] At the National Conference for a New Politics in Chicago in 1967, for instance, after radicals Shulamith Firestone and Jo Freeman had stayed up all night writing a women's resolution to be put out to the floor, meeting chair William Pepper ignored them. "Cool down, little girl," he told Firestone. "We have more important things to do here than talk about women's problems."[20] A few years earlier, around the time that SNCC activists Mary King and Casey Hayden circulated a position paper on women's status in the civil rights movement, chair Stokely Carmichael jokingly clarified the "progressive" male opinion on the position of women with his legendary response: "The only position for women in SNCC is prone."[21]

Sometime around 1967, radical women began meeting together in small groups to discuss their experiences of sexism within these liberation-oriented organizations supposedly committed to social justice. Naomi Weisstein, an early organizer of Chicago's Westside Group, couldn't wait to go to meetings. "[W]e talked ecstatically about everything," she recalls. "We talked about the contempt and hostility we felt, not only walking down the street, but from our male friends in the New Left. We talked about our inability to speak in public. We asked ourselves what we should call the thing that was squelching us. Male supremacy? Female subordination? Capitalist debris?"[22]

In 1967 and 1968, radical women faced a split. While some blamed men and male supremacy for women's oppression and felt the newly forming women's groups should focus exclusively on women's issues, others blamed capitalism ("the system") and felt that women's groups should also commit themselves to antiwar activism and antiracism and work side by side with their male comrades in the New Left. Those who believed that men were the enemy derisively called those who believed the problem was capitalism the "politicos." "Politicos," in turn, called those who blamed men the "feminists." In the beginning, politicos dominated. But eventually, the feminists—or radical feminists, as they came to call themselves—would prevail.

Defining women's oppression as a problem of national significance and not at all confined to their struggle for personal liberation within the movement, these women extended their comrades' critique of the separation between public and private life to the power struggle between women and men. The critique spread. In November 1969, disparate groups that were part of the expanding women's movement gathered at a Congress to Unite Women in New York City. For three days straight, over five hundred women from a wide range of groups and organizations representing different and often opposing viewpoints debated issues of men, women, and power. The mood was rowdy. Rebellion was in the air. In an article appearing in the November 28, 1969, issue of a new publication called *Woman's Monthly*, the female rebels heralded the formation of "a women's political power block to fight for women's liberation": "We now expand the definition of political to include women's 'personal' lives, meaning both the structure of government in the present society, and new alternatives on which

women unite. While we demand representation on all such bodies in proportion to our numbers (presently 51 percent), we see this only as a means
to an even larger end—the total liberation of women by every avenue available."[23] Their framework was borrowed, but by equating the personal and
political in a gendered way, they were about to launch something new.

Soon personal politics was no longer the purview of women in the New
Left alone. Ordinary women started talking about their lives like revolutionaries. Ideas traveled from pamphlets and position papers to the bedrooms and kitchens of American households and into more public arenas.
"The Personal Is Political" meant that—suddenly!—sex, family life, household chores, and, indeed, everyday interactions between men and women
were not simply private matters of individual choice but involved the exercise of institutional power. It meant that a refusal to fetch your male boss
coffee might be part of a collective movement based on the human right
to fulfillment. It meant questioning the assumption that *his* job mattered
more than *hers,* or that *her* role was to do the dishes while *he* watched TV.[24]
The slogan meant that wanting more out of life than being a mother,
daughter, or a wife could be a political position. With its powerful implication and bumper-sticker-like brevity, the slogan fundamentally altered
the way many Americans thought about the politics of private life.

The slogan heralded a broader revolution in language. New words entered the lexicon—*Ms., chairperson, sexism, male chauvinist pig.* New
spellings materialized too—most famously, womyn. Steinem wrote in an
essay about words and change: "A handful of women have even exchanged
their *patriarchal* names for *matriarchal* ones ('Mary Ruth*child*'), or followed the black movement tradition of replacing former owners' names
with place names or letters (for instance, 'Judy *Chicago*' or 'Laura *X*')."[25]
Just as the juxtaposition of "personal" and "political" was new and shocking, other words were coming together in equally startling combinations:
Sexual harassment. Domestic violence. The feminization of poverty. Situations and scenarios that had previously been called "just life" now had
deeper meaning—and condemnatory labels to describe them.

With the new language came sweeping consequences. Armed with a
new vocabulary, white, middle-class American women, many of whom had

described themselves to census survey takers only a few years before as "just a housewife," began taking unprecedented action. Countercultural students in granny glasses and jeans and glamorous establishment wives alike found themselves confronting their professors, supervisors, and mates. Recent college grads who tooled around New York City in tobacco suede miniskirts paired with ribbed poor-boy turtleneck sweaters and knee-length brown leather boots had never participated in a demonstration until they joined the women's liberation movement. One woman described how she quaked at her first picket—a protest held during July 1968 outside the *New York Times* truck-loading entrance on 43rd Street to force the paper to stop categorizing help-wanted ads by sex (Help Wanted: Male, Help Wanted: Female). "The New York Times is a sex-offender!" protestors chanted. As more and more women joined the demonstration and reporters turned up in droves, the woman stopped quaking. She and others were determined to lie down in front of the trucks to prevent delivery if they did not get an affirmative answer from management by evening. But, to their astonishment and delight, the newspaper's managers capitulated quickly to the women's demands. "[W]e were spared getting our demonstration frocks covered in crankcase oil. . . . We had won our first battle, and didn't even have to miss dinner."[26] The woman, Anselma Dell'Olio, would soon become a public spokeswoman for the movement, appearing with three others in a segment called "Four Angry Women" on the nationally syndicated *David Susskind Show* in 1968.

By the end of that year, four New York City newspapers—the *New York Times, Post, Daily News,* and *Village Voice*—would integrate their Help Wanted advertisements. Suddenly, masses of bold women were dragging their infants to sit-ins and rallies, demanding rights, dignity, and day care—and getting results. Wrote Steinem, "Ten years ago moving up the economic ladder for a few women meant becoming a doctor not a nurse, a boss not a secretary: a token not a movement. Now, nurses are striking, secretaries are organizing, and there is an uprising in the pink-collar ghetto."[27] There were "nude-ins" at Grinnell College in Iowa to protest campus recruitment by *Playboy* magazine and guerrilla theater at a fraternal "Men's Day" event at the University of Washington in Seattle, where chanting women with bags on their heads were eventually dragged off the stage. The Women's Liberation Rock Band played in halls around the nation, their lyrics chronicling women's workaday frustrations in a song called "Secretary": "Get up, downtown / don't you wish you could get out of this? / no trust / big bust / doesn't all the mumbles ever bother you?"[28]

Women were waking up en masse. Wrote Steinem in an essay called "Sisterhood," "I have met brave women who are exploring the outer edge of human possibility, with no history to guide them, and with a courage to make themselves vulnerable that I find moving beyond the words to express it."[29] Among the women Vivian Gornick canvassed for an article published in the *New York Times Magazine* in January 1971 were a legal secretary in a lower Manhattan office, a forty-year-old mother in a Maryland suburb, and a factory worker in Toledo, Ohio, all of whom clearly possessed an awareness of the political meaning of their personal lives. None of these women was a feminist, wrote Gornick. None was a member of the women's liberation movement. And yet each of them was "drawing on a linking network of feminist analysis and emotional upchucking" that was beginning to suffuse the social-political air.[30] Each was beginning to feel the effects of considering her personal experience in a political light.

Meanwhile, fresh theories cropped up daily within what was now coming to be known as the radical feminist movement—a number of loosely affiliated groups, or "cells," many of which were made up of civil rights and New Left exiles concentrated in major U.S. cities.[31] At the same time that radical feminist groups were forming, socialist feminists—those who saw race and class, among other relationships, as producing forms of domination that could not be summed up simply by the term "male supremacy"— agitated around bread-and-butter issues like equal wages, day care, and union organizing. Socialist feminists advocated a more European-style social-democratic politics and were less concerned with theory than the radicals. The socialist feminists outnumbered the radicals and dominated in San Francisco, Chicago, Boston, and many smaller cities. They tended to be less academic, less publicity-oriented, less sectarian, and less hyperbolic in their claims.[32]

But the women who called themselves radical feminists captured—and courted—major media attention. Like today's celebrities and politicians, a number of early radicals were savvy manipulators of the press. Some of the better-known women had their start as writers and editors—and there was even a former actress. Before editing the influential anthology *Sisterhood Is Powerful*, and, later, the magazine that became known as the movement's mouthpiece, *Ms.*, Robin Morgan was an editor at Grove Press and, well before that, a child actress on the television show *I Remember Mama*. Before she wrote her groundbreaking bestseller, *Sexual Politics*, Kate Millett was a doctoral candidate in English and comparative literature and a master of rhetoric. And, of course, there was Gloria Steinem, with her gift for words.

Steinem may have retained her rock star–like status across the decades, though even her name seems to be diminishingly recognizable to a younger generation now coming of age. Unlike celebutantes such as Paris Hilton or Nicole Richie, however, most of the names of those most instrumental in crafting radical feminism are largely unknown to college students today, many of who are more likely to associate the title *Daring to Be Bad* with a rap group than a history of radical feminism in America. Among the movement's more influential and less-known architects, for one, was Kathie Amatniek, a peace activist from Radcliffe who grew up in a left-leaning middle-class family loving Pete Seeger and Paul Robeson renditions of folk songs and freedom songs. In 1964, Amatniek became an organizer for the Summer Voter Registration Project in Mississippi. She was beginning a career as a film editor in New York when she was swept up by women's liberation and changed her last name to Sarachild. There was Pamela Allen, a former SNCC organizer who married a black activist, Robert Allen, in 1965 and later became active in Chicago Women's Liberation, where she organized with the help of Shulamith Firestone, who had previously been active in a socialist Zionist group. Heather Booth was a Brooklyn native who dropped out of her cheerleading team, which discriminated against blacks, after hearing Martin Luther King Jr. speak. Naomi Weisstein was an experimental psychologist and a dynamic activist involved with both SDS and the Congress on Racial Equality (CORE), and Roxanne Dunbar was an Oklahoma native who grew up idolizing Annie Oakley. After the assassinations of King and Kennedy and Valerie Solanas's attempt on Andy Warhol, Dunbar was inspired to move to Boston, where both the nineteenth-century antislavery and feminist movements had been centered, in order to start a radical feminist group of her own.[33]

If such names are little known among a younger crowd, the names of activist women of color from the time are generally even less known—in spite of the fact that the civil rights movement was a major stimulus and catalyst for so many women, black and white. Just as women leaving the New Left had expanded on the New Left's notions of class and social justice, so women of color activists quickly expanded on radical feminism to include not just gender but race. Their contributions would profoundly shape future generations of feminist writers and thinkers, as we'll see in chapter 5. But women of color played a critical role in the formation and widening of the second-wave women's movement, too—much more so than modern scholars tend to acknowledge.[34]

Early radical feminist groups tended to be racially homogenous (white), and many women of color who attended early meetings felt unwelcome. Some, like Shirley Geok-lin Lim, attended early radical feminist meetings but decided not to return when they realized that members were not interested in confronting their own unexamined assumptions about class and race. Elizabeth (Betita) Martinez participated in a radical feminist group until King was assassinated, and no one at her women's meeting that night thought it should take precedence over their usual business. "It was a night to realize that if the struggle against sexism did not see itself as profoundly entwined with the fight against racism, I was gone."[35] Martinez went on to work with other Chicanas, challenging sexism within the Chicano movement.

Many feminists of different racial/ethnic groups—black, Chicana, Asian American, Native American—went on to establish independent organizations, separate from the primarily white radical feminist groups that organized primarily along the axis of gender.[36] Among these, for instance, were the Third World Women's Alliance, Black Women Organized for Action, the National Alliance of Black Feminists, the National Black Feminist Organization (NBFO), and the Combahee River Collective. There were smaller, and more localized, groups, as well. Writer Michele Wallace and her mother, artist Faith Ringgold, founded Women Students and Artists for Black Art Liberation, which staged protests and "art actions" at museums in New York City, while Daphne Busby founded the Sisterhood of Black Single Mothers. Such groups emerged in response to the marginalization of women of color in existing social justice movements, stereotyping in popular culture, and misrepresentation in public policy. Using feminist theory as one tool among others, they tackled issues including reproductive rights, rape, prison reform, sterilization abuse, violence against women, health care, racism within the white women's movement, and, at root, sexism within black liberation. In the "Statement of the National Black Feminist Organization," the organization's founders urged their brothers to remember, once again, that "there can't be liberation for half a race," and declared that "sexism is destroying and crippling us from within." Along the left margin of the document ran an image of the female symbol with a twist: in the center, reminiscent of the Black Power movement, was a clenched fist.[37]

In spite of their separate roads, feminists from different backgrounds and of different ethnicities overlapped and intersected. When Steinem began speaking to audiences across the country, she often paired with African American activists Dorothy Pitman Hughes, Margaret Sloan, or Florynce Kennedy—the latter an older African American lesbian lawyer who cowrote an early book on abortion as a feminist right and would later run for president on the Feminist Party ticket in 1972. Frances Beal, a former SNCC activist who called attention to the fact that certain "women's issues," such as reproductive rights, had been historically tainted by racism, wrote a widely influential essay, "Double Jeopardy: To Be Black and Female," first published in *The Black Woman: An Anthology* and reprinted in Robin Morgan's popular anthology, *Sisterhood Is Powerful* in 1970. Also appearing in that widely visible collection was an essay by Eleanor Holmes Norton titled "For Sadie and Maud." Norton, at the time an adjunct assistant professor at New York University Law School, supplemented Beal's critique that women's liberation was fast becoming a white women's movement because it insisted on organizing around gender alone, while women of color shared more intersecting concerns.[38] Theorists like Angela Davis and Toni Cade Bambara provided still further analysis and debate.

Just as white women were hardly the only women raising radical and feminist questions during this time, manifestos were not the only genre of radical writing in circulation. Novelists, poets, and playwrights of color—Toni Morrison, Alice Walker, Audre Lorde, June Jordan, Ntozake Shange, and many others—simultaneously applied a radical feminist analysis to white patriarchal culture and explored the roots of the oppression of women of color through these more literary forms.[39] Their works had profound and lasting effects, reaching far beyond immediate circumstances and shaping the consciousness of a generation yet to come.

Still, the version of feminism that captured the public's attention was that promulgated by white women, whose groups had colorful names that reflected the energy and vision of the women who founded them. In Boston, there was Bread and Roses, a city-wide group whose name came from a women's labor song written during the Lawrence, Massachusetts, strike of 1912 ("Hearts starve as well as bodies. Give us bread but give us roses!") as well as the enigmatically named Cell 16 (the status of cells one through fifteen was unknown). Radical Feminists 28 took Kansas, Missouri, by storm, while in Berkeley there was Women's Liberation. The Furies (a lesbian-feminist collective) amassed in Washington, D.C., along with D.C. Women's Liberation. In Chicago, there was the Chicago Women's Liberation Union and the Westside Group. In New York, there were the Feminists, New York Radical Feminists, New York Radical Women, the Redstockings, the Women's International Terrorist Conspiracy from Hell (WITCH), and the short-lived but influential Radicalesbians. Radical lesbian groups, though small in numbers, were highly visible and vocal, spearheaded by particularly charismatic leaders (such as novelist Rita Mae Brown).

These groups were loosely affiliated, circulating their writings among each other and every so often coming together for a national gathering in Maryland, Chicago, or New York.[40] Together, radical feminist cells participated in a free-flowing exchange of strategies and ideas. Information circulated through a variety of formats and in a range of genres. Mimeographs and meeting minutes, pamphlets, newsletters, and journals were passed along underground, the most popular of these anthologized in aboveground books that reached far beyond the original groups. Members of some cells published newspaper and magazine articles in the mainstream press. Others went on to produce edited collections or single-authored books, a number of which—to their authors' shock and delight—made the nation's bestseller lists.

The precise origins of radical feminist ideas are difficult to trace by name, and highly influential articles were often group-authored or anonymous. Most famously, perhaps, a group known as the Boston Women's Health Collective together wrote the pamphlet that would become *Our Bodies, Ourselves.* Cells existed in a continual state of flux, with members frequently leaving one group to start or join another. The traffic in members, like the circulation of ideas, flowed in multiple directions at once. But one practice united almost all, as common as it was controversial: "consciousness raising" or, in shorthand, "CR."

CONSCIOUSNESS RAISING: POLITICS, BITCH SESSION, THERAPY?

Carol Hanisch's slogan-inducing article was itself, in part, a defense of "consciousness-raising"—the facilitated awakening of women who had been brainwashed into mindless, floor-mopping automatons or, in the case of New Left women, pliant defenders of male political privilege. The practice of consciousness-raising spread quickly, educating women much as the Vietnam teach-ins had educated individuals and raised awareness during the antiwar movement. Women across America met in kitchens, living rooms, and church basements to discuss common experiences of oppression in their daily lives. But CR was more than what some would call a simple bitch session. Anselma Dell'Olio described it using language that invoked spiritual and erotic catharsis: With an opening of the mind, she explained, came an opening of the heart. She was in a state of "quasi-hysterical delight and excitement all the time," due to the "ecstasy of relief" from a tension she had always felt between who she was and who she thought she was supposed to be.[41]

Despite its instant popularity, CR was loaded with controversy. Early practitioners felt obligated to validate their practice as a revolutionary tool over and over again. Hard-line politicos still active in the New Left accused feminists of creating a movement that was no more than group therapy. Speaking, in part, to an "invisible audience" of male New Leftists while simultaneously convincing themselves, as well, the earliest articulators of the practice—and slogan—defended themselves against the charge. Wrote Hanisch, "I want to stick pretty close to an aspect of the Left debate commonly talked about—namely 'therapy' vs. 'therapy and politics.' Another name for it is 'personal' vs. 'political' and it has other names, I suspect, as it has developed across the country." Throughout her essay, Hanisch justified CR in light of the New Left "debate" by writing about what CR was *not*. The "analytic sessions" that took place through the consciousness-raising groups were not therapy, she explained, but "a form of political action." CR, she argued, was not merely another psychologically-based fad where participants were encouraged to merely "change their heads" but a revolutionary movement that deserved to be taken seriously.[42] After 1969, when explanations of the relationship between "the personal" and "the political" began to appear frequently in print, nearly every radical feminist manifesto rehearsed a similar legitimizing disclaimer (the "not-therapy" defense), giving the slogan a distinctly defensive ring.

Although to these women consciousness raising was novel, the practice itself was not entirely new. It borrowed tactics and language from the civil rights movement ("speaking truth to power") and the Chinese revolution ("speaking bitterness") as well as from Marxism ("false consciousness")—movements in which the airing of words and experiences played a key role in naming and shaping reality. In a sense, however, CR was a rejection of the idea that there could be such a thing as "false consciousness," for the CR principle claimed that all women's perceptions were valid if one understood them fully—it was possible, in other words, to get past ideology and lay bare women's most internal truths. In a widely circulated article titled "The Small Group Process," Pamela Allen codified CR as a four-step process of "opening up," "sharing," "analyzing," and "abstracting."[43] But most important, she argued, the disclosure and analysis of personal experience would "liberate" participants and pave the way for a wider politics of engagement. Steinem translated this idea for a lay audience when she later wrote in *Ms.,* "In this wave, words and consciousness have forged ahead, so reality can follow."[44]

At the same time that radicalized women were offering disclaimers about what CR was not, they were also offering assertive explanations of what it *was.* As Steinem explained, whether at speak-outs, consciousness-raising groups, or public hearings, the goal was "*Tell your personal truth, listen to other women's stories, see what themes are shared, and discover that the personal is political—you are not alone.*"[45]

To radical feminists, consciousness raising was political strategy. From this equation sprang a number of significant assumptions that would make their way into books, and none would be more far-reaching and influential than a soon-to-be bestseller written by that long-haired doctoral student from Minnesota, Kate Millett.

SEX AND POLITICS

In 1970, at age thirty-five, Kate Millett was a PhD candidate at Columbia University and a sculptor of some repute. A noted work of hers that year consisted of a wooden cage housing a porcelain toilet with a U.S. flag in it, titled "The American Dream Goes to Pot." Taking a break from art, Millett was putting the finishing touches on her dissertation about love, literature, and relations between the sexes. Combining a literary analysis with a sociological and anthropological approach, Millett attacked patriarchy, romantic love, and monogamous marriage in western society and, most notably, in literature. Her ideas about sexual domination in the works of Freud, D. H. Lawrence, Henry Miller, and Norman Mailer—all "counter-revolutionary sexual politicians," in her words—would spark an intellectual fire.

If most early writings invoking "The Personal Is Political" struck a defensive note, Millett's argument put an unambivalent and assertive spin to the phrase. When Doubleday agreed to promptly publish her dissertation, titled *Sexual Politics*—a publishing feat that rarely occurs without years of revisions today—a landmark treatise on how male supremacy worked to make what was political seem "just personal" took radical feminism public. On August 31, 1970, *Time* magazine ran a sensationalized cover story on Millett. In the same issue appeared an article by Gloria Steinem optimistically titled "What It Would Be Like If Women Win." It was a winning week for women's liberation. (Steinem was infuriated to learn later that she had been paid less for her piece than the male reporters had been for articles of similar length.)

Sexual Politics reached a wide audience, aided, no doubt, by laudatory reviews. Yet many reviewers were only dubiously impressed. Hailed as "a rare achievement" and "the Bible of Women's Liberation" by the *New York Times* and "the first scholarly justification for women's liberation" by *The Christian Science Monitor,* the book, though an instant bestseller, was not without critics. Jonathan Yardley of *The New Republic* called it "too much of a literary-anthropological-sociological-historical-psychological grabbag to be a clear success," its "regressions" into "Women's Lib rigidities" diminishing its otherwise "splendid" inquiries into sexual attitude. The *New Yorker* called it "partly brilliant and partly silly," while the reviewer for *Time* warned that "nice guys"—the ones who volunteer to wash the dishes and change the baby—may feel "an inkling of what it must have been like for a moderate Southerner caught between protest and bigotry for the past 15 years" when they read her book. There will always be a few men, he added, who will want to invite Millett outside to settle the question of women's liberation "in a manly manner."

On one thing, reviewers agreed: The book would have an impact. As readers learned from *Time,* "[I]f it has not already happened at your house, braless converts to the Women's Liberation Movement are poised to leap right off the panels of the TV talk-shows and play hell with your pipe and slippers. Sooner or later they will probably all be armed with a copy of Kate Millet's *Sexual Politics.*"[46]

Reading *Sexual Politics* today, I am struck by Millett's versatility. She wrote with a scholar's conviction and an activist's passion, making clear how sexuality, family life, and relations between men and women involved transactions of power: "We are not accustomed to associate patriarchy with force. So perfect is its system of socialization, so complete the general assent to its values, so long and so universally has it prevailed in human society, that it scarcely seems to require violent implementation."[47] Supplying example upon example of how patriarchy played out in literature and in life, Millett melded her training as a critical reader with knowledge gained in the women's liberation movement to which she now belonged. She identified "patriarchy" as a socially conditioned belief system masquerading as nature; she demonstrated in devastating detail how its attitudes and systems penetrate literature, philosophy, psychology, politics, and life. Her incendiary work rocked the foundations of the literary canon by castigating time-honored classics for their use of sex to degrade and undermine women. Norman Mailer? A prisoner of the cult of virility. Henry Miller? A pathetic neurotic. D. H. Lawrence? A quasi-religious worshipper of the cult of phallus.

Like the underground memos, manifestos, and articles, Millett's book extended and critiqued theories born of the New Left. Taking a broadened definition of politics as her starting point, Millett introduced her title by asking whether the relationship between the sexes can really be viewed in a political light. The answer, she suggested, depends on how you defined politics.[48] Rejecting the *American Heritage Dictionary*'s definition, Millett advocated broadening the definition beyond state affairs to include "a set of stratagems designed to maintain a system."[49] Departing from an understanding of politics as the narrow and exclusive world of meetings, chairmen, and parties, she laid out her terms: "politics" meant arrangements whereby one group of persons was controlled by another, and "patriarchy" was an institution perpetuated by techniques of control.[50]

Millett's argument presented a fresh understanding of power relations for the feminist movement. In highlighting power arrangements between men and women, *Sexual Politics* popularized the idea that "male supremacy" was a political institution. The insight would echo throughout other early manifestos. Wrote Frances Beal in "Double Jeopardy," expanding the analysis to include a consideration of race as well, "[T]o live for the revolution means taking on the more difficult commitment of changing our day-to-day life patterns. This will mean changing the routines that we have established as a result of living in a totally corrupting society. It means changing how you relate to your wife, your husband, your parents, and your co-workers."[51]

For Millett, those relations went straight to the bedroom, and so, therefore, should the women's movement. The point was further brought home in 1970 by Shulamith Firestone in *Dialectic of Sex*, in which she famously wrote, "A revolutionary in every bedroom cannot fail to shake up the status quo."[52] The sentiment complemented well the undercover exposé penned by Steinem in a bunny suit. Women began to talk about sex and politics in ways their mothers and grandmothers would never have imagined. With *Sexual Politics* on their bedside tables, more and more women became revolutionaries overnight.

Coupled with *Sexual Politics* and *Dialectic of Sex* and *Sisterhood Is Powerful* on bedside tables that year was *The Female Eunuch*, written by Australian-born, London-based academic Germaine Greer, which made a splash, as did the author, who, with her high cheekbones, lack of inhibition, and talent for self-promotion, took the United States by storm. Greer liked to call herself an "Intellectual Superwhore." She claimed that the suburban, consumerist, nuclear family repressed women sexually, in effect devitalizing them and rendering them "eunuchs."[53] Other voices added virtuoso contributions to the rising sexual din. In "The Myth of the Vaginal Orgasm," a much-circulated essay of the same year, New York Radical Feminists cofounder Anne Koedt called for the exploration of new sexual techniques that would maximize women's sexual pleasure, while Erica Jong's 1973 bestseller *Fear of Flying* chronicled the guiltless sexual adventures of her adulterous heroine Isadora Wing and introduced the term "zipless fuck" (sex without emotional involvement or commitment, particularly between strangers) to the lexicon— the precursor, perhaps, to chick lit–inspired and *Sex and the City*-style adventure today.

Taken cumulatively, the activity during this period was dizzying. Writing that grappled with new ideas was one of feminism's popular means of expression, but litigation, fundraising, and grassroots organizing on the part of thousands of women across the country together made the revolution real. At the same time that women were becoming sexually radicalized and buying their first vibrators, theorists were crafting their manifestos, and newly radicalized activists across the country were organizing forces on the ground. While New Left women postulated, many others created women's schools that taught everything from auto mechanics to silk screening to childbirth. At the first statewide AFL-CIO Women's Conference in Wisconsin, two hundred women convened to discuss the status of women in unions. An enormously successful women's health movement mobilized around clinics; challenged existing medical practice, diagnoses, and treatments; worked toward the inclusion of women in drug trials and health surveys; and introduced the notion that women, as informed health consumers, could be catalysts for social change. Activists worked to transform sex education both in and out of schools, to create free and safe space for lesbians, to make sexual harassment and violence against women far less acceptable, and to persuade courts and the public not to blame women for rape. Women launched widespread campaigns for child care. On campus, activists fought for women's studies programs in colleges and universities. Others organized women workers in many occupational categories including, notably, clerical and health, and organizations like 9-to-5 organized women workers on the job.

The changes were breathtaking—difficult, perhaps, for someone who didn't experience them as part of personal cultural history to understand. In 1969 alone, the first accredited women's studies course appeared in the spring curriculum of Cornell University, and San Diego State College offered a ten-course program of women's studies—the first full program and most comprehensive in the country at the time. After sixty years, the journalism society Sigma Delta Chi admitted women to membership. The National Coalition of American Nuns came together to support the civil rights and antiwar movements and to pressure the Catholic Church for women's equality. The producers of the highly acclaimed children's television program *Sesame Street* made changes after feminists criticized the show for its stereotypical portrayal of women and girls.

The gains were not merely cultural but political. Shirley Chisholm became the first African American woman elected to the U.S. House of Representatives. In 1970, in a change from a traditional pattern, none of the women who ran for Congress was a widow campaigning to fill a seat vacated by the death of her husband. During these early years of the second wave, Congress initiated the first federal family planning program, Title X of the Public Health Services Act. For the first time in history, the House held hearings on education discrimination. The biennial conference of the American Civil Liberties Union adopted a strong policy recommendation supporting women's rights. The Equal Rights Amendment—which had been introduced in every session of Congress between 1923 and 1970 but had never reached the floor of either the Senate or the House of Representatives for a vote—was passed by the U.S. House of Representatives by a vote of 354 to 24 and later in the Senate by a vote of 84 to 8. The ERA, which stated that "[e]quality of rights under the law shall not be denied or abridged by the United States or by any State on account of sex," was finally presented to the state legislatures for ratification in 1972. (That same year, Helen Reddy's "I Am Woman" went gold and hit number one on the charts.)

These combined activities brought about sweeping change and a tremendous sense of optimism among women on the cusp of their movement. Women inside and outside the New Left started seeing themselves as "sisters"—allies in a struggle against a common set of oppressions and oppressors. Sisterhood was proving not merely contagious, but powerful. But for women at the red-hot center of the radical feminist movement, sisterhood was also proving contentious. It would soon become clear that when it came to theorizing and codifying feminism, sisterhood, in fact, could be a bitch.

CHAPTER 2

RADICALS AGAINST THEMSELVES

The connections between and among women are the most feared, the most problematic, and the most potentially transforming force on the planet.

—Adrienne Rich

On a clear, sunny day in September 1968, Peggy Dobbins, dressed in a stockbroker's traditional buttoned-down garb, stood on the wooden boardwalk outside of Convention Hall in Atlantic City and auctioned off an effigy in the shape of a woman: "Gentlemen, I offer you the 1969 model," she hawked. "She's better every year. She walks. She talks. She smiles on cue. *And* she does housework!"[1] Dobbins was one of a hundred young radicals who had traveled by bus, car, and plane from New York, Massachusetts, Washington, D.C., Michigan, New Jersey, and Florida to take part in what would become the first widely broadcast "zap action" of the women's liberation movement: a protest of the Miss America Pageant. The protest served a double purpose. It was an attack on the age-old American icon of male-defined femininity and on the notion that American women were objects to be consumed. It was also a carefully planned publicity stunt.

Four decades later, with reality television series like *The Bachelor* and *Who Wants to Marry a Millionaire?* broadcasting the notion that modern women are actually more than willing to be bought for a price, and on prime time, the spectacle of beautiful women competing for male attention and reward has become so ubiquitous as to be mundane. To younger women today, popular series like *America's Next Top Model* (now in its eighth season) hardly seem worth a demonstration. But in 1968, for radical twenty-somethings who were seeing with new eyes, Miss America, the über–beauty pageant icon, brought into high relief the pervasive power that male-defined standards of beauty held over ordinary women's lives. In the days leading up to the pageant that year, members of New York Radical Women, who spearheaded the action, spread the word about their intention to protest "the degrading mindless-boob-girlie symbol" and an image that has oppressed women.[2] A flyer promised a range of actions and activity— "Picket Lines; Guerrilla Theater; Leafleting [and] Lobbying Visits to the contestants urging our sisters to reject the Pageant Farce and join us." The flyer called for "a Boycott of all those commercial products related to the Pageant." There was to be a huge "Freedom Trash Can" into which protestors would chuck "instruments of female torture": bras, girdles, curlers, false eyelashes, wigs, and issues of *Cosmopolitan, Ladies' Home Journal,* and *Family Circle.* At midnight, the media was promised a "Women's Liberation rally" at the moment Miss America was to be crowned on live television. The preparatory flyer encouraged participants to add "other surprises" of their own.[3] Organizers prepped protestors to speak only to female reporters.

On the night of the big event, the media showed up en masse, and the rebels rose to the occasion. They trotted out a sheep, paraded it on the boardwalk, and crowned it Miss America. Protestors waved antipageant and anticontestant placards that read "Miss America Sells It!" "Miss America Is A Big Falsie!" "Up Against the Wall, Miss America!" Some chained themselves to a large red, white, and blue Miss America dummy propped up on the boardwalk to dramatize, guerrilla-theater style, how women were enslaved by beauty standards. Others ceremoniously threw their so-called instruments of torture into the trash. Inside the glittering Convention Hall, sixteen radicals, disguised as pageant viewers, smuggled in a large banner inside an oversize handbag. They took their seats in the balcony near the stage and, as the outgoing Miss America sashayed to the microphone to deliver her billowy farewell address, four stood and unfurled their banner over the railing. In large letters, it read: "Women's Liberation!" The sixteen women chanted "Freedom for Women!" and "No More Miss America!" as onlookers turned their heads in surprise. Miss America reportedly trembled.[4]

It wasn't long before burly policemen in riot gear bounded up the stairs and hustled the radicals out of the hall. But the protesters were elated: Mission accomplished. The television cameraman trained his lens on the chanting women, and viewers across the country caught the first glimmers of women's liberation, right there, live, on network TV.

The next morning, news that Miss Kansas had been crowned Miss America ran alongside news that a women's liberation movement was loose in the land. But much of the national press coverage portrayed the protest in ways that made the fledgling movement seem ludicrous and frivolous. Instead of foregrounding the protestors, *New York Times* reporter Charlotte Curtis—a woman, no less—called attention instead to some alleged "650 generally unsympathetic spectators" watching from the sidelines.[5] The *Times* salaciously referred to "bra-burnings" though in fact no bras were actually burned. (Organizers were careful to follow the Atlantic City police's request not to endanger the wooden boardwalk by lighting anything on fire.) Feminist insiders worried that the negative press coverage, with its titillating emphasis on charred bras, spelled disaster for their newborn movement. Others realized the movement's day had come. "The news about the first Miss America protests . . . galvanized us," recalls then-emerging radical Barbara Winslow, who got the news in Seattle. "Women's Liberation existed across the nation. We had sisters everywhere."[6]

No longer just a fringe fad, women's liberation was on the map. Following the Miss America protest, women across the country were energized by the spectacle. New York Radical Women was flooded with mail and new members. The media followed developments closely. "Every day in a woman's life is a walking Miss America contest," declared Rosalyn Baxandall on nationally syndicated TV.[7] *Newsweek, Time, Life,* and *The Nation* profiled emerging leaders like Millett, Steinem, and Betty Friedan in their pages. In New York City, Norman Mailer refereed a high-profile Town Hall discussion on feminism with writers Jill Johnson and Germaine Greer. Toni Morrison's *Sula,* a novel centered on the friendship between two adult black women, became an alternate selection for the Book-of-the-Month club, with excerpts published in *Redbook.* The spate of nonfiction books by and about women became top sellers, delivering feminist slogans and concepts straight to the neighborhood bookstore.

Following the Miss America protest, radical feminists who had been busy theorizing the movement from within their individual cells quickly woke up to the fact that this was a movement worth fighting for on a large scale. Unfortunately, as is often common among visionaries of start-up movements, they also did a great deal of fighting among themselves.

The minute sisterhood became powerful, radicals seeking to liberate women also sought to control the form and direction that liberation would take. The more women who joined the fight, the more difficult it became to control collective actions and efforts. Outside of New York City and the few other urban centers where radical theorists tended to cluster, conflicts within women's groups were far less intense, and activists forged ahead with concrete actions, protests, and campaigns. But on the East Coast in particular, individual radical feminists vied for visibility and influence—despite the general ethos of women's liberation that there should be no leaders.

The Miss America protest was a success, but the negative publicity it garnered sparked heated internal disagreement over what kinds of activities and behaviors counted as feminist, and why. In those early days, feminism was intricately connected with action. With the success of their movement in the balance, radicals struggled intensely to define the meaning of politics and identify the "correct" blueprint for mass liberation. "The Personal Is Political" became not merely a slogan but an ideology—a key to setting the course for the cause.

BLUEPRINTS FOR ACTION

So eager were the new feminists to carry forth their vision, the impetus to succeed was intense. After the initial flush of excitement around the Miss

America protest began to cool, feminist solidarity took its first blow as some activists started to criticize others who had participated in the protest for making what they thought were poor choices. Carol Hanisch, for one, spoke out against the "antiwoman" tactics of those who had displayed posters verbally attacking the female contestants. In "A Critique of the Miss America Protest," an article published in an influential collection of radical writings titled *Notes from the Second Year,* Hanisch argued that such woman-hating tactics were not feminist, political, or a promotion of sisterhood. "[C]rowning a live sheep Miss America sort of said that beautiful women *are* sheep," she wrote, with disdain.[8] She further argued that by failing to make it clear that women are forced by men and a system of male supremacy to play the Miss America role—and not by beautiful women themselves—the protest came off as an attack against beautiful women in general and the contestants in particular. Others were annoyed by the "do-your-own-thing," free-form nature of the protest and lamented the fact that not all actions had been cleared by group planners. In an unauthorized action that surprised many demonstrators, Peggy Dobbins had mischievously sprayed Toni home-permanent spray (or was it a stink bomb?) around the mayor's box in the auditorium. Toni was one of the pageant's sponsors. Dobbins was arrested and charged with disorderly conduct (and, amusingly, for "emanating a noxious odor").[9] Some felt that her action and arrest hurt the movement's credibility. But everyone involved with the protest agreed that they had succeeded in destabilizing the pageant, which had been the goal. In the aftermath, Pepsi-Cola withdrew its sponsorship. Pageant officials considered taping the show without a studio audience in the future to avoid another embarrassing disruption. Radical Judith Duffett even wondered whether continued pressure from the movement might force the pageant to fold.[10]

The tactics of the Miss America protest prompted a theoretical debate that went beyond noxious hair spray and live sheep. "What counted as a sufficiently 'political' act?" the radicals asked themselves. Being "on the streets" was important to many, but, according to radicals including Hanisch, it was *not* a political act to be "out in the streets demonstrating against marriage, against having babies, for free love, against women who wore makeup, against housewives, for equality without recognition of biological differences, and god knows what else." Such acts, Hanisch claimed, were merely "personal solutionary"—that is, they assumed that women's problems could be solved on an individual level alone.[11]

By contrast, many radicals insisted that feminist action was not at all about personal choices and solutions but collective action for a collective solution. It was a core disagreement that didn't stop there. As their writings reveal, radicals committed to the principle of collective action fervently disagreed about what kind of action was politically radical *enough*. These debates took shape, for example, on August 26, 1970, during the Women's Strike for Equality.

The strike—initiated by Betty Friedan, founder of NOW, who we'll hear more about in chapter 3—brought together a coalition of women from various groups and organizations and was to be a commemoration of the fiftieth anniversary of the ratification of the women's suffrage amendment. After much wrangling, strike organizers agreed to call for the right to abortion, child care, and equal opportunities in jobs and education.[12] In its publicity-savvy management, the national strike was a redux of the Miss America pageant's publicity actions, but with different tactics—ones the radicals ultimately felt were not "political" enough, as they were defining the term.

On this day, a smattering of women across the nation actually went on a daylong "strike," refusing to work at their jobs or at home. Posters in New York City egged them on: "Don't Cook Dinner—Starve a Rat Today!" "Don't Iron While the Strike is Hot!" Strike organizers urged women to boycott four products whose advertising, they charged, offended and degraded women: *Cosmopolitan* magazine, Silva Thins cigarettes, Ivory Liquid soap, and a "feminine hygiene" spray named Pristeen.

The strike was an impressive show of feminist solidarity. In small towns and large cities across the nation, women marched, picketed, held teach-ins and rallies, and performed guerrilla theater, skits, and plays. In New York City, where an estimated 20,000 to 50,000 women marched together down Fifth Avenue, radical feminists marched with NOW organizers, suburban housewives linked arms with domestic workers, mothers walked with their teenage daughters. Establishment wives in buns and heels and hippie students with long hair flowing joined elderly suffragists dressed in traditional white as they followed the same route taken by first-wave feminists over half a century earlier. A group of women built a makeshift child care center on the grounds of New York's City Hall. Others draped an enormous banner with the words "Women of the World Unite," over the Statue of Liberty, while still others invaded Manhattan advertising agencies with medals inscribed "This ad insults women." In Rochester, women smashed teacups to protest a lack of female participation in government. On Boston Common, they distributed contraceptive foam and whistled at and taunted construction workers. In Dayton, Ohio, women on welfare and hospital union members gave public talks. There were teach-ins on women's issues at the *Washington Post*.

As with the Miss America protest, the strike made headline news: "Women Rally to Publicize Grievances," declared *Newsweek*. "Women March Down Fifth in Equality Drive," ran a headline in the *New York Times*.[13] Once again, coverage was mixed. *Newsweek* described the movement behind the strike as a "shaky coalition of disparate groups" and doubted that it "will ever be able to unite women as a mass force." The *Times* similarly downplayed the strike, declaring that "For Most Women, 'Strike' Day Was Just a Topic of Conversation." It failed to feature or profile in depth any of the thousands of demonstrators who joined in the day's activities, but again it succeeded in capturing the sentiments of those who decided to sit the strike out. One woman from the advertising firm Doyle, Dane, and Bernback said she was spending the day in "the most liberated way possible": She was taking the day off to play golf. A sidebar headlined "Leading Feminist Puts Hairdo Before Strike" snidely highlighted the fact that Betty Friedan was twenty minutes late to her first scheduled appearance because of a "last minute emergency appointment with her hairdresser," trivializing the seriousness of the strike by focusing on her coiffure in a move foreshadowing the later media fascination with Hillary Clinton's hairband. The next day a leading editorial in the same paper condemned the demonstrations as "publicity seeking exhibitionism" and "attention getting antics." *Time* suggested that the Fifth Avenue march provided "some of the best sidewalk ogling in years" and seemed disappointed that there were no "charred bras." But more to the point, the movement was squarely on the nation's radar. A CBS News poll conducted nine days later found that whether they were in favor of it or not, four out of five people over eighteen had read or heard about women's liberation.[14]

Yet despite—or perhaps because of—the organizers' success in generating publicity, in its aftermath, the organizing coalition rapidly fell apart. A number of radical feminists ended up walking out of the coalition that had organized the event. The reason? Among other things, coalition members who walked out felt that the feminist actions being pushed were too conventional. To radicals, the strike narrowed the idea of politics to mere demonstrations and strikes, eclipsing the broader idea that "politics" was also a way of being, thinking, and interacting.

In a flurry of internal papers and articles that circulated immediately following the strike, radical feminists returned to the old New Left issue of how "politics" should be defined. Among the coalition's inner circle, the dominating view of "politics" was based on a much more old-fashioned—even "male"—definition than they had anticipated: electoral politics, that is, running for office in a system they wanted to overthrow, not join. To radicals committed to attacking the system at its roots, such political strategies seemed conservative and outré. For women whose definition of activism included guerrilla theater and other sensational and outrageous "zap" actions, the emphasis by march leaders on cooperative, disciplined, finely choreographed forms of protest seemed unimaginative—and worse, ineffective. Radicals questioned the value of these tamer actions and contended that they may actually be detrimental to the furthering of feminist goals.

But what exactly was real action? Where, practically speaking, should the uprooting process begin? Such questions belie an attention to philosophical questions that may sound like hair-splitting today. But at the time, for radical insiders who felt themselves on the cusp of changing the world, theories were more than words; they were maps to a postpatriarchal future.

Depending on where one located the roots of women's oppression, "The Personal Is Political" could be understood as a call to an externally focused revolution, an internally focused transformation, or something in between. It was like debating the difference, perhaps, today between the effectiveness of a Hillary Clinton (who uses government channels to effect more systemic change) and an Oprah Winfrey (who encourages viewers to transform themselves). And those who adhered strictly to either end of the continuum increasingly found themselves at odds.

For some, the slogan was a call to lesbianism—which, lesbian feminist groups insisted, was not merely a sexual alternative but a political choice. Lesbians were in the vanguard of the revolution, argued Jill Johnston in *The Lesbian Nation: The Feminist Solution.* In contrast to those who were "stranded" between their personal needs and their political persuasions, Johnson wrote, the lesbian was the woman who united the personal and the political in the struggle to free herself from "the oppressive institution"—meaning marriage.[15] While many radicals experimented freely or came out as lesbians during this time, others were skittish if not downright hostile toward lesbianism—and homophobic. Many dismissed lesbianism as sexual rather than political and similarly dismissed lesbians' issues and concerns.

Radicals who favored the internal focus thought electoral politics and reform within the existing structure had their place, but were not enough. Wrote members of Radicalesbians in 1970 in an article reprinted in *Notes from the Third Year,* "On a . . . political/psychological level, it must be understood that what is crucial is that women begin disengaging from male-defined response patterns"—such as always needing to please, or apologizing for outspoken behavior. Once this disengagement is achieved, "all else will follow, for ours is an organic revolution."[16] Added Johnston, "As for reform within the structure itself, we root for our Bellas [Abzugs] and our [Shirley] Chisholms but we know that true revolution is a glacial process of unknown cell structures that will evolve out of shared bits of profoundly internalized consciousness."[17]

Robin Morgan likened it all to a "ripple effect." It started with individual women gaining self-respect and power over their own bodies and souls, then within their family, on their blocks, in their towns, states, and beyond. "This is a revolution in consciousness, rising expectations, and the actions which reflect that organic process," she wrote from the pages of *Ms.*[18] For Morgan, personal knowledge and self-esteem were keys to transforming the world. Although the process might be slow and the outcome not always visible, such was the formula for change. For Kathie Sarachild, the radical feminist movement was based on the assumption that a mass liberation movement would develop as more women begin to perceive their situation "correctly." To facilitate the correction in women's self-perception, Sarachild maintained, the primary task was to awaken women's consciousness of themselves as a class, on a mass scale.[19]

On the other side of the debate were those radicals who rejected the singular focus on what seemed to them a revolution from within. Critiques of the ideas of revolution as primarily a matter of self-esteem, awakenings, and changing perceptions were as sharp as they were biting. Some radicals openly mocked their sisters for targeting consciousness as the primary realm for transformation. Roxanne Dunbar of Cell 16 recalls, "Our group was contemptuous of what we called their 'T-groups,' which we considered touchy-feely self-indulgence. We thought that we were more revolutionary. . . ."[20] In Chicago, the Westside Group's Amy Kesselman felt conflicted about spending so much time sitting around just talking. "Although some of the time we sensed the importance of our discussions, we often felt guilty about not being 'on the streets.'"[21] These women and others feared that the emphasis on consciousness raising and personal growth was creating a movement that would turn so inwardly on itself, it would ultimately disappear.

These critics of internal revolution had a point. In some cases, consciousness-raising groups became so insular as to disengage from the outside world altogether. The world outside receded as the small group became an end rather than a means. In such groups, members tended to withdraw from externally focused actions and create a separate reality all their own. A number of groups and individuals took it further, committing to a program of personal politics that advocated changes in individual lifestyle above all else—similar to some of the religious movements of the time. Rallying around the practice their critics would later put down as "cultural feminism," participants focused on building a separate "women's culture," one that provided an alternative to the patriarchal world in which women currently lived. This cultural legacy resurfaced—though many no longer called it feminism—in the late-1990s music festival known as Lilith Fair, and continues today through women's bookstores, art galleries, and women-only spaces like the feisty knitting circles known as Stitch 'n Bitch. Back then, this embrace of women's culture included the goddess/spirituality movements and cultivation of women's health clinics, art, restaurants, and music (culminating in the annual Michigan Women's Music Festival)—all elements of separatism, whether temporary or permanent, in which the act of separation was, in and of itself, the revolution.[22]

When detractors said "cultural feminism," they meant no compliment. Indeed, among more external-action-oriented radicals, the term raised hackles and ire. In concentrating exclusively on the cultivation of separate, "alternative" lifestyles, these critics charged, so-called cultural feminism lacked the capacity to support a revolution on a mass scale, and the movement, they feared, risked going down in history as merely another psychospiritual fad. Radical Jennifer Gardner blamed consciousness raising itself for this unfortunate development, calling the small group "a counter institution" that diverted women's energy from revolutionary activity.[23] A radical named Brooke Williams charged a number of feminist groups with falsely spreading the belief that "if our lifestyles are pure enough and we set up enough 'alternative' situations, the revolution will magically arrive, and everything oppressive will automatically collapse through accumulated good vibes."[24]

Hovering over these debates was the specter of the now-apparent failure of the New Left. As many radical feminists would attest, the New Left's failure to sustain itself as a mass movement was a blueprint for how *not* to succeed. Fearful of repeating history, many radical women were anxious to prevent their movement from following the same course.

By the early 1970s, the organized New Left had largely fallen apart. A number of its key leaders, including Rennie Davis and Sharon Jeffrey, had abandoned radical politics for a spiritual quest. In a 1971 article, Gail Paradise Kelly wisely called for a middle ground, noting that the New Left's preoccupation with the cultural revolution had led that movement to a stalemate. Feminists needed to form a synthesis of the diverging sides to revolution.[25] Having learned the lessons of the failed New Left, Weisstein and Booth similarly reminded women's liberationists that "without a movement to support it, consciousness veers off, turns inward toward self-hatred or destructive mysticism, and finally dies."[26] They saw the rise of "cultural feminism" as detrimental to the movement's longevity. If women tried to change their lives without changing their social conditions, they argued, they would fail.[27] And to a degree, history proved them right. Calling attention to the precarious situation of the movement, Weisstein and Booth gave their article the ominous yet prescient title, "Will the Women's Movement Survive?"

THE SOURCE OF WOMEN'S OPPRESSION

At the heart of debates between radical feminists who prioritized institutional transformation and those who emphasized individual change was a fundamental disagreement about the sources of women's oppression. Today women argue over the question of *whether* women are oppressed, but in the late 1960s, this was a given. The question was not *were* women oppressed, but who, and what, was to blame.

Opinions varied. Wrote the authors of the Redstockings Manifesto, "We . . . reject the idea that women consent to or are to blame for their own oppression. Women's submission is not the result of brainwashing, stupidity or mental illness but of continual, daily pressure from men."[28] It was men, and not women, they felt, who needed to change. In an article titled "False Consciousness" that circulated a few months earlier in the October 1969 issue of the journal *Tooth and Nail,* Jennifer Gardner called the theory that women oppress themselves "insidious."[29] Those who believed that women were their own worst enemy, Gardner suggested, were encouraging a state of mind that would ultimately cause women more harm than good.

In the case of poor women and women of color, the argument seemed repugnant. Blaming women who were fighting racism both institutionally and in their homes—where incidents of domestic violence were statistically higher—for their own oppression seemed particularly insulting. In an August 1970 issue of the journal *It Ain't Me Babe,* Barbara Leon of Redstockings suggested that the emphasis on "brainwashing" and other psychologically oriented theories developed through consciousness raising merely perpetuated the class and racial bias of the movement.[30] Leon's critique echoed what a number of women of color, including Celestine Ware, Toni Cade, and Pauli Murray, were articulating both inside and outside radical feminist circles: For many women, the luxury of focusing exclusively on changing one's personal and internal life was a privilege, limited to women who were white and middle-class.[31] For women who daily experienced material as well as psychological forms of oppression, whose daily experiences of disempowerment were not limited to the unconscious adoption of "male-defined response patterns" but included obvious physical patterns of oppression—poverty, domestic violence, racism—the idea that overcoming oppression was simply a matter of changing one's mind was offensive. Those who emphasized psychological transformation as the goal of revolution, according to their critics, demonstrated a blindness to the circumstances in which nonwhite, non-middle-class women lived.

Those who believed that individual liberation could never be anything more than a means to an end felt that anyone who did not agree relied on an inaccurate understanding of how power worked. Wrote Brooke Williams of Redstockings, "Individual changes, no matter how many people make them, cannot go beyond minimal changes unless the larger political and economic structures of male supremacy are changed, too."[32] Without its externally oriented focus on changing social structures and power relations in the material realm, such women feared, feminism would simply devolve into a useless discourse of self-blame.

The infighting among radicals was impassioned, but it was nothing compared to their attack on more mainstream feminists during the mid-1970s. A good number of those fighting for the meaning of their movement shared a common enemy: the populist organ of the movement, *Ms.* magazine. And nowhere did the tension between a view of feminism as self-transformation and a view of feminism as a militant movement to eradicate patriarchy at the roots play out more tangibly and more publicly than in the radicals' attack on *Ms.*—and ultimately on its founder, Gloria Steinem.

RADICALS VERSUS *MS.*

Ask a younger woman today what she thinks of *Ms.* and she may respond with a flinch. Nestled between stylish, updated magazines with names like *Bust, Bitch,* and *Fierce, Ms.* can be perceived by the younger generation as out of touch and outdated. Among those not predisposed to identify as feminists, *Ms.* can be perceived as touting a too-out-there, too-radical, old-fashioned feminism. But at the magazine's beginning, it was cool—and, to early 1970s radicals, not radical enough.

After months of unsuccessful efforts to raise money for a new magazine intended to take feminism into the mainstream, Steinem had been presented with a remarkable opportunity by her friend and editor, and *New York* magazine founder, Clay Felker. Felker offered Steinem the opportunity to publish a piece of a sample issue in *New York,* which always published a double issue at the end of the year. The preview issue of *Ms.* thus debuted as a thirty-page insert in the December 20, 1971, issue of *New York,* with a circulation of 300,000. The cover featured an eight-armed woman, each arm holding a symbol of the many tasks that make up an "ordinary" housewife's day—an iron, a frying pan, a feather duster, a steering wheel, a telephone, a typewriter, a clock, a mirror—an image reinvoked thirty-four years later, perhaps, on a July 24, 2006, *New York* cover that featured a woman lifting a baby in the air. On the 2006 cover, thought bubbles—"I never wanted this baby" and "I know my husband is cheating on me" and "Anyone else in a sexless marriage?"—circle the woman's head, while inside, an article about the mommy Web site UrbanBaby.com reveals how New York City mothers today confess their ambivalence and discontent about their lives to each other, anonymously, online.

On the 2006 cover, the woman is smiling—misleadingly. On the *Ms.* cover, she is visibly overworked, and in tears. But headlines on the 1971 cover promise the answer to her woes: "Sisterhood" (by Gloria Steinem), "Raising Kids without Sex Roles" (Letty Pogrebin), "The Housewife's Moment of Truth" (Jane O'Reilly), "Women Tell the Truth about Their Abortions" (Barbara Lee Diamonstein). Inside, readers could learn "Why Women Fear Success" (Vivian Gornick), ask each other "Can Women Love Women?" (Anne Koedt), learn why "I Want a Wife" (Judy Syfers), and learn that "Welfare Is a Woman's Issue" (Johnnie Tillman). The magazine—and the movement it sought to represent—offered a collective solace to ordinary women's woes.

This preview *Ms.* generated a response beyond the editors' imaginations. Designed to stay on newsstands for three months, the issue sold out in eight days. More than 20,000 reader letters poured in. (By comparison, a typical *McCall's* issue, with a circulation of 7 million around this time, drew only 200 letters.) Twenty-six thousand subscription orders for *Ms.* followed. In July 1972, the first official issue again sold out almost as soon as it hit the stands. By the eighth issue (February 1973), circulation was up to 350,000. By April 1976, 450,000. And by November 1976, it reached half a million.

Ms. was quickly becoming the magazine of record for American feminism, and, as with many tenets of women's liberation, the spread of *Ms.* was viral. Wrote a reader from Pennsylvania, "*Ms.* was as illuminating and supportive as a successful consciousness-raising session and if I can find enough newsstand copies, I'll send them in lieu of Christmas cards."[33] Similar to the experience of a CR group, but on a much larger scale, the experience of reading *Ms.* offered individuals—many of whom were living in rural or suburban isolation—solidarity and support. Lurking subversively among the other monthly women's magazines lined up neatly in bins at the grocery store checkout line, *Ms.* sneakily reeled women in. Observed Onka Dekkers, a writer for the feminist journal *off our backs* in 1972: "*Ms.* is making feminist converts of middle class heathens from academia to condominium ville [*sic*]. A slick reputable looking magazine breaks down defenses and lets the word worm its way into the brain. *Ms.* is almost in violation of Truth in Packaging laws. There is a female mind-set on those glossy pages slipping into American homes concealed in bags of groceries like tarantulas on banana boats."[34] While many on the Left welcomed the influx of these tarantulas into America's kitchens, others were less sanguine about the new dissemination vehicle for women's liberation. The growing New Right condemned the magazine as antifamily. Nancy Reagan, then first lady of California, felt *Ms.* was "very dangerous as far as the country is concerned."[35] Conservative columnist James J. Kilpatrick agreed that the magazine struck the wrong note—like a "C-sharp on an untuned piano" or "nervous fingernails" that screech across a blackboard. He called *Ms.* bitchy and petulant, castigating its writers for making high tragedy out of the mere picking up of a husband's sock.[36]

Described by Gloria Steinem in 1971 as a "how-to magazine for the liberated female human being—not how to make jelly but how to seize control of your life,"[37] *Ms.* focused on personal transformation—but not the kind hawked by the usual women's magazines. As Steinem told a reporter from the *San Francisco Examiner, Ms.*'s service features offered instruction on "how to change the world instead of how to disguise hamburger eighteen different ways."[38]

In stark contrast to the idealized, glamorous, and glossy world of *Cosmopolitan* or *Mademoiselle,* where "seizing control" meant weight loss, fashion overhauls, and kitchen makeovers, *Ms.* writers and editors urged women to wake up and join the revolution. Articles appearing in early issues carried titles like "Down with Sexist Upbringing!" "How to Write Your Own Marriage Contract," and "Child Care Centers: Who, How, and Where." In the cover story highlighted in the preview issue, "The Housewife's Moment of Truth," Jane O'Reilly drew on personal anecdotes to illustrate feminist conversion: "In New York last fall, my neighbors—named Jones—had a couple named Smith over for dinner. Mr. Smith kept telling his wife to get up and help Mrs. Jones. Click! Click! Two women radicalized at once."[39] Readers sent in letters detailing their own awakening "clicks" and signing off "just a housewife"—a response that became a tradition for letter-writers to the magazine.

Ms. advised its readers in practical terms, offering a feminist version of self-help. Regular columns featured advice on mechanics, revised etiquette, child raising, and health. A column called "How to Make Trouble" offered articles on subjects ranging from how to start one's own consciousness-raising groups to how to begin a nonsexist, racially diverse child care center. Through this combination of personal awakening, self-transformation, and targeted activism, readers were exhorted to work, as the magazine's subtitle suggested, "For a Better World."

But *Ms.*'s image of that better world was not nearly radical enough for radicals who prioritized systemic overhaul. Many of the architects of radical feminism felt that Steinem and some of her collaborators did not have radical "cred." Steinem herself had not taken part in the radical women's movement until 1969, when she attended a Redstockings speakout on abortion. (Her earlier activism had been on behalf of farmworkers and the movement to end the war in Vietnam.) Steinem and the other early *Ms.* editors agreed with radical activists about the need for fundamental change at the roots, but many felt that some "reformist" short-term tactics could also have significant and sufficiently transformative long-term results. Articles that focused on external change generally limited antisexist activism to activities an individual woman could take on while working within the current political and economic order. Despite forays into discussions about poverty and welfare, *Ms.* generally avoided critiques of male domination that linked those forms of oppression to the economic system at large.[40] And this, not surprisingly, was where *Ms.* and radicals parted ways.

Ms. was in a tricky position. In order to be a sustainable commercial venture, the magazine operated within the capitalist system, accepting advertisements from various industries. The fact that the magazine accepted ads depicting skinny, rich, successful women angered radicals. Ads often projected messages that equated the rhetorics of liberation and consumption. The notion that a woman could become "free" simply by buying New Freedom Pads, for instance, or the idea that ordering Drambuie over Ice was a "courageous move" seemed to many a crass perversion of feminist principles. In selling feminism, many radicals believed, *Ms.* was selling it out.

Their hostility toward *Ms.* stemmed from multiple sources. There were those who were angry at *Ms.* from its inception for going outside the inner circles of the women's liberation movement for its writers and editors. Susan Brownmiller, Nora Ephron, and Sally Kempton had struggled earlier to establish a mass-circulation feminist magazine named *Jane* and had failed to raise the seed money. Steinem, in turn, had received seed money from Felker.[41] With the successful launch of *Ms.*, the telegenic Steinem had catapulted to media stardom. Her frequently referenced beauty and glamour triggered hostile reactions among radical insiders who disavowed leaders and hierarchy and called her "a "middle-class nice girl," "bourgeois," and "uptown."

But members of Redstockings took their critique of the magazine—and its founder—to another level. On May 9, 1975, Redstockings called a press conference at a convention sponsored by the journalism review *MORE* and accused Steinem of having conspired in a government plot to displace and eliminate the radical feminist movement through *Ms.* "It is widely recognized that one major CIA strategy is to create or support 'parallel' organizations which provide an alternative to radicalism," the accusation read, insinuating that *Ms.* was a CIA front.[42] Although their criticisms may sound paranoid to younger women today, their fears were not unfounded. The CIA was known to have funded the National Student Association and had thereby tried to control the student movement. It was not impossible, the radicals feared, that the CIA might try to control the women's movement as well. In 1969 the FBI had actually initiated an investigation of the women's movement for possible subversive activity, though this was not confirmed until eight years later, when information about the surveillance was disclosed by an inquiry under the Freedom of Information Act.[43]

Steinem's accusers dredged up her previous relationship with the Independent Research Service (IRS), an organization that had indirectly received funds from the CIA. Steinem had helped found the IRS and served as its director in 1959 and 1960. The organization encouraged American students to participate in the communist-dominated World Festivals of Youth and Students for Peace and Freedom. Redstockings alleged that the CIA established the IRS to organize an anticommunist delegation of Americans to disrupt the festival, and they accused Steinem and the IRS of gathering information on foreign nationals attending the festivals.[44]

Steinem's relationship with the organization was hardly news. She herself had made public her association with the IRS years before in newspapers and magazines. But Sarachild, Hanisch, and others now brought it up to insinuate that Steinem's relationship with the CIA continued. They questioned *Ms.*'s "curious financing"—Warner Communications had put up most of the money for the venture, relinquishing corporate control by taking only 25 percent of the stock—and urged the magazine's editors to come forward with more information about their "unusual stockholders."[45] They alleged that the formation of *Ms.* had given Steinem a strategic position from which "feminist politics can be influenced." And they alleged that, through Steinem and *Ms.,* "information can and is being gathered on the personal and political activities of women all over the world."[46] Redstockings gave no hard evidence to support these charges. And they threw in some more eyebrow-raising claims: that Wonder Woman (who graced a *Ms.* cover) reflected "the anti-people attitude of the 'liberal feminists' and matriarchists"; that *Ms.* undercut Simone de Beauvoir's contribution as a "feminist pioneer"; and that *Newsweek* and the *Washington Post* were all in on the conspiracy.[47]

Along with these public accusations, Carol Hanisch, Kathie Sarachild, and Ellen Willis wrote and circulated accusatory articles condemning "The Liberal Takeover of Women's Liberation" by *Ms.*—which, they pointed out, was far more than a magazine. *Ms.* was a political organization, charged Willis. There were *Ms.* books, a Ms. foundation, a *Ms.* TV show, and other related organizations, projects, business ventures, and political causes now connected to the magazine.[48] Many women, Willis pointed out with concern, viewed *Ms.* as a center for leadership for the movement. And that center, in her view, was far too connected to the state.

For two years, Willis, a rock critic for the *New Yorker,* had been a part-time contributing editor at *Ms.* In time, she came to feel that she was the only "true" radical working there. Later Willis clarified that while she never expected *Ms.* to be a spearhead of radicalism, she had high hopes that the magazine would change as it grew and be open to more radical ideas. But by 1975 Willis turned on her sisters, and quite publicly.

Willis's attack echoed debates then going on inside radical circles. She slammed the publication for "[t]he continual implication that we can liberate ourselves individually by 'throwing off our conditioning,' unilaterally rejecting our traditional roles, etc."[49] Such an emphasis, she believed, "denies the reality—that men have *power* over women, and that we can only liberate ourselves by uniting to combat that power." In her view, the emphasis on attacking sex roles rather than male power propagated the false idea that "We don't need to avoid men, only our conditioning. We don't need to attack the economic system; we too can make it." Willis faulted the magazine for its "obsession" with electoral politics and its refusal to acknowledge the need for "militant resistance" against an oppressive system. She further criticized the magazine for avoiding basic economic issues and taking upper-middle-class privileges and values for granted.

Just as younger women of the 1990s would later lambaste their foremothers for mandating a "politically correct" ideal of feminist behavior that they felt was impossible to live up to, Willis charged *Ms.* with creating a new image for women to live up to: "the liberated woman." This image simply replaced that of the perfect homemaker, she insisted, resulting in a new harmful ideal and making *Ms.* no different from other women's magazines. Misrepresented as feminism, this fantasy would mislead some women, convince others that women's liberation had nothing to do with them, and play into the hands of those who oppose any real change in women's condition, she feared.[50]

Willis resigned from her job at *Ms.* on June 30, 1975. She explained in her statement of resignation that the Redstockings' accusations augmented (but did not initiate) her decision to leave. Rather, after two years of working on the magazine, she was resigning because of political differences. She publicly rejected what she felt was the "conservative and anti-left feminism" of the magazine.[51]

The feminist press went wild in response to the Redstockings' charges and called on Steinem to respond. Reporter Lucinda Franks wrote a piece for the *New York Times* repeating the accusations, which was syndicated and circulated throughout the country. Betty Friedan, never a big fan of Steinem's (their looks were constantly compared in the press, with Steinem "the beauty" and Friedan "the beast"), joined in, implying that a paralysis of leadership in the movement could be due to the CIA. She demanded that Steinem respond and brought the story even more mainstream publicity by discussing the charges in the *Daily News* and at the International Women's Year Conference in Mexico City.[52] Personally devastated by the accusations and the unsisterly nature of the attack, Steinem declined interviews. Three months later she issued a six-page letter to the feminist press, published on September 6. In it, she noted that she had been told about the CIA as an indirect funder for some of the people who were working on the festivals and that she "naively believed then that the ultimate money source didn't matter, since, in my own experience and observation, no control or orders came with it." She admitted that it was "painfully clear with hindsight that even direct, control-free funding was a mistake if it couldn't be published," but that she "didn't realize that then."[53]

While Redstockings' main point of contention was the magazine's collusion with the system, behind the charges was an underlying theme, expressed in no uncertain terms: *Ms.* had co-opted radical feminism. Read the accusatory statement: The popularity and groundbreaking successes of women's liberation preceded "the installation of Gloria Steinem as the movement's 'leader' by the rich and powerful." The situation, they felt, was dire: "Today all the trappings of the radical upsurge remain, but the content and style have been watered down. We have reached a point when the movement must have a revival of radical ideas and leadership which marked its early growth and success."[54] Threatened by the prominence of a less radical vision, radicals were poised to reradicalize feminism and take their movement back.

WHO OWNS FEMINISM?

The hostility toward Steinem stemmed not merely from radicals' fears of CIA co-option, but from their suspicion of a woman who used the media so adroitly—and who was used by it to speak for the movement at large. Radicals showed deep antagonism to anyone who assumed leadership or who consciously used the establishment press (which Steinem did, and skillfully) to advance her cause.

Steinem had star power. At first a reluctant spokeswoman, she worked hard, and graciously, to share the spotlight. Yet some who worked equally hard but were not as publicly recognized resented Steinem for stealing the show. They were outraged by seeing the media turn hard-won, original insights developed by others in anonymity into, as Susan Brownmiller put it, "Gloria Steinem pronouncements," "Gloria Steinem ideas."[55]

While the radicals' antileader stance was both a conscious reaction against the charismatic leadership of the civil rights and antiwar movements and a principled attempt to practice egalitarianism and reject hierarchy within their own movement, their antimedia stance grew out of their general distrust of mainstream media. And Steinem, according to the radicals, had hijacked their ideas. Of all the Redstockings' accusations, perhaps the most significant was the charge that *Ms.* was "blocking knowledge of the authentic activists and ideas" of the "original" women's liberation movement.[56] The commercial success of *Ms.* and the rise of cultural feminism had raised challenging and theoretical questions. But the battle over blueprints had taken over, corroding the battle over meaning into a battle for control.

It wasn't just about Steinem. As the press continued to cover cultural feminism and some of its more esoteric and fringe practices with an air of mockery and amused disdain, offhandedly lumping together feminism, spiritualism, and gay liberation, the movement had a problem with image control. Believing the very future of their movement at stake, a number of radical "sisters" indulged in name calling and "trashing," furthering already fierce divides.

The lack of structure and the disavowal of leadership in many groups contributed to their ultimate collapse.[57] Some group members had been "purged" from their consciousness-raising groups for attempting to assert leadership; other cells disbanded over other personality conflicts and serious political disagreements. As groups fragmented, feminist solidarity became increasingly elusive. Radicals recklessly blamed each other for things that were often not fully under their own control.

To a young woman previously unacquainted with this history, the fact that feminists ultimately attacked each other—rather than the establishment they were trying to change—may seem disappointing, even surprising, a case of the sisters doing it to themselves. But powerful, intensive movements like this one are rarely cohesive or long lasting. By 1975, the year historians identify as the "end" of the organized radical feminist movement, this particularly explosive burst had burned itself out. Like many visionaries with radical ideas, the early agitators lacked some of the flexibility and practical skills needed to create a movement that would endure. The radical feminist movement became known for its infights, but its instigators were hardly alone in history. The early civil rights movement was as divided as the women's movement. Soon after its formation, the liberal coalition that had secured passage of the Civil Rights Act of 1964 and the Voting Rights Act of 1965 began to fray. When understood in this larger context, the breakdown of radical feminism was perhaps an inevitable phase.

As the radical movement fell apart, its architects grew increasingly self-reflexive about the reasons why. A number of key players had already offered their own analysis of what went wrong. Carol William Payne blamed the early creators (herself included). As she bemoaned in "Consciousness Raising: A Dead End?" in 1973, "We never resolved the question of what a women's liberation group was supposed to do." The constant conflict between those who favored the strictly personal, psychological approach and those who felt that the personal insights gained by participating in a small group should be linked to collective political action was left unresolved.[58] For others, the downfall was due to a loss of definitional control. Women's liberation slogans were used to push ideas the slogans were never meant to push. As Williams wrote in 1975, radical feminist phrases like "consciousness-raising" and "the personal is political" were distorted beyond recognition, the original definitions and source papers forgotten or ignored.[59] The farther words and phrases traveled from their original meanings, the less "radical" they became and the less they meant. Carol Hanisch agreed, reminding women that "the personal is political" had meant that experiences previously thought of as "individual" were in fact the experience of women "as a class" and resulted from men having power over them. Such experiences had to be taken out of the realm of private problems with private solutions. But the cultural feminists were arguing for a return to the private realm once again.[60]

Not everyone saw the general dispersion and internal dissent as bad. As early as 1971, the editors of *Notes from the Third Year* had put a positive spin on the movement's diffusion, interpreting the conflicting pleas of the movement as natural, a case of both/and: The women's movement was "not only an organized political force but a state of mind as well." Rather than signaling disorganization or failure, some argued, the explosion of ideas was a sign of a tremendous grassroots success.[61] But more often, radicals felt that the dispersal of the movement's focus had led to its demise. For Sarachild, for instance, to widen radical feminism was to spread it too thin, lessening its original power.[62] Whether the result of inexperience, internal squabbles, a hostile media, or the growing opposition and defeats that the movement was beginning, bit by bit, to encounter from the outside, this thinning, according to Sarachild, went hand in hand with a historical forgetting. And origins, she felt, mattered.

Sarachild was not alone in believing in the power and significance of the source. In fact, in a different realm but at the very same time, a parallel battle over origins and ownership was heating up, spearheaded by one of the movement's fiercest mainstreamers.

Her name was Betty Friedan.

CHAPTER 3

THE BATTLE OF BETTY

[I]f you are serious about anything in America, to make it fashionable helps.

—Betty Friedan, It Changed My Life

One early fall day in 1968, Betty Friedan was slated to speak on television about the nascent women's movement. Appearing along with her were Roxanne Dunbar of Cell 16 and Rona Jaffe, a novelist affiliated with NOW. Tensions in the green room were heavy that day as a result of recent news events—the feminist fiasco known as the Solanas affair.

Valerie Solanas, the disturbed artist who penned the S.C.U.M. Manifesto and shot and wounded Andy Warhol, blamed men for every evil under the sun. Her manifesto had argued for men's collective annihilation. Warhol in particular peeved her; he had refused to produce her play, titled *Up Your Ass,* and she blamed him for her personal marginalization as an artist. Her nonfatal shot hit him in the gut. According to witnesses, she had aimed lower.

While most thought Solanas insane, a few prominent feminists had turned her into a cause célèbre. Solanas's supporters argued that the shooting of a prominent male avant-garde figure was a bold political statement offered in the name of women's liberation. Roxanne Dunbar was one of the women who identified with Solanas's explosive rage. In August 1968 Dunbar visited Solanas at the New York Women's House of Detention, where she was being held until her hearing. All she could make out clearly were Solanas's piercing black eyes. Solanas's act of lawlessness, Dunbar later wrote, had preempted her own.[1]

Dunbar was not alone in her embrace of the woman in detention. Ti-Grace Atkinson, Friedan's colleague and the president of the New York chapter of Friedan's NOW, embraced Solanas as a heroine of the movement. But Friedan herself was not at all sympathetic to Solanas's plight. When Flo Kennedy, a black civil rights lawyer and prominent NOW member, agreed to be Solanas's attorney in the trial, Friedan grew irate. She cared deeply about maintaining the movement's public image as respectable and legitimate and feared that this militant, "man-hating" stance would taint the public's perception of feminism—and of NOW.[2] To Friedan, Solanas's action was worse than criminal; it was bad publicity.

Such was the context leading up to Dunbar and Friedan's joint television appearance. When Dunbar showed up at the station that day wearing white cotton army surplus trousers, a plain white masculine shirt, and no makeup, Friedan was incensed by her combative, unfeminine appearance. In the studio's dressing room, as the women prepped for their interview, Friedan implored Dunbar to put on some makeup. But Dunbar stood her ground. Friedan told Dunbar that "scruffy feminists" like her were giving the movement a bad name.[3] Dunbar accused Friedan of being afraid of losing her celebrity leadership position to a movement of women committed to collective action without leaders. Friedan called Dunbar an anarchist, which was, perhaps, the only point on which the two women agreed.[4]

Makeup was not the real issue, of course. In Friedan's opinion, radicals like Dunbar were leading the movement astray with their "crazy" talk of sexual politics and their vocal refusal to work within the system and side by side with men. For Friedan, "politics" meant activities that went on in the proverbial City Hall, not the bedroom. Friedan was convinced that radical feminist politics would fail to gain converts in the heartland: Peoria, Illinois.

Peoria was nationally symbolic. In the vaudeville era, comics and other performers tried new stage productions in Peoria to measure audience acceptance. If the show was a hit in Peoria, it was ready for Broadway. Hence the phrase "If it plays in Peoria, it will play anywhere." It was Richard Nixon who reportedly imbued the phrase "how will it play in Peoria?" with new meaning—as a litmus test for how his politics would go over with so-called regular folks living in regular towns. For Friedan, "playing in Peoria" had special meaning. Peoria was her hometown.

Betty Friedan (née Bettye Goldstein) grew up in a big red brick house on the top of a hill in the conservative town whose name, as her biographer notes, was a byword for provincialism. The town was flanked by the Illinois River, which connected it to the Mississippi River and Chicago and the world beyond. Born in 1921, the year after women got the vote, Friedan grew up in comfort along with a brother and sister, a nursemaid, a cook, a butler-chauffeur, a jeweler father, and a mother who had given up her job as an editor of the women's pages of the local newspaper to become a homemaker. Friedan identified strongly with her midwestern roots, despite the fact that she would spend much of her adult life on the East Coast.

In 1963 Friedan would make history with her book *The Feminine Mystique,* which depicted the stultifying, stifling roles of women in modern American society and, in particular, the numbing plight of the full-time homemaker role—a theme uncannily repeated, though now the numbness comes from trying to combine it all, in novel after novel today. *The Feminine Mystique* argued that an internal, psychological crisis of identity, a "false consciousness" (though Friedan shied away from that abstract Marxist term), kept women from realizing their full potential: "It is my thesis that the core of the problem for women today is not sexual," Friedan wrote, "but a problem of identity—a stunting or evasion of growth that is perpetuated by the feminine mystique."[5] The feminine mystique was fed by social institutions like Freudian psychoanalysis and originated in the larger society, Friedan argued, such that women internalized its values and engaged in self-limiting behavior. The mystique crippled women's individual potential and stunted their growth by prescribing their role in life as mothers and wives.

The book hit a nerve among white, Middle American, middle-class housewives. Although *The Feminine Mystique* made top-seller lists in major coastal capitals, Friedan's target audience remained suburban. To continue to have relevance and impact, Friedan believed, feminism must continue to appeal to this crowd. Women outside the largely coastal urban areas where radical feminist groups were most prominent, women Friedan vaguely referred to as "the mainstream," "Middle America," and "middle class," were, in her view, the key to the movement's success. Such women were often conservative in their outlooks and their dress, married, suburban, and largely college-educated. They were PTA mothers and society wives. They were precisely the demographic that these radicals, with their wild hair and wilder ideas, were turning away, Friedan feared.

In 1968, the year of her television appearance with Dunbar, Friedan was a public figure, known not only for her bestseller but for her role as the founder of NOW, which was, at the time, two years old. Not one to keep opinions to herself, Friedan went public with her concerns in her published writings and in her speeches, insisting that the movement's leaders define their mission and mandate in a way that would ensure the continued acceptance of feminism by this crucial demographic of nonradical women. In the late 1960s, as radical feminists captured the media spotlight with sensationalized "zap" actions, Friedan found herself reminding sister organizers not to alienate the heartland. She later gave voice to this insistence, writing that she "continually had to fight attempts to narrow the appeal, to take positions and stands couched in the radical jargon that was okay for the East Village in New York or counterculture San Francisco, but not for the breadth of women throughout America wanting their own political voice." It wasn't the same voice, she implored.[6]

Some radicals themselves shared Friedan's concern. Carol Hanisch, in particular, worried that revolutionary language might repel otherwise potentially sympathetic women. "Stop using the 'in-talk' of the New Left/Hippie movement (Yes, even the word FUCK!!)," she warned fellow radicals. "We can use simple (*real*) language that everyone from Queens to Iowa will understand and not misunderstand." Robin Morgan turned the critique on herself: "I pepper my language with -isms and -ations . . .

this is still the style coming out of the New Left. . . . I'm not reaching . . . these women in their little Iowa dresses." She subsequently cleaned up her act.[7]

Cleaned up or not, the voice Friedan herself equated with radical feminism struck a singular chord. Collapsing their various notes and strands into a single unwieldy screech, Friedan understood radical feminists to be advocating a program of far-out sexual expression and "orgasm politics." She was convinced that this "ideology"—her derisive term for the ideas behind radicals' words—was a dangerous diversion.[8] Women in Peoria proverbial and real would never fully embrace the vision of these "crazies." And it was her duty as the woman who had initially sold feminism to Peoria, Friedan believed, to fashion a feminism that would continue to play among ordinary women in her hometown who were not about to abandon their husbands for vibrators.

As one of NOW's primary architects, Friedan wielded great influence over the documents that shaped the organization's mission and agenda during its formative years. During the years between the founding of NOW (1966) and the publication of her third book, *The Second Stage* (1981), Friedan's battle with radicals unfolded in slow motion.

If radicals were feminism's theoreticians and Gloria Steinem its media-annointed spokeswoman, Betty Friedan was the women's movement's consummate mainstreamer. Scholars have criticized Friedan for the exclusivity of her focus and the derivative nature of her work. But in truth, Betty Friedan was one of the most effective popularizers and savvy marketers of the women's movement. The history of Friedan's life has been written and rewritten; the significance of *The Feminine Mystique* is well known. And yet, in all the commentary around her death in 2006, one important legacy was completely ignored. In recent decades, younger generations of women have been replaying—without necessarily realizing it—Friedan's battle for feminism's soul. Although younger women may think themselves far beyond the plight of their movement mothers, in certain ways, as we'll see in part II, they are still very much in the thick of debates similar to that which took place between Dunbar and Friedan on a 1968 green room floor.

THE MAKING OF BETTY FRIEDAN

What drove a housewife from Peoria to midwife—and mainstream—a social movement? In contrast to younger radical women, whose feminism grew out of their participation in the civil rights and student movements of the 1960s, Betty Friedan came to both feminism and politics from a more practical and unassuming place. A prominent member of the older, more liberal (or "reformist") women's rights–oriented branch of the movement that sought to work within the existing political structure, rather than overthrow it, Friedan's brand of feminism was deeply informed by the liberal optimism of the early 1960s that characterized Kennedy's New Frontier and Johnson's Great Society. Her passion for social justice and her skills were profoundly influenced and shaped by her involvement in the labor movement of the 1940s as well.[9]

Like many of the women who would eventually play a central role in the establishment of the liberal, rather than radical, arm of the women's movement, Friedan grew up in an era of democratic progressivism. The daughter of first- and second-generation Jewish Americans, Friedan developed early on a commitment to issues of social justice and a profound awareness of the devastating effects of anti-Semitism. Her family's collective experience, combined with the sweeping changes implemented through Franklin Delano Roosevelt's New Deal, would deeply impact young Betty's developing sense of the world and her role in it. Her early concern for issues of social justice became the prominent theme of her writing life. Friedan began her writing career as a labor reporter for the *Federated Press* and the *UE News,* the official organ of the United Electrical, Radio, and Machine Workers of America. At the time, the UE was among the most progressive of the labor unions.

While personal and social history provided an entry point for her writing career, it was the study of psychology that offered Friedan an entry point into politics. As a college student at Smith during the 1940s, Friedan had argued that psychology (her major) provided the basis for a progressive political philosophy. Combining democratic ideals with an optimism rooted in psychological discourse, Friedan believed that psychology offered the possibility that people could shape their own worlds. Later, as a graduate student at the University of California–Berkeley, she studied how social structures limited human potential. Influenced by the theories of psychologist Abraham Maslow, she embraced the notion that, once basic biological needs were met, the fundamental human drive was the need to grow and reach one's full potential. Maslow's theories fueled Friedan's growing belief that reigning definitions of femininity were antagonistic to human growth.[10]

The Feminine Mystique began as an ill-fated women's magazine article Friedan wrote following her fifteenth college reunion. In 1957 Friedan conducted a survey of Smith College graduates. Mulling over her fellow alumnae's comments about their education, their subsequent experiences, and their satisfaction with their present lives, Friedan noticed a common theme: discontent. In 1958 she submitted an article based on her findings to a number of women's magazines, but editors rejected it. Friedan decided to try another route and expanded the article into a book. In 1963, fourteen years after the publication of Simone de Beauvoir's *The Second Sex* and the same year Gloria Steinem published "I Was a Playboy Bunny" in *Show* magazine, Friedan's *The Feminine Mystique* became a smash success. It was the bestselling nonfiction paperback of 1964, selling 1.3 million copies in its first edition alone.

Friedan's famous articulation of what kept women down had little to do with later New Left interpretations of power relations. In the final sentence of the book, Friedan cast the revolution as a battle between the internal and the external: "The time is at hand when the voices of the feminine mystique can no longer drown out the inner voice that is driving women on to become complete."[11] If only women would listen to their "inner voices," Friedan maintained, self-realization, growth, and personal fulfillment would be theirs.

As in radical feminist circles, the tension between change as internal and change as institutional animated Friedan's writings throughout her career. For Friedan in *The Feminine Mystique,* the problem (and hence the root of the revolution) began in the psyche, while concrete and measured change was to be fought for in the outside world. In 1964 Friedan extended her position on the internal root cause of women's oppression in a speech entitled "The Crisis in Women's Identity." Also that year, around the same time as *The Feminine Mystique* appeared in paperback, Friedan spoke at conferences held by government agencies and state commissions on the status of women. In these talks, Friedan hinted that women may in fact be oppressing themselves: "It is not laws, nor great obstacles, nor the heels of men that are grinding women down in America today." Rejecting the more openly critical stance of many radicals, who argued that the problem was, indeed, laws and men and systems and institutions, Friedan reiterated that the cause of women's oppression was an internalized and self-limiting blockage.

Friedan of course recognized that in order for women to achieve personal independence, society would have to change as well. No matter how psychologically independent one was in one's mind, in other words, women as a group would not see "real" gains in status unless changes in the outside world accompanied these profound changes from within. As she wrote a few years later, in an editorial published in *NOW Acts* in 1968, "For women, as for black people, self determination cannot be real without economic and political power."[12] In this respect, as with the radicals, the civil rights movement served as her model.

Although she herself did not directly participate, as had many radical feminists, in the civil rights movement, Friedan was deeply influenced by it. She reworked civil rights–based paradigms about group identity to apply to women, much as the suffragists did with abolitionist rhetoric. In a talk before the organizing conference of the National Women's Political Caucus in Washington, D.C., Friedan claimed that women had to have some economic, psychological independence—"our new consciousness of ourselves as people"—in order to exert any real political power. To use the vote in their own interests as women, for instance, they first had to come into awareness of themselves as a group.[13]

For Friedan, feminism was a natural extension of American democratic values, a continuation of the American Revolution. Rooted in the best of American traditions, feminism was not a countercultural program of dismantling and overthrow but a realization of one's rights as a citizen, and as

American as Mom and apple pie. As she later explained, "The logic was inexorable. Once we broke through that feminine mystique and called ourselves human—no more, no less—surely we were entitled to enjoyment of the values which were our American, democratic human right."[14]

To engage in "politics," therefore, meant to run for a town committee or for Congress, or go to law school and become a judge.[15] "Politics" meant legislation, elections, civil service. It was not how you lived but who you voted for. "Political power" meant influence within the legal arena. And the problem with political power, according to Friedan, was not that it was intrinsically corrupt; the problem was that not nearly enough women had it.

BETTY'S BATTLE

In the early twenty-first century, almost every major newsweekly has run a cover story examining the relationship between women and power, from bedroom to board room.[16] Some of these stories argue that women today have it, and others argue that they don't, but they all share a common fascination with the question of what women do with power once they achieve it. Forty years ago, however, this was not the debate. For the most part, the only power many women held was in the home. But even there, power was limited. Spousal rape was legal. Divorce often left women materially bereft and without recourse, since no laws yet existed regarding the equal division of common property. A woman couldn't even get a credit card in her own name. And until 1964, women still lacked the right to equal employment and legal protections from sex discrimination on the job.

In the early 1960s, women's second-class status was increasingly documented. In 1961 Pauli Murray, an African American legal scholar and a member of the President's Commission on the Status of Women Committee on Civil and Political Rights, compiled a list of all the laws that discriminated against women.[17] Murray stressed discrimination in employment as among the most serious forms of discrimination that women faced. In 1964 the pending Civil Rights Act had been broadened to include "sex" as well as race in the section concerning equal employment opportunity (Title VII), and the Equal Employment Opportunities Commission (EEOC) had been established to handle complaints. By 1965 working women were flooding the EEOC with Title VII grievances.

In 1966, as younger, radical women poured their talents and energies into the student movements of the New Left, Murray, Friedan, and a handful of others decided to build what many at the time referred to as an "NAACP for women." The idea that American women needed their own civil rights organization—first articulated by Addie Wyatt, an African American leader of the United Packinghouse Workers of America and the NAACP—had been spreading among professional civil servants and others who risked their government jobs to promote women's issues within the nation's capital.[18] The need for a national organization became more pressing to members of this feminist underground when it became clear that the EEOC was refusing to take women's charges of sex discrimination on the job seriously in spite of its founding mandate.

In the summer of 1966 delegates from the state commissions for women established by President Kennedy gathered for the Third Annual Conference on the Status of Women in Washington, D.C. When it became clear to the delegates that their efforts to force the EEOC to protect women's rights—and specifically to enforce Title VII's injunction against sex discrimination—were in vain, Friedan discussed the situation with other well-positioned attendees. Pauli Murray; Aileen Hernandez, an African American woman who was about to leave her position as a member of the EEOC; Catherine East of the Women's Bureau of the Labor Department; Mary Eastwood, a former member of the President's Commission; Esther Peterson; EEOC commissioner Richard Graham; Congresswoman Martha Griffiths; Kay Clarenbach, head of the Wisconsin Commission on the Status of Women; and Dorothy Haener agreed with Friedan that something had to be done.

With Friedan at the helm, the National Organization for Women held its founding conference on October 29, 1966, in Washington and its first national convention in 1967, attended by 300 women and men. Chapters sprang up across the nation. At the founding meeting of the New York chapter, Flo Kennedy and Muriel Fox—two middle-aged dames decked out in full makeup, suits, and hats—greeted newcomers as if at a tea party. Many attendees had never before attended a political gathering of this kind. Friedan charismatically took the floor, reeling off Labor Department statistics documenting the political, social, and economic discrimination against women in the United States. It was a powerful juxtaposition.

Revolution may have been in the air, but NOW's founders enacted their revolution in an orderly fashion: disciplined, polite, and, above all, respectable. The organization lobbied legislators, collected petitions, sent mass mailings to the White House to pressure government officials, and formed special task forces. While NOW waged many of its high-profile battles in the courts, its members also educated, marched, picketed, and protested to publicize feminist issues. The organization's first target, of course, was the EEOC. In 1967 NOW forced the EEOC to rule that sex-segregated want ads were discriminatory. Prior to this, "His Girl Friday" ads appeared in one column, while managerial opportunities ran in another. NOW also supported a sex discrimination suit brought by flight attendants—then called stewardesses—that year. When the EEOC ruled in NOW's favor in both cases, President Lyndon Johnson issued an executive order barring discrimination by federal contractors. The message was clear: NOW had arrived.

From the beginning, the organization was guided by the principle, perpetually invoked by Friedan, that "Participation in the Mainstream is the Real Revolution."[19] Indeed, as NOW's founding slogan conveyed, revolution had nothing to do with overthrowing the power elite or reformulating what was meant by "political," as radical feminists were suggesting. Rather than overthrow the system, the women who formed NOW wanted to join it. NOW's board was made up of university professors and administrators, state and national labor union officers, local and federal government officials, business executives, physicians, and members of religious orders. Whereas the radical feminist movement was a reflection of women's disillusionment with the male-dominated New Left, the so-called reformist or women's rights branch of the movement was a product of early

1960s liberal optimism. The "reformists" grew disillusioned with it, but they never fully deserted the mainstream political system.

The NOW Statement of Purpose, which Friedan played a lead role in writing, clearly articulated the organization's commitment to participation in that system. NOW's stated mission—"to bring women into full participation in the mainstream of American society now, exercising all the privileges and responsibilities thereby in truly equal partnership with men"—recalled language from *The Feminine Mystique.* Women must have the chance to develop their fullest human potential, the statement read. As human beings and as Americans, such was their natural right.[20] The founders agreed that "by acting now, and by speaking out in behalf of their own equality, freedom, and human dignity," women would ultimately develop confidence in their own ability to shape their lives and their world.[21]

And men, they argued, were necessary.

From day one, Friedan rejected rhetoric and actions that encouraged women to lash out at men. A group of mostly married, middle-age, professional women, NOW's founders made it clear that the organization would welcome male participation. Freidan reminded NOW's constituency of this mandate in her President's Report of 1967: NOW members should not be afraid or ashamed to be called feminists. But they are a new breed—not battle-axes nor man-haters. "Indeed, there are men in our own ranks," she made clear.[22] She reinforced this principle in her correspondence around the Solanas affair. Friedan's often militaristic language suggested the seriousness with which she perceived the threat. Solanas' act was entirely irrelevant, indeed antithetical, to NOW, and Kennedy's defense of it, by extension, was treacherous.

Even with all of NOW's civility, sisterhood was no less contentious here than it was in radical feminist circles. In the earliest days, influential NOW members disagreed on a number of other key points. What, for instance, counted as a legitimately "feminist" issue? Battles of this ilk came to a head as the prospect of the Equal Rights Amendment (ERA) and the debate on reproductive rights advanced. At the 1967 NOW Convention, the organization passed an agenda supporting the ERA and advocating the repeal of antiabortion statutes. A host of members resigned. Labor union women left NOW because they saw the ERA as undercutting legislation protecting women workers. (Labor women ultimately changed their minds and fought strongly for the ERA.) Others left NOW because they felt that reproductive freedom was too radical an issue for the American public to accept.[23] Some of these latter dissenters went on to found the Women's Equity Action League (WEAL), described by its founders as a "conservative NOW" with the goal of achieving equality through strictly conventional means, primarily lobbying and lawsuits. Without the more labor-focused and conservative opposition among their ranks, NOW subsequently pushed the ERA campaign and abortion rights to the forefront of its plank.

Around certain issues, including abortion, and in at least some of their tactics, NOW activism resembled that of the radicals, so much so that as NOW grew in membership and credibility, in influence and visibility, some embittered radicals began to fear that NOW was ripping them off. Beginning in 1967, less than one year after NOW's founding, a certain wilder spirit of protest had entered the organization, in part because a number of the younger members were involved simultaneously in radical feminist groups and organizing.

But cross-pollination was inevitable. Inspired, perhaps, by radicals, three prominent NOW-NYC members organized an event explicitly designed to garner media attention one week in 1967. Staging a demonstration outside the swank Park Avenue headquarters of Colgate-Palmolive (a company NOW was suing for sex discrimination), protestors orchestrated what was probably the nation's first "Flush-In."[24] On posh Park Avenue, they flushed toothpaste and other Colgate products in a make-shift commode to protest discrimination in hiring practices, carrying picket signs that read "Down the Drain with Ajax," "The White Knight Is a Dirty Old Man," and "Cold Power Versus Woman Power." The toilet was sculpted by none other than Kate Millett.

There was more. Later that year NOW members demonstrated in front of the White House on Mother's Day for "Rights, Not Roses," demanding that the ERA be brought before Congress for a vote. Adding a touch of the theatrical, they dumped piles of aprons on the White House lawn. Also in

1967, NOW board members staged an ad hoc protest at Biltmore Men's Bar and Grill when, after a lengthy meeting at the Biltmore Hotel, they were refused service in the all-male club. The board members had intended to hold a sit-in, but someone's mole-ish husband allegedly tipped off the management, who closed the bar early at 4:00 p.m. The women picketed anyway and decided to hold a national day of action against sex discrimination in public accommodations on Susan B. Anthony's birthday. This was a time when women could be refused entry in some places if they were wearing pants. With television cameras capturing the drama, NOW members gracefully participated in sit-ins at the Stouffers Grill in Pittsburgh, the Polo Lounge at the Beverly Hills Hotel, and McSorley's Old Ale House and the Oak Room at the Plaza in New York.

Some of the younger NOW members were also active in radical feminist circles, even though their philosophies about revolution were seemingly at odds. Some, like Jo Freeman, snuck off to NOW meetings behind her comrades' backs, fearing their radical sisters would think they were selling out. She kept her NOW membership a secret. Once she left women's liberation, however, she could be "out" as a member of NOW.[25]

Instead of peaceful coexistence, a rivalry began, and charges of co-optation were fierce. "NOW more and more used the radical slogans, organizing and action ideas to build its ranks—without acknowledging it," accused Redstockings member Kathie Sarachild.[26] Friedan denied the charge. In 1969 she had put out feelers to the radical women's groups and, at Susan Brownmiller's invitation, attended a small consciousness-raising group. Friedan was less than impressed. "As far as I'm concerned, we're *still* the radicals," she quipped. "We raised our consciousness a long time ago."[27] Just as radicals were charging NOW with ripping off their slogans and ideas, Friedan blamed them for perverting and distorting the idea that "The Personal Is Political," a concept she took credit for first bringing to light.

In the fierce battle for control over the early women's movement, Friedan faced a losing month in November 1968. NOW had gathered over 500 women from disparate groups from the expanding women's movement at a Congress to Unite Women staged in a grungy public high school on West Seventeenth Street in New York City. Friedan felt deeply alienated by the forms of protest that took place.

The conference aimed to fuse moderate and radical feminist interests, and there were at least three other similar regional conferences in San Francisco, Los Angeles, and Chicago. But on the first night of the three-day gathering in New York, the rowdy, irreverent spirit of younger, radical women—electric and full of charge—dominated the meeting's mood and agenda. A group of radicals from Boston took the stage and performed a bit of hallmark guerrilla theater: They formed a semicircle around one of their members, who proceeded to cut off the luxurious long blond hair of another, to chin length. The women explained to the audience that the cultivation of stereotypical feminine appearance (long hair) had political implications. Short hair, they explained, was a rejection of the conventional feminine image and therefore a revolutionary act. The audience was riveted. Pandemonium ensued. "Don't do it!" cried one woman in the audience. Some shouted that long hair was both beautiful and countercultural. Others denounced long hair as the sign of the hipster movement "chick." And then, a shout from the stands: "Men like my breasts too; do you want me to cut them off?" The room went still. Friedan looked on, aghast.[28]

Describing the hair-cutting incident a few years later, Friedan (with strikingly sexist language) called it "a hysterical episode."[29] She was appalled at the idea that feminists were trying to push the message that "to be a liberated women [sic] you had to *make yourself ugly*."[30] That same night, she reported, other NOW members who had come in from Syracuse, Buffalo, and the suburbs of Westchester, Long Island, and New Jersey shared her disgust. Media coverage of the women's movement was continuing to cast it as out of touch with and hostile to the majority of American women. "The angries" became synonymous with "feminist." An article titled "The New Feminists: Revolt Against 'Sexism'" that appeared in *Time* magazine in November 1969 reported that "[m]any of the new feminists are surprisingly violent in mood, and seem to be trying, in fact, to repel other women rather than attract them."[31]

The hair-cutting spectacle went deep; to a certain extent, it symbolized the differences that philosophically and stylistically separated women young and old, radical and Establishment. Whereas a number of the young radicals believed that individual actions (like short hair, or organizing a session at a conference to discuss orgasms) mattered profoundly, Friedan and her NOW peers believed that individual actions mattered little until women also occupied positions of political power. "I didn't think a thousand vibrators would make much difference—or that it mattered who was in the missionary position—if unequal power positions in real life weren't changed," she wrote. It was a critique echoed three decades later by second-wave veterans who would accuse third-wave sex-positive feminists of once again elevating the orgasm gap over the wage gap as the primary object of their concern.

Friedan believed that *economic* imbalance subverted sex, making sex itself into a power game where no one could win.[32] Furthermore, she knew, the sexual and stylistic emphasis would hardly keep the interest of women in Peoria. And it wasn't helping matters that nearly every time a television station aired a segment on the women's movement, the piece ended with images of frightening-looking women learning karate.

In 1970, just as Millett's *Sexual Politics* climbed to the top of the bestseller charts, Friedan declared rhetorical war on radical feminism. She went public with her critique, condemning its language as "the new abstractions," "the new feminist ideology," and "pseudo-radicalism." Earlier she had limited her critique to feminist venues. But in January 1969 she delivered a hostile talk at the Cornell University Intersession on Women, entitled "Tokenism and the Pseudo-Radical Cop Out: Ideological Traps for New Feminists to Avoid." Her comments were largely a response to Millett, who had given a talk at Cornell the previous November, titled "Sex, Politics, and the New Feminism."[33]

Although previously reluctant to voice her dissent outside feminist circles, Friedan changed her tune when it became clear that Millett's book, which she dismissively dubbed "the ideological Bible for the new feminism," was having a significant influence beyond radical feminist circles.[34] Friedan granted that Millett had mixed some "brilliant insights" in with her rage. But when others espoused Millett's rhetoric of sex warfare, she charged, it was rage without brilliance. And this, she feared, was dangerous. In 1970 Friedan was asked why she thought the new "trend"—the new bedroom politics—was catching fire. "[B]ecause it's sexy; it suits the communications media, the TV," she quipped. "It's more glamorous than talking about jobs and discrimination and women in politics" and made for kickier headlines indeed than child care centers or abortion reform.[35] But as Friedan also noted, sensational headlines were also a way for the media to dismiss the entire movement as a dirty, silly joke.[36]

In a critique of sexual politics for *Social Policy* magazine that indirectly attacked Millett,[37] Friedan deplored "the orgasm talk that leaves things unchanged, the rage that will produce a backlash—down with sex, down with love, down with childrearing" and concluded that the "highly verbalized sexual emphasis" was distracting women from collective political action.[38] Casting sexual politics as a "fruitless impotent reaction" that ultimately would lead the movement to "sterile dead ends," Friedan implied that if radicals had their way, the fledgling movement would prematurely abort. "Real" women, she suggested, would ultimately choose a feminism that supported the traditionally feminine values of family, life, and love. Reinforcing the opposition between her vision and radicals' through rather loaded metaphors—fertility versus sterility, life versus death, patriotism versus anti-Americanism—Friedan drew on language that would eventually resurface, ironically, in the antifeminist rhetoric of the New Right.[39]

Friedan's deepest fear, no doubt, was lesbianism.

By 1972, the gay-straight divide would hit a number of women's groups, but it hit earlier in NOW due in large part to Friedan's blatant and open mistrust. Outside of NOW, lesbian feminist groups seemed disproportionately influential because they wrote hard-hitting and often shocking articles that provoked a great deal of debate within the movement. Within the organization, lesbian women came out of the closet and began to agitate for official recognition of rights, which were not included in the original NOW charter. "Lesbian is the one word that can cause the Executive Committee [of NOW] a collective heart attack," wrote lesbian NOW member Rita Mae Brown in a statement detailing the homophobia within the organization.[40] Friedan infamously referred to lesbians within NOW as the "lavender menace."[41]

To Friedan, this lavender menace (a play on the Red Menace of communism in the 1950s) went hand in glove with the orgasm-feminism, "man-haters," and "anti-family" feminists. Rita Mae Brown responded to Friedan's diss by forming a guerrilla group that staged an invasion of the Second Conference to Unite Women wearing lavender T-shirts with "Lavender Menace" emblazoned across the front.[42] At the opening session of the congress, the "Menaces" cut the lights, grabbed the microphone, and seized the stage. They took the organizers to task for not including out lesbians on the program and handed out their manifesto, "The Woman-Identified Woman," which argued that because lesbian women were at the forefront of the struggle for women's liberation, support for lesbians and an open commitment to lesbian liberation was essential to the movement's fulfillment and success. The divisiveness at the gathering led some women to call it the "Congress to Divide Women."

To Friedan, such divisiveness spelled disaster. On other occasions, Friedan had derided lesbianism as a "red herring." If feminism continued to go in this direction, she warned, it would "boomerang into an era of sexual McCarthyism that might really paralyze the women's movement, and hurt *them* [lesbians] and everyone."[43] Coining a controversial term to describe the threat, Friedan invoked the scare tactics of an earlier era, all the while insistently denying that she was homophobic. She was just a "square" from Peoria, she claimed, and a reflection of "the mainstream." (In 1977 she finally admitted her homophobic feelings both to herself and to the large audience of women gathered at the National Women's Conference in Houston, where her words apparently brought down the house.[44])

In the end, Friedan conceded that her antilesbian campaign was ineffective. "I didn't succeed in convincing them," she lamented.[45] Ultimately, however, Friedan may have lost this battle but won the war. Many lesbian women felt alienated from NOW and left the organization, "purged" by Friedan's assaults.

In the years that followed, "The Personal Is Political" became, for some, a call to NOW's leadership to recognize lesbian rights as civil rights both within and beyond the organization—functioning much as the slogan had for the women of the New Left. For others, the slogan became shorthand for the political infighting within NOW that was often very personal in nature. For Betty Friedan, it remained a powerful phrase, one that had been sorely—but not, she hoped, irretrievably—corrupted.

REFASHIONING FEMINISM

The lavender menace fiasco—and the lack of a concerted focus on issues Friedan felt were truly important, such as child care—left NOW's founder feeling alienated from the organization she had brought to life. Perceiving her organization to be co-opted, Friedan took her politics elsewhere, always searching for ways to broaden the appeal.

In 1970 during a two-hour "farewell address" at NOW's Fourth National Conference in Des Plaines, Illinois, retiring president Betty Friedan surprised everyone by taking it to the streets. It was during this address that she called for the "Women's Strike for Equality" (detailed in chapter 2). From Friedan's vantage point, the strike was a public relations campaign. In her memoir, she described her motivation for organizing it. By staging what she called "a serious action," she hoped to get the focus off sexual politics and back to the fight for equal opportunity in jobs, education, child care, and women's right to control their own bodies—issues that were finally being addressed.[46] Friedan urged the organizing coalition to make sure that the day would not be dominated by radicals, and indeed, recall, the coalition defined "politics" as she did. Her stamp was particularly evident in New York City, where the strikers had ended their day with a rally at City Hall, the symbolic center of political power.

After it was over, Friedan publicly called August 26, 1970 "a political miracle experienced personally by the women who made it happen" and animatedly instructed the crowd gathered in Bryant Park: "This is not a bedroom war. This is a political movement, and it will change the politics."[47] Friedan used the occasion to remind her audience that women's self-denigration, and not men, was the enemy. She wanted heterosexual women to be able to identify as feminists without having to question their intimate connections with men. Her words were picked up by national newspapers, including the *New York Times*.

According to Friedan, the strike did something more than help many women take a first step toward developing the self-confidence they needed to become fully actualized human beings; it made them feel radiant. Describing the impact of that late-summer day on countless lives, Friedan would often quote from letters women had sent her in which they described the way the strike had made them feel: "It made all women feel beautiful." "It made me feel ten feet tall."[48] By giving women a collective jolt of self-confidence, Friedan maintained, the march was a turning point for the movement. On August 26, she wrote, it suddenly became both political and glamorous to be a feminist.[49]

Starting in 1971, and fully aware of the irony, Friedan began writing a regular column for *McCall's*, "Betty Friedan's Notebook," in which she continued her effort to refashion feminism into something more classically "feminine."[50] She also wrote for *The New York Times Magazine, Saturday Review, Harper's, Newsday, TV Guide, Mademoiselle, Ladies' Home Journal, True Magazine,* and *Family Circle*—but nothing symbolized her transition from movement insider to commercial marketer more than her tenure at *McCall's*, which lasted until 1974.

Friedan's media-savvy was prescient. In 2002 actress Ashley Judd wore a T-shirt with the words "This is what a feminist looks like" to a photo shoot for *Glamour* magazine, and *Ms.* subsequently invited her to appear on the cover of its spring 2003 issue, along with fellow feminists Margaret Cho, Whoopi Goldberg, and Camryn Manheim, to show a new generation that feminists were not all axe-wielding and frumpy. In writing "Betty Friedan's Notebook," Friedan basically did the same thing. The column was an attempt to replace one image of feminism with another. While Friedan publicly described her engagement with *McCall's* as a way of "bowing out . . . of the power struggle," a space in which she might "try to come to new terms with the political as personal, in my own life," these columns were her mass-scale rebranding campaign.[51]

Friedan was fully aware of the irony that the author of *The Feminine Mystique*—an exposé of how women's magazines (among other forces) helped keep women down—was now writing for a magazine once considered a cause of the problem that she had given a name. Yet she wisely recognized the significance of a women's magazine as a vehicle for dissemination—much as the youth voting campaign, Rock the Vote, recognizes MTV as an effective partner because of its appeal among the audience they wish to reach.

Although addressed to "the movement at large," Friedan's columns were specifically targeted to 8 million readers, the suburban housewives, women with children and/or jobs, married and divorced, who still had to deal with housekeeping, meals, and laundry.[52] Calling attention to her own background, Friedan fashioned a voice she thought *McCall's* readers would accept as their own. "I am a revolutionary," she explained to her readers. "I also happen to be an American pragmatist, 'Middle American,' if you will, since I did grow up in Peoria, Illinois."[53]

Friedan was merciless in her condemnation of the radical feminists who had usurped her and NOW. Many of her entries bore titles that emphasized the necessity of moving "Beyond Women's Liberation" (August 1972). Others viciously trashed radicals: "The Anti-Man Extremists Are Not the True Radicals—They Are the Enemy of Change" (May 1972). Still others ("The Need for Love" [June 1972], and "We Don't Have to Be That Independent" [January 1973]) reassured *McCall's* readers that identification with the women's movement did not require renunciation of one's dependence on men.[54] "Femininity is being a woman and feeling good about it, so the better you feel about yourself as a person, the better you feel about being a woman," she wrote. "And, it seems to me, the better you are able to love men."

The *McCall's* publicity department played up and magnified the battle between Friedan and radicals. In July 1972, the magazine issued a press release to call attention to the following month's issue, heralding "Betty Friedan Denounces 'Female Chauvinist Boors' in Women's Movement: Says 'Sexual Politics' Can Cause Dangerous Backlash." The authors of the press release went further in calling attention to Friedan's disagreement with radicals. The second line read: "In McCall's Article Reappraising Goals and Methods, Founder of Women's Lib Defends Marriage and Family; Calls Male Conspiracy Non-Existent, Female Sexists 'Freaks.'"

Shuttling between personal anecdote and political reflection, Friedan interspersed political matters with diarylike installments about her personal life: shopping trips with her daughter, feelings about turning fifty, and other musings appropriate for a women's magazine. In the one column, Friedan awkwardly combined the discourses of feminism and fashion in an attempt to help her readers come to terms with the meaning and the benefits of "liberation." Her columns stressed a revolution grounded in consumption, beauty, and self-esteem and presented a vision of personal politics that was decidedly less focused on external change than the one she had presented back when she was founding NOW. Although she had accused radicals of overemphasizing lifestyle change at the expense of real political engagement, in her columns she was doing exactly that. If in her *McCall's* columns the founder of NOW did not quite place feminism back in the bedroom, she certainly domesticated it by directing it away from City Hall and back in the house.

In *McCall's,* this lighter, gentler feminism, however, served its purpose. Redefining empowerment in language befitting a magazine about housekeeping, meals, and clothes, Friedan made feminism feel familiar to women who were not predisposed to strike, boycott, or march. The feedback she received from readers confirmed her sense that her words were hitting their mark. A number wrote to tell her that her articles about women's liberation put them much at ease.

When Friedan's stint with *McCall's* came to an end in 1974, she returned to her roots as a writer of books. In her next two books, she would shift back and forth between her emphasis on self-esteem and legislative political activism.

In 1976 Friedan published an assortment of her columns, articles, and essays—*It Changed My Life*—that recounted the history of the movement thus far. Retelling the story of where things went wrong, she once more sought to intervene and set the movement straight. Hopeful that her words would again appeal to a wide swath of American women, she warned her readers of the misguided zeal of radical feminism. She concluded the book with an "Open Letter to the Women's Movement," in which she declared that the time had come for feminists to "say no," once and for all, "to sexual politics and to the vicious and divisive power struggles within the movement" and focus instead on the restructuring of institutions. Although the book had neither the depth nor the initial impact of *The Feminine Mystique*, it shared its predecessor's close analysis of the relationship between rhetorical authority and ideological control. Friedan continued this theme in a third book, *The Second Stage*, published in 1981, which was an extended call to restructure the workplace and to make this restructuring part of the American political and economic agenda—a version of feminism that would take on vital relevance for the soon-to-be career women of the 1980s, and one that remains at the heart of contemporary debate about women, work, and life.

Friedan wrote that the personal was both more and less political "than our own rhetoric ever implied." She argued that women now had to break through a new mystique, come to terms with their new realities, and move into the "second stage." In a play on the title of the book that had made her a celebrity, Friedan coined a new term, "*feminist* mystique," to describe the myth being perpetuated and disseminated by her more radical sisters.[55] If women were to continue to move forward in their march, Friedan maintained, they would have to expose and successfully shatter this new mystique just as they had the feminine mystique a decade ago. Little did Friedan know that a decade later, feminism's daughters would come of age only to turn their backs not merely on the radicals' brand of feminism, but on hers as well.

Part II

Daughters

CHAPTER 4

POSTFEMINIST PANACHE

It is out of the deep belief that some feminisms are better than others that I have written this book.

—*Katie Roiphe,* The Morning After

Once upon a time in the 1990s, a precocious, curly-haired twenty-five-year-old Princeton grad student with a B.A. from Harvard and a famous second-wave feminist mother wrote a controversial essay in *The New York Times.* What if the rape-crisis movement was a crock? she suggested. What if all the antirape marches—where hundreds of college coeds marched arm in arm, carrying candles and beating drums, through the streets of Princeton, Cambridge, and Ann Arbor shouting "No Means No!" and "Women Unite! Take Back the Night!"—dramatized a problem not in society at large but in women's heads? What if women weren't perpetual victims by definition—what if one woman's date rape was just another woman's bad night?

To card-carrying feminists of the second wave who had fought long and hard to get rape taken seriously, Katie Roiphe with her controversial thesis—presented not only as a *New York Times* op-ed but also in a lengthy *New York Times Magazine* article and as a book, *The Morning After: Sex,*

Fear, and Feminism on Campus—was an abomination. Second-wave feminists had criminalized rape and raised public awareness so that women like Roiphe might live in a safer world. Beginning in the late 1960s, they fought for legal reforms that made rape a prosecutable crime. Susan Brownmiller, a leader of the antirape movement and later founder of Women against Pornography, electrified the nation with her surprise bestseller in 1975, *Against Our Will: Men, Women, and Rape,* in which she argued that rape was the central mechanism by which men oppress women throughout history and all over the globe. "[R]ape is nothing more or less than a conscious process of intimidation by which *all men* keep *all women* in a state of fear," she wrote.[1] Scholars like Catherine MacKinnon made breakthroughs in the legal sphere. In 1979 MacKinnon argued that sexual harassment is a form of sexual discrimination under Title VII of the Civil Rights Act of 1964; her argument was adopted by the United States Supreme Court in 1986 in *Meritor Savings Bank v. Vinson.* (The next year she would take on the issue of pornography in *Feminism Unmodified,* along with Andrea Dworkin, whose book *Intercourse* famously argued that heterosexual sex expressed patriarchal oppression, although it did not argue, as has often been assumed, that all sex is rape.) Second-wave feminists had successfully criminalized not only sexual harassment, but date rape—legally considered as rape or nonconsensual sexual activity between people who are already acquainted, be they casual acquaintances, lovers, or two people on a date, where consent is either absent or given under duress. Their work resulted in thousands of prosecutions and convictions of rapists over the years.[2]

By the late 1980s, the anti–sexual violence movement had hit the campus: Take Back the Night marches and speak-outs against date rape became staples of college life. Student-run women's centers, rape-crisis hotlines, workshops, and peer-counseling groups were as common as Jansport knapsacks and milk-crate shelves. The impact of the antirape movement on college campuses was tangible. Many campuses installed special lights and emergency telephones. The campus felt like a safer—or at the very least a better lit—place.

Then: Roiphe. Two decades after Brownmiller's cutting-edge tome established the feminist position on rape, Roiphe's ideas could not have seemed more heretical. "In classrooms and journals, in lectures and coffee shops, academics everywhere are talking about rape," began Roiphe in her November 1991 op-ed, provocatively titled "Date Rape Hysteria." "While real women get battered, while real mothers need day care, certain feminists are busy turning rape into fiction. Every time one Henry James character seizes the hand of another Henry James character, someone is calling it rape." Far from gratitude or solidarity, Roiphe's take on the work of older feminists was irreverent—even condemnatory. The "neo-puritan preoccupation" with women's "victim status," Roiphe wrote, was fueled by an outdated model of sexuality, one in which men want sex and women don't. He pushes, she resists. Such a model infantilized modern women by treating them like children who weren't responsible for their actions—and she believed that certain feminists were to blame.[3]

Roiphe followed her op-ed with an even more aggressive and strident—some might say feminist-bashing—4,700-word essay in the *New York Times Magazine* that proclaimed "Rape Hype Betrays Feminism." It included a damning (and hotly contested) interpretation of rape statistics. Roiphe pointed out that in a 1985 survey undertaken by *Ms.* magazine and financed by the National Institute of Mental Health, 73 percent of the women categorized as rape victims did not initially define their experience as rape—rather, the psychologist conducting the study did. Furthermore, if there were really a crisis, if one in every four women is raped, as posters on college campuses claimed, if 25 percent of Roiphe's women friends were being raped, wouldn't she know it? Roiphe described her shock when a college senior told her that she thought one in four was too conservative an estimate, that it was closer to one in two. This was the true crisis, Roiphe felt: that young women were walking around believing that 50 percent of women were raped, "a hyperbole containing within it a state of perpetual fear."[4]

In addition to challenging rape statistics, the *New York Times Magazine* piece made an unfavorable comparison between second-wave feminists and nineteenth-century Victorians: Second wavers, in Roiphe's view, were as old-fashioned and constraining as corsets and stays. Things were different now. It was time to wrap up certain ideas in mothballs and put them on the shelf. Because some feminisms, like the kind that urged women to stop thinking of themselves as passive and helpless innocents, as Roiphe suggested in the introduction to her book, were better than others.

Roiphe's argument was notable not so much for what she argued (which was not as original as it was hyped to be, as we will see) but because it sparked a war between—and also among—generations of feminists. Second wavers responded with fury to her claims. That Roiphe and her friends may not have been raped themselves did not mean that rape was not a serious problem, argued Brownmiller and company. What was more, they countered, only by the very privileges granted her by the women's movement had Roiphe been able to attend Harvard and Princeton (both all-male schools at the time of her birth). Because of the antirape movement itself, Roiphe and her friends could walk to class in an environment of relative safety compared to the past. And if not for feminism—by which of course they meant *their* kind—Roiphe would have been unlikely to publish a book at all, let alone one dismissing the prevalence of sexual coercion and rape. Many women Roiphe's age who had themselves experienced sexual coercion shared their elders' appall.

But Roiphe had tapped into something powerful. Much to the old guard's dismay, her argument caught a wave. Roiphe was smart, appealing, young, and pedigreed—two Ivy League degrees, famous parents (her mother, Anne, a high-profile feminist novelist), and a platform in the *New York Times*. What was more, she possessed rebel panache. Her argument was embraced by an array of supporters, including some on the Right (who Roiphe later insisted could not possibly have read her book). It was as if she'd given feminism—or was it antifeminism?—a face-lift. *The Morning After* garnered hundreds of reviews, interviews, and features. *The New York Times* hailed it as "one of those books that defines the Zeitgeist."[5] On the cover of the book, conservative George Will called it "a bombshell." It was one of the most talked-about titles of the year. Roiphe herself even appeared in an ad for Coach, wearing a pricey leather handbag and a smirk.

If it were only Roiphe garnering attention for these sorts of ideas, perhaps Brownmiller and others might have been less distraught. But more and more, young women who called themselves "feminists" seemed to be distancing themselves from the second wave—or at least their image of it—and writing books that publicly chastised the women's movement for allegedly imagining women as fragile flowers. Still in her twenties, Naomi Wolf had appeared on the scene in 1991 as a strong new voice of what Roiphe might have called "old school" feminism. In her bestseller *The Beauty Myth,* Wolf had argued that the beauty industry oppressed women with profitable double standards that were impossible to live up to. Wolf carried on the second-wave legacy while giving it a much-needed makeover. But in 1993 she came out with *Fire with Fire,* in which she identified the old-school approach as "victim feminism" and argued that women who flaunted women's victim status made themselves impervious to the power actually available to them. "Victim feminist assumptions about universal female goodness and powerlessness, and male evil, are unhelpful in the new moment for they exalt what I've termed 'trousseau reflexes'—outdated attitudes women need least right now," Wolf wrote, angering the old guard even as she continued to advance some rather classic feminist claims.[6] Then, in a book dubbed the sequel to Roiphe's, a young, streetwise, amateur boxer from Portland named Rene Denfeld called older feminists "New Victorians"—prudes on a moral crusade who advocate political helplessness. The New Victorianism, Denfeld argued, was why women in their twenties and thirties were abandoning the women's movement in droves.

Older women who called themselves feminists were attacking the movement as well—and academic feminism in particular. Christina Hoff Sommers, a professor of philosophy at Clark University, suggested that feminism had betrayed women. Noretta Koertge, a professor at Indiana University, and Daphne Patai, a professor at the University of Massachusetts–Amherst, coauthored an exposé of the nefarious world of academic feminism, offering, their subtitle promised, some "cautionary tales." They described Women's Studies classrooms where indoctrination was thinly disguised as pedagogy, where militant students bullied the rest, and where the teacher's emphasis on "support" and "finding one's voice" turned group discussions into therapy sessions. In a second book, *Heterophobia,* Patai slammed feminist ideologues for creating a repressive atmosphere in universities and documented cases in which faculty members (mostly men) had had their careers ruined by false allegations and frivolous, opportunistic complaints. Meanwhile, Emory University humanities professor Elizabeth Fox-Genovese penned a book-length tirade against campus Women's Studies departments with the damning subtitle *How Today's Feminist Elite Has Lost Touch with the Real Concerns of Women,* in which she insisted that feminists were out of touch because they spoke in abstractions and posed solutions that seemed to lead to the disintegration of the family rather than its reconstruction.

The new reclaimers were mainstreamers in the tradition of Betty Friedan. They wanted to take the movement back. And though popular understandings of where and why feminism went wrong had certainly proliferated since Friedan's time, the message these latter-day mainstreamers delivered was strikingly the same: They believed that feminists, with their offputting rhetoric and excessive claims, were responsible for alienating women from their own cause.

While these new spokeswomen disagreed over the corrective, they all agreed that the old feminism was far too removed from everyday women's lives to be effecting real change. They attacked the language and the terms of academic feminism—"pig latin," Wolf called it—much as Friedan had attacked the "abstract," "intellectual" language of the radical feminists on the coasts. Yet unlike Friedan (who was at least *from* Peoria), the new reclaimers purporting to tout a populist feminism often did so from a more distanced perch. College-educated, articulate, and graced with access to prominent publishing houses and other media outlets, the younger among them (born between 1960 and 1980) were fortunate members of a generation that could afford to take feminism and its gains for granted. These were women who had grown up empowered and who identified, many of them, with people in power. Some were arguing that because enough women like them had made it, "certain" kinds of feminisms no longer had currency for anyone at all. The professors, however, were women who clicked in the 1970s but clacked, so to speak, in the 1990s; they felt disconnected from a movement that they had helped create.[7]

Both groups of women—the young upstarts and the turncoat professors—took a cue, to various degrees, from University of the Arts Professor Camille Paglia, who, in 1990, published a book that refuted central aspects of Kate Millett's *Sexual Politics*. In her erudite tome *Sexual Personae,* Paglia argued that men are inherently violent, agreeing with Millett. And sex, she claimed, is risky. Yet unlike Millett, Paglia was uninterested in changing the way men and women related—especially around sex. "There is a daemonic instability in sexual relations that we may have to accept," wrote Paglia. "Feminists, seeking to drive the power relations out of sex, have set themselves against nature."[8]

Dazzling and polished, and as subtle as a tornado, Paglia set off a storm of controversy with her charge that old-school feminists were basically unnatural. Her premise, a fundamental reversal of the logic behind *Sexual Politics,* riled feminists inside and outside the academy—many of whom had spent the previous twenty years building institutions and careers dedicated to the analysis and redistribution of power and the eradication of sexual inequity. But *Sexual Personae* was a popular success, the paperback from Vintage Books appearing on the *New York Times* Best Seller list for a full five weeks.

Paglia's challenge to the classic feminist view of sexual dynamics, her belief in women's innate power, and her feisty, rebel posture set a precedent. Even if she herself was uninterested in reconstructing the movement, her defiance paved the way. Together, these hot new spokeswomen created what many old-school types took as an atmosphere of blame. Rejecting some of second-wave feminism's most foundational premises, messages, and accomplishments, some embraced ideas once considered retro but now reimagined as cutting edge. Besides their aversion to "old-school" feminism, one of the themes that linked the new feminists was the idea that women bear more responsibility for their own lives than old-guard feminists would currently own up to. Whether in bed, at home, or at work, women brainwashed by the "old" feminism were falsely blaming others for their discontent, when the real problems now lay within. To this brazen new wave of reclaimers, the feminist cult of victimology was the new evil to overcome.

To her opponents, Roiphe, a skilled polemicist albeit one who might benefit from a bit more empathy for her less-privileged peers (not to mention her feminist elders), seemed to be calling for a return to a day when "oppression" was just called life. "If there is any transforming to be done," Roiphe argued, "it is to transform everyday experience back into everyday experience."[9] Karen Lehrman, author of a book titled *The Lipstick Proviso: Women, Sex, and Power in the Real World,* whose glamorous jacket photo shows her giving the camera a classic come-hither look, agreed. "Under real feminism," wrote Lehrman, "women had ultimate responsibility for their problems, happiness, and lives. The personal is no longer political."[10]

Lehrman's sentence captured a full-circle irony: A wave of women had empowered their female offspring only to be rebuffed by them. For many old-school feminists, the women they were fighting for and those they were fighting against had become one and the same: their daughters—the so-called postfeminists.

THE 1980S AND EARLY 1990S

The term "postfeminist" is itself rife with paradox. Resurfacing in the early 1990s to describe the belief that feminism was dead because it was no longer needed, the word was also used to describe the new coterie of media-annointed spokeswomen who identified in some way with feminism but made their reputations attacking it.[11] Small in numbers but high in visibility, they positioned themselves as not only after but in some ways against core principles of the second wave. They were, in effect, postfeminism's feminists.

One of the reasons the public battle between visions was so acute during this time is that interest in feminism during the 1980s had waned. Signs that the movement as a whole was weakening appeared by the mid-1970s. By the 1980s, the movement practically moved underground. As Pulitzer Prize–winning journalist Susan Faludi had documented in *Back-lash,* feminism and feminists had been publicly flamed and blamed in the media during this decade for everything from harried career women's burnout to infertility epidemics among the miserable and unwed. Popular culture was rife with portrayals of independent, professional women as insane malcontents—like Glenn Close's character in *Fatal Attraction,* a hysterical single editor who stalks her married lover and boils his family's pet rabbit. In 1984 a young law student named Mona Charen published an article titled "The Feminist Mistake" in the *National Review,* in which she argued that while women's liberation had given her generation "high incomes, our own cigarette, the option of single parenthood, rape crisis centers, personal lines of credit, free love, and female gynecologists," it had in return "effectively robbed us of one thing upon which the happiness of most women rests—men."[12] Equality, it seemed, was causing women deep pain.

Meanwhile, a handful of victories for women in the 1970s were slowly being undermined. In many respects, the organized women's movement began to lose momentum and coherence following the success of *Roe v. Wade* in 1973. In the fall of 1975, NOW, rife with internal dissension, had been publicly exposed for voting fraud at the organization's national conference in Philadelphia. After the breakup of radical feminism's most active cells, proponents of women's liberation had retrenched. With new editors at the helm of *Ms.,* feminism's flagship magazine began to drop its focus on political change, running articles that instead emphasized individual professional mobility, such as "Exactly What to Say to Get the Salary You Want" and "How to Know When You're Stuck and Other Career Tips." As the 1970s rolled into the 1980s, women entered—and reentered—the workforce in record numbers and needed advice on how to make it professionally in a man's world. No longer the voice of revolution, the magazine appealed to the reader concerned with getting ahead. It was an era of me-first feminism—at least as popularly conceived.

In November 1975 the Equal Rights Amendment—first introduced in Congress back in 1923—was defeated in a number of key progressive states. The defeat was notable because only a few years earlier, the amendment's passage had seemed a sure thing. (It passed the House in 1971 and the Senate in 1972, but was then killed during the state ratification process, three states short of passing, thanks in large part to the anti-ERA activism of conservative poster girl Phyllis Schlafly and her Eagle Forum.)

Except in its defeats, feminism was no longer making headlines in mainstream newspapers and magazines. No more glamorous Gloria Steinem gracing the cover of *Life*. No more Kate Millett scowling from the cover of *Time*. No more Miss America protests, flush-ins, sit-ins, or national strikes making the evening news. Instead, headlines sounded death knells: "Does the Women's Movement Still Have Clout?" "Can Feminism Survive the ERA Defeat?" "Is NOW on the Brink of Then?" "Is Feminism Finished?" and the cruelest: "Is Gloria Steinem Dead?" These would be neither the first nor the last obituaries for the movement. But they would set the tone for decades to come.

As would Ronald Reagan. The election of Reagan to the presidency in 1980 introduced a host of new threats to the fragile gains the movement had achieved. At the same time, the New Right was gaining strength, moving into the public spotlight, and talking politically about sexuality— abortion and lesbianism in particular. Members of the New Right openly declared their opposition to abortion and homosexuality and affirmed the "natural" fit between women's nature, homemaking, and motherhood. In 1975 the Right to Life movement took hold. New groups rallying under that name called a massive march on Washington in an attempt to roll back *Roe v. Wade*. Two years later the Hyde Amendment, the first of a series of legislative efforts to whittle away the right to abortion, cut off federal Medicaid funding for abortion, guaranteeing that it would be available only for those who could afford to pay. In addition to eliminating women's access to abortion, the new regime's domestic programs sought to restrict sex education, contraceptive services, and feminist-inspired programs such as battered women's shelters with the so-called Family Protection Act.

With opposition rising and the fate of the ERA on the brink, internal battles among feminist writers and thinkers were pushed aside. As the mainstream political climate became increasingly hostile, many prominent feminist thinkers retreated from overt activism and dispersed into the academy and other professional enclaves, turning feminism into a career. But feminism as a popular movement went off radar. To the "average" American woman trying to get ahead, or get by, the women's movement no longer seemed relevant.

Out of the limelight did not mean dead, of course. With the academy becoming a central location for feminist activity, debate shifted from popular magazines and trade books published by large publishing houses to academic journals and scholarly tomes published by university presses. The feminist journal *SIGNS,* which debuted in 1975, and *Feminist Studies,* which began in 1972, published seminal works of feminist scholarship throughout the 1980s, solidifying feminism as a critical theory and practice in the academy. For those who had been active feminists in the late 1960s and 1970s, the 1980s was a decade of integration, solidification, and institution building. Much of the theorizing at this time circulated around two general themes: the experiences of women of color and issues of sexuality; conversations, conferences, publications, and debates around these issues were among the advances feminism made while allegedly "dead."

The feminism of women of color emerged as a substantial force in scholarship, as theorists built on the principle articulated in the 1977 Combahee River Collective's "Black Feminist Statement" that the most radical politics are those that stem from one's identity, that is, from working to end one's own oppression rather than someone else's. Fashioning a feminism that took into account their own experiences of multiple oppression, women of color produced an outpouring of scholarship in a wide range of fields, founded the first autonomous U.S. publisher for women of color (Kitchen Table: Women of Color Press), and held conferences of their own. The National Council on Black Women sponsored the First National Scholarly Research Conference on Black Women in 1979, while other organizations similarly organized symposia in Chicago, New York, Houston, and Indiana. An influential anthology published in 1983, poignantly titled *This Bridge Called My Back: Writings by Radical Women of Color,* took white feminists to task for talking primarily to and about issues affecting white women. If they only referred to the white experience, then whose personal experience was "political?" Scholars and writers theorized prolifically around questions of difference. Activists and authors Barbara Smith and Beverly Smith (twin sisters) asked what the "click" experience—that moment that Jane O'Reilly had first identified and named in the pages of *Ms.* when a woman realizes her oppression as a woman—had to do with women of color. Middle-class white women may have been slowly coming to an awareness of their oppression as a group, but the "day-to-day immediacy of violence and oppression" had been clicking and clucking for poor women and women of color on a daily basis for decades. Challenges from black, Latina, Asian American, and other feminists took place outside academe as well. In 1986 Alice Walker withdrew her name from the *Ms.* masthead in an act of protest. She was tired of seeing primarily white women's issues featured in articles, she explained, and few women of color gracing the cover. When Michele Wallace, author of *Black Macho and the Myth of the Superwoman,* had been photographed for the cover of *Ms.,* in which her book was being excerpted, she was asked to take out her braids.[13]

Alongside these discussions about the color and face of feminism, another important—and more publicly visible—set of debates emerged around issues of sexuality. Younger women of the new millennium often lay claim to inventing "sex-positive feminism," but it was the "sex debates" and pro-sex activism of the 1980s that paved the way. During this decade notoriously known as the backlash years, activists and academics were busily fashioning a forward-looking sexual politics that took women's pleasure—and not just endangerment—into account. Their strokings laid the groundwork for the generation of sexual revolutionaries to come.

These earlier "sex-positives" were responding to party-line feminist sexual politics, which had focused primarily on protection from oppression. Members of the highly active and vocal group Women against Pornography saw pornography and sadomasochistic sex as patriarchal mechanisms to keep women passive objects in sex as in life. Group members demonstrated, organized conferences and exposé slide shows, and gave tours of sex industry outlets in Times Square to broadcast their message that pornography contributed to violence against women. Some of the more extreme antipornography feminists presumed a world in which men were always violent and women always vulnerable, although the debate was generally more complex.[14]

Although positions were often more varied, the media cast antiporn ideology as the accepted—and only—feminist position on sex. Antiporn feminists were buttressed by the media—and by unlikely bedfellows: members of the Republican Right who were at the time pushing a politics of sex that many found homophobic, sexist, and sexually repressed. The combination of the Right's regressive stance, together with the highly visible work of antipornography feminists, alienated a rather significant (to put it mildly) cross-section of women who actually liked heterosexual sex—and not only when they were on top. Such a killjoy platform was a turnoff to women for whom sexual liberation had been, in their minds, integral to feminist politics from the start.

Such was the backdrop when, in the spring of 1982, faculty at Barnard College organized a forum on this rift: "The Sex Conference" (officially titled "Toward a Politics of Sexuality"). Shortly before the Barnard conference, the feminist journal *Heresies* had devoted an issue to the sexual dissidence. Coming together now to flesh it all out, scholars and activists gathered for a full day at the all-women's college and debated a sexual politics that emphasized sexual agency, variety, and pleasure. They built on the earlier arguments made by Anne Koedt, Erica Jong, and Germaine Greer. (While some feminists in the 1970s had focused on protecting women from male aggression, remember, these women and others had been busy challenging the "accepted" notion that women didn't like sex.) Why shouldn't liberated women be liberated sexually? pro-sex feminist pioneers of the 1980s now asked again, continuing this thread.

At the Barnard conference, participants questioned the assumption that women were powerless and challenged the conservative view—which meshed with the antiporn feminist view—that women were innocent victims in need of protection. Their talks had sexy titles. Activist, artist, writer, and community organizer Amber Hollibaugh closed with "Desire for the Future: Radical Hope in Passion and Pleasure." Anthologies resulted, bearing titles—*Powers of Desire* and *Pleasure and Danger*—that themselves sounded a bit like the titles of highbrow porn flicks. Kate Millett was there, as was Ellen Willis and fellow members of No More Nice Girls (a group that began as an abortion rights group in 1977 and coalesced in the early 1980s to oppose the antipornography campaigns). What were feminists doing legislating women's sexuality? pro-sex feminists of the early 1980s asked. Shouldn't women be not only liberated *from* sexual oppression but also liberated *to* express themselves freely in bed? Didn't women have a right to enjoy porn and S&M, if that was what turned them on?

While these debates were hot on campus and profoundly influenced intellectuals, artists, and gay activists, to the general public—and notably to younger women who were just coming of age—the women's movement had developed a reputation for being a bore—a doctrinaire set of rules and codes hawked, in some version of the popular imagination, by righteous, hairy-legged women's studies professors. Although there were certainly sexy models of feminism out there—like the group of feminist artists called Guerrilla Girls who, beginning in 1984, appeared in gorilla masks, miniskirts, and fishnet stockings and used guerrilla tactics (especially guerrilla art) to promote women in the arts—feminism in general had yet to acquire its fishnets. Antifeminist jokes on late-night talk shows were de rigueur. (Question: How many feminists does it take to screw in a light bulb? Answer: One, and that's not funny.)

The stereotype was heightened by feminism's association with the political correctness (PC) movement. Toward the end of the 1980s, feminism fell under attack, along with other -isms, for advocating PC behavior. A powerful network of Right-leaning scholars who felt that both the civil rights and the women's movements had gone too far faulted these movements—together with postmodernist theory—for challenging Enlightenment values like objective Truth and for trashing the Dead White Male. In his 1987 bestseller *The Closing of the American Mind,* University of Chicago political philosopher Allan Bloom lamented the decay of the humanities, the rise of cultural relativism (the refutation of the belief that any one culture had the monopoly on the highest art and values), the decline of the family, and students' spiritual rootlessness. Four years later, in his provocative *Illiberal Education: The Politics of Race and Sex on Campus,* former White House domestic policy analyst Dinesh D'Souza would take the "liberal academy" to task for pushing a multicultural curriculum at the expense of "real" knowledge and for advancing affirmative action policies that he believed promoted, instead of defended against, racism. Meanwhile, the conservative movement poured dollars and zeal into conservative student organizations and newspapers nationwide.

By the late 1980s campus activism revolved around these confused and misguided debates. Divides between students who identified as progressive and conservative ran deep. In 1991 the first President Bush delivered a controversial commencement speech at the University of Michigan on the topic of "political correctness"—a so-called trend on campus. Broadcasting the conservative position, he condemned the liberalization of the academy and called for a return to standards. He lamented the so-called assault on free speech, called political correctness a "movement," and denounced it for replacing old prejudice with new ones.[15]

While politically conservative student groups continued to receive funding from conservative think tanks, progressive-leaning students operated largely on their own. Political debates came down to liberals versus conservatives, pro-life versus pro-choice, and all of these versus a silent majority that seemed not to care about politics at all. Campus newspapers faced off on such issues as abortion, affirmative action, the necessity of women's studies departments, and funding for minority extracurricular groups on campus, but progressive student groups were often disjointed—and inept at responding effectively to these opposing points of view.

Weakened, fragmented, and underfunded, the organized feminist movement seemed shut down—reactive and responding defensively to setbacks. Public feminist activism on and off campus focused on countering the rise of the New Right, the nomination of Robert Bork to the Supreme Court, and setbacks in abortion policy at the national and state levels.

And then came Anita Hill.

Anita Hill galvanized those predisposed to embrace classic feminist ideas and drew in some new believers. Hill's battle with the Senate Judiciary Committee in 1991 framed a younger generation's understanding of women, politics, and power. When Hill charged her former boss and Supreme Court nominee, Clarence Thomas, with sexually harassing her—pressuring her to go out with him, commenting that his penis was like a porn star's, joking to her about finding a pubic hair in a Coke can—and nearly prevented his rise to the Supreme Court, it riveted a generation of young people for whom sexual politics had seemed a snoozy, low-stakes topic. That these accusations could be taken so seriously—by the most important men in the nation, and aired on national television—seemed to shake latent feminists out of their slumber. Because of Anita Hill, scads of younger women realized that some of the rights they had taken for granted were tentative at best and that accused sexual harassers could get promoted to Supreme Court Justice, while the women who accused them got discredited and disgraced.

But Hill not only galvanized supporters; she also ignited an opposition. For some women, Hill's testimony against Thomas before the all-male Senate Judiciary Committee and her subsequent humiliation and villification turned them off to feminism with a vengeance. In other words, Hill's testimony was a catalyst for another backlash. Women who already felt empowered experienced the Hill affair as a setback. Some formed an ad hoc group known as Women for Judge Thomas. Others felt massively disempowered by the spectacle of a woman—a black woman, no less—capturing national attention by speaking out against the second African American Supreme Court nominee. There was no doubt: The symbolism of a black man being charged by a black woman in front of an all-white jury of all-male senators was eerie. That Hill's accusations could make or break this historic appointment was a disgrace, many black women in particular felt, to women and, more so, to feminism. Some women, unsympathetic to Hill's complaints, felt she was an outspoken "uppity woman" who gave all women trying to make it in a man's world a bad name. Antifeminist fervor ran strong. Radio host Rush Limbaugh threw out whoppers: "Feminism was established to allow unattractive women easier access to the mainstream," he declared. "Women were doing quite well in this country before feminism came along."[16]

Anita Hill had an impact. Because of Hill, "sexual harassment" became a household term. Women spoke out en masse about their own experiences of being sexually harassed by male bosses while on the job. (According to the National Organization for Women, between 1990 and 1995, sexual harassment cases reported to the Equal Employment Opportunities Commission rose by 153 percent.[17]) Groups with names like African American

Women in Defense of Ourselves channeled women's outrage at the Hill-Thomas hearings into activism. But other organizations with names like the Independent Women's Forum and the Women's Freedom Network sprang up as well, their founders hoping to harness the Hill opposition and counter the swell of post-Hill feminist activity. These groups criticized sexual harassment laws and exploited the legal "gray area"—the subjective definition of "hostile environment" that girded the law. One woman's sexual harassment, they argued, could be another woman's tasteless joke. Suddenly, an innuendo, a moment of ogling, one leer, and a man could be out of a job. If we start legislating relations between the sexes this way, asked Hill's opponents—echoing Roiphe, who was saying similar things about date rape—what's next?

The growing debate reached a bizarre peak in 1993, when a small liberal arts college in Ohio made headline news with its "Sexual Offense Prevention Policy." According to the code, students at Antioch College who wanted to kiss and grope would give and get verbal consent before each new level of physical and/or sexual contact/conduct. The Antioch policy also outlined six categories of offense, ranging from persistent sexual harassment to rape. Violators would be brought before the campus judicial board for disciplinary action. At a time when the women's movement was getting heat from the Right and in the press, the college's unusual sexual offense policy came to represent, for some, feminism's pedantic, excessive, regulatory Victorian, PC, authoritarian tendencies—especially on college campuses. This was the same year Roiphe's book hit the shelves, and the controversy around who were the righteous torch-bearers of feminism and who were the Benedict Arnolds made for gossipy headlines. In October and March respectively, *New York Magazine* and *Newsweek* ran exposés of young women who cried date rape and then recanted, bolstering Roiphe's claims.[18] Many criticized the easy, excessive regulation of the fuzzy line between tasteless joke and sexual harassment, and farther down the continuum, from verbal coercion to out-and-out rape. They protested the blurring of the line between mere verbal pressure and physical force. Meanwhile, the media had a heyday with the attention-grabbing stories that too many young women may be crying rape, that the talk of "roofies" (slang for Rohypnol, the temporarily incapacitating "date rape drug") on campus was overblown, and that vintage sex codes were coming back in style like a new fall fashion that ironically turned back the clock on the sexual revolution.

A series of other high-profile sex-related cases in the early 1990s only added to the media frenzy and the raging national confusion around issues of sex and power. Socialite doctor William Kennedy Smith and sports giant Mike Tyson were on trial for rape in 1991 and 1992 respectively. In June 1993 Lorena Bobbitt, a housewife from Virginia, cut off her sexually abusive husband's penis with a kitchen knife while he was sleeping and subsequently drove off and threw it out the car window. White House intern Monica Lewinsky had an affair with President Clinton and almost got him impeached. These cases were fodder for daytime talk shows and late-night television, the watercooler, and the neighborhood bar.

The nation was divided: Who were the victims in these instances and who were the perps? Tyson and Clinton were heroes to many. Was Monica a victim or a tramp? Lorena became an emblem of female aggression gone wrong—a kind of latter-day Solanas. Many thought she was insane. Or was she simply a desperate victim of domestic violence?

In a nation abuzz with talk of Anita, Lorena, Monica, and Antioch, feminism became an easy movement to hate. The feminist rebellion against sexism had somehow been rerouted, perceived by many as a war against sex. If you were for Lorena, you must therefore be a victim-mongerer and a man-hater. If you sympathized with Anita, you couldn't take a joke. If you were expansive in your views against rape, you must be against sex and, therefore, a prude. On many campuses, "feminist" became a label most younger women no longer wanted to wear. Instead of the avant-garde movement that once promised less restriction and more fun, feminism had become conflated with victimology, sexual protectionism, humorlessness, and rules.

There was another reason for the so-called rejection of feminism among the younger generation. If you grew up believing you were equal, then wasn't the term "feminist"—with its implication of battles yet unwon—itself a threat to your sense of social standing? It was all this and more against which women like Roiphe—women just coming into their own nascent power—rebelled.

REVAMPING THE "F" WORD

In the early 1990s, popular culture stoked our imaginations with images of unconventional, empowered heroines—women who ran with wolves, as the 1993 bestseller by Jungian analyst Clarissa Pinkola Estes called the woman who followed her gut instincts. Saucy working-class television mom Roseanne and single-mom career woman Murphy Brown blurred the line between off-screen and on-screen confidence and power—particularly when single-mom Murphy mocked Vice President Dan Quayle's old-fashioned disapproval of her unmarried status in an episode titled "You Say Potatoe, I Say Potato." Hollywood stories like *Fried Green Tomatoes* and *Thelma and Louise* projected worlds in which sisterhood trumped marriage. In the 1980s, in box office hits *9 to 5* and *Working Girl*, brainy career women had bested their bosses, but in the early 1990s, *Silence of the Lambs* showed us Jodie Foster as a tough, smart FBI agent, flipping the traditional horror movie model and giving rise to a whole generation of droll, unflinching female investigators and forensic experts on American prime time. The same year that Jodie went head-to-head with Hannibal Lecter, Linda Hamilton, playing a buff, combat-ready female action heroine, vied for the spotlight with Arnold Schwarzenegger in *Terminator 2*.

Images of powerful women were rampant. But "young" and "feminist" were two words one rarely saw together in a sentence. By 1992, a study of the most empowered female generation to date—women on college campuses—showed that most young women no longer wanted to be associated with feminism. According to a *Time*/CNN poll, while 77 percent of women thought the women's movement made life better, and 94 percent said it had helped women become more independent, and 82 percent said it was still improving the lives of women, only 33 percent of women identified themselves as feminists. Although over half (57 percent) of the women interviewed said they believed there was a need for a strong women's movement, nearly two-thirds (63 percent) said they did

not consider themselves feminists.[19] "I'm not a feminist, but . . ." became the mantra of the day.

When young women said "I'm not a feminist, but . . . ," they often
went on to add something suspiciously feminist sounding in the rest of
their sentence. What many of them meant by the hallmark disclaimer was,
"I may believe in women's equality, but I'm not uptight." Feminism's new,
end-of-the-millennium reframers gave this so-called uptight feminism
many names—establishment feminism, orthodox feminism, ideological
feminism, gender feminism, resenter feminism, victim feminism, The New
Victorianism, official feminism, upscale feminism, elite feminism—and
wanted to reanimate it with relevance, meaning, family-friendliness, and,
above all, sex appeal.

New feminists came up with new names for everything. They wanted to
refurbish the language, the ideas, and the face. New names were necessary—
strong and edgy names. Most famously, perhaps, was "power feminism"—
the alluring name for a feminism where women were in control. Power
feminism, explained Naomi Wolf, who coined the term, meant identifying
with other women through shared pleasures and strengths rather than
through shared vulnerability. In place of a sentimental fantasy of cosmic sisterhood, power feminists imagined a network of alliances based on economic self-interest and economic giving back. It was not about being weak
but being strong. It was not about hating men but hating sexism.[20]

Although power feminism also had to do with harnessing the resources
of the wealthy and mobilizing the mass power of the poor, what the media
most picked up on was its implication of power through sex. Power feminism—the sexed-up kind—made its way into the popular men's magazines
Esquire, where writer Tad Friend coined what may be the oxymoron of the
movement—or not?—"do-me feminism" in 1994. In the wake of the rape
debates, that term said it all. (Friend wholeheartedly supported the do-mes'
fight for a woman's right to get laid—and a man's right to lay her, taking
the phrase "asking for it" to a new level.)

But the "new feminist" had other, more buttoned-up names too. An
"equity feminist," according to Christina Hoff Sommers, was one who
fought for full civil and legal equality rather than the total abolition of gen-

der roles. A "family feminist," according to Elizabeth Fox Genovese, was one who trusted women to set their own priorities, based on the facts of their lives, rather than try to live up to an unattainable ideal.

In addition to the offputting rhetoric and unattainable ideals, many reclaimers felt that "old" feminism did women a disservice because at the end of the millennium, American women were no longer very oppressed. Wolf and Daphne Patai, among others, faulted the old guard for going against progress. "Men are seeing their empire begin to crumble; their world is indeed dying," observed Wolf in *Fire with Fire*.[21] And in 1993 it made sense that Wolf would write this, for women—and especially feminists—*had* made unprecedented gains.

Despite popular declarations of feminism's demise, women were organizing again—and voting with their pocketbooks. Organizations such as EMILY's List—a national network of political donors that began seven years earlier with a gathering of twenty-five women with Rolodexes in founder Ellen Malcolm's basement—had helped elect four new pro-choice Democratic women senators and twenty new congresswomen.[22] (EMILY stood for "Early Money Is Like Yeast.") Membership in the organization had grown more than 600 percent in 1992, with more than 23,000 members contributing over $6.2 million to recommended candidates—giving new meaning to the power of the purse.[23] Indeed, *Time* magazine declared 1992 the Year of the Woman. (Sniped Senator Barbara Mikulski in response to this popular declaration, "Calling 1992 the Year of the Woman makes it sound like the Year of the Caribou or the Year of the Asparagus. We're not a fad, a fancy, or a year."[24])

Women had become a powerful voting block. Forty-five percent of those voting for Clinton had been women. As a result of the 1992 election, the number of women in the Senate increased from four to seven and the number of women in the House jumped from twenty-eight to forty-seven.[25] Carol Moseley-Braun, the Democrat from Illinois, became the first African American woman to win a major-party Senate nomination and the first woman of color to serve in the U.S. Senate.

With the advent of the more liberal Clinton-Gore era—and the novel presence of openly feminist Hillary Rodham Clinton in the White

House—traditional women's movement issues returned, for at least a moment, to national attention. On April 5, 1992, more than 750,000 pro-choice women and men joined Planned Parenthood, the National Organization for Women, and other organizations in the "March for Women's Lives" in Washington, D.C. In 1993, pushing President Clinton to honor his campaign promise of making his cabinet look like America, feminist leaders remained determined to regain lost ground. Clinton's cabinet included five women—the most of any presidential cabinet in United States history. The veteran state prosecutor from Miami, Janet Reno, became the nation's first woman attorney general, joining Donna Shalala, secretary of Health and Human Services; Hazel O'Leary, secretary of the Department of Energy; Madeleine Albright, ambassador to the United Nations; and Carol Browner, director of the Environmental Protection Agency. Judge Ruth Bader Ginsburg became the second woman—and the first self-described feminist—confirmed to the United States Supreme Court. Dr. Joycelyn Elders—an unabashed supporter of abortion rights, sex education, family planning, AIDS prevention, school-based clinics, and preventive health care measures—was the first African American woman to become Surgeon General of the United States. With this partial shattering of the political glass ceiling came significant legal gains: Anti–abortion-clinic–violence bills were passed in several states. The unpaid Family and Medical Leave Act was finally passed into law by Congress and signed by the president. From a certain vantage point, it felt almost as if in every realm, the feminists were finally having their day.

Why, in the face of such evidence, reclaimers asked, would feminists still insist that women were oppressed?

Statements about patriarchy crumbling now sound overly optimistic, even wistful, in the wake of remarks by then Harvard president Lawrence Summers in 2005 about women not having what it takes to be scientists, for instance, or President George W. Bush's failure to replace Sandra Day O'Connor with another well-qualified female judge, or the persistent reality of the wage gap in the United States in 2007. Even in 1993, though, public evidence of patriarchal forces was well at hand. Clinton's struggle to appoint a female attorney general, for instance, revealed the double standard still in play for female nominees. Clinton's first two nominations for the position, Zoe Baird and Kimba Wood, were both withdrawn when the arrangements they had made for undocumented domestic employees became a national, federal case—and one that seemingly affected only high-powered women who hired domestic help to "replace" them in the home so that they could pursue their careers. Their choices came under undue scrutiny that no man appointed to a cabinet-level position has ever had to endure. While Baird was publicly flamed for her late payment of Social Security taxes, Secretary of Commerce Ron Brown was quietly allowed to pay back taxes on Social Security for his domestic employees.[26] Notably, Janet Reno was unmarried and without kids and posed no problem of this sort.

But the reclaimers of the 1990s made an important point: In focusing solely on the gaps, and not the gains, were feminists themselves perhaps playing a role in holding women—psychologically at least—back?

In a universe where so many women had essentially made it, where women finally had some clout, this argument ran, old-school feminists were failing to take advantage of an open moment. "By the beginning of the 1990s, just when women's position seemed to be improving decisively, the feminist elite was sounding dire alarms," complained Elizabeth Fox-Genovese in *Feminism Is Not the Story of My Life,* implying that those who still harped on women's victim status were anachronistic spoilsports. Women in the United States were neither subjugated nor oppressed, wrote Karen Lehrnman, who went on to name the real problem: "What [women] very well might be, though, is overwhelmed and confused."[27]

In blaming feminists for modern women's confusion, reclaimers invoked Susan Faludi's *Backlash* and Wolf's own *Beauty Myth*—1991 bestsellers in which the authors had acknowledged the inroads women had made during the 1980s but forcefully insisted that the war against patriarchal institutions of domination and control was far from won. Faludi's book suggested that male anger over women's increasing demands for autonomy had created a popular backlash, whereby women were continuously being punished for having gone "too" far. Calling attention to the systemic roots of women's continued oppression, Wolf's earlier book had insisted it was men's institutions and institutional power that were responsible for perpetuating the beauty myth. Reclaimers who disagreed that American women as a group were still personally and politically oppressed charged these authors with perpetuating damaging falsehoods about women's social reality and exaggerating the strength of a patriarchal power elite.

Like modern-day Bettys, the new mainstreamers conceded that "The Personal Is Political" had once meant something good and real; it had had its time and its place. They acknowledged the role this slogan had played in sensitizing the legal system to issues such as sexual harassment and marital rape and in helping individual women understand that they were not alone in suffering from problems with social causes. But somewhere along the way, reclaimers insisted, the catchphrase became perverted in the grip of what they saw as lesser minds, making "feminist" something most women didn't want to be.

Although each offered her own version of the slogan's eventual excesses and subsequent fall, all agreed that the slogan's meaning had been corrupted with the passing of time. When and how the distortion occurred seemed subject to debate. Lehrman vaguely suggested that it was "sometime during the seventies" that "the interpretation of this phrase went haywire." Sommers squarely located the distortion in the writings of Kate Millett—which, she argued, taught women "that politics was essentially sexual and that even the so-called democracies were male hegemonies," a premise that sparked a number of wrongheaded theories based on misguided assumptions about relationships among women, men, and power. Sommers also blamed cultural feminists, who, she claimed, had adapted the slogan to celebrate women's "victim" status in patriarchal society. Roiphe located the problem in both the early writings of second-wave feminists and in the slightly later writings of Catherine MacKinnon, who, she argued, spawned a "cultural obsession with sexual violation."[28] Although Roiphe took issue with MacKinnon's equation of sex and rape, she saw the real perversion in the loose process by which MacKinnon's ideas traveled through American culture at large. As the ideas became cocktail-party conversation, Roiphe argued, radical premises were progressively amplified and rendered common—too common. The result was that what once had seemed "radical" no longer seemed radical at all. Instead, radical became "chic." And meaningless.

For Wolf, who alone seemed to straddle the "old school" and the "new," the problem was not a matter of misguided amplification but of sloppy translation. Theories that emerged in the 1970s translated poorly into popular conversation, she said. While the theories revolutionized the way women and men thought about gender, they circulated through catchphrases that ranged "from the preposterous to the threatening."[29] As in the child's game "telephone"—where a phrase is whispered into one ear to the next until it is distorted beyond recognition—epiphanies of liberation had been reduced quite quickly to victim-mongering, wallowing, and manhating. Like Friedan before her, Wolf, and Roiphe too, worried that these distortions and misinterpretations had irreversibly alienated the mainstream over the years.

Others, like Rene Denfeld, located the perversion of personal politics in more recent times. According to Denfeld, the once-useful slogan had been distorted by contemporary feminist "extremists" who had crossed the line. The phrase had come to mean that all aspects of a woman's personal life, including sex, are appropriate matters for feminist direction. "What we do in bed is seen as just as important, if not more, than how we vote," she lamented.[30] Denfeld's critique of sexual politics delivered a by now time-worn argument, just repackaged in 1990s garb.

In a similar repackaging, Lehrman and Patai argued that by adopting the expanded understanding of "the political" born of the New Left in the 1960s, the "bad" (outdated) feminists had rendered the term "politics" virtually meaningless. Wrote Patai in *Heterophobia,* "The feminist slogan, 'The personal is political' has transmuted into its opposite, 'The political is personal,' which in turn has come to mean that where everything is political, nothing is." A surplus of meaning had paradoxically resulted in no meaning at all. "To get feminism back on . . . track, we need to first return the word 'political' to its conventional definition: state action."[31]

For Friedan, the insistence on a state-based definition of politics had gone hand in hand with her attempt to fashion a less radical feminism, one that would play to women in Peoria (and those who read *McCall's*). But for the new reclaimers writing during a more conservative era, the call for a narrowed definition of the political was ironically congruous with the rhetoric of a still-powerful (if not officially in power) force: the well-entrenched American Right.

In the 1990s, "conservative" was no longer a word associated solely with the Right. Even with the Clintons in the White House, a socially conservative ethos together with attitudes about minimal government intervention in daily life exerted considerable influence on American culture and politics (an ethos that continues today). Welfare reform—pushed by conservatives but adopted by Clinton—replaced Aid to Families with Dependent Children (AFDC) with Temporary Assistance for Needy Families (TANF) and welfare-to-work requirements. Republicans pushed hard for reductions to, and conditions on, the Earned Income Tax Credit, which affected the married poor as well as single mothers. Even in the midst of what many called a progressive presidency, calls for less government dependency and more personal responsibility rang through loud and clear.

To many of feminism's new reclaimers, as to many of those who advocated rolling back social programs that helped the underprivileged and poor, personal and political life were best maintained as separate spheres. Reversing, in effect, the second-wave logic that had led to legal edicts around issues such as rape, domestic violence, and sexual harassment, Fox-Genovese, for instance, insisted that Americans were not accustomed to making personal relations between women and men matters for state control and that now was not the time to begin. Others claimed that the broadening of "the political" had resulted in a world in which government was often called on to do the fixing when the real responsibility lay with women themselves. Instead of attacking the state, some reclaimers charged old-school feminists with enlarging the state and attacking individual autonomy. Denfeld wished for a movement that truly addressed women's concerns "while keeping its nose out of women's private lives."[32]

Just what such a movement would look like remained unclear. The reclaimers' strategies for effecting change were generally limited to the private arena. Instead of litigation, Lehrman advocated peer pressure, reducing movement strategies to high school tactics. Wolf, again the exception, advocated a more externally proactive plan, proposing "ad campaigns, consumer clout, 900 numbers, health clubs and sororities, charity dollars, and women's magazines, to make prowoman action in this decade, and into the next century, something that is effective. . . ."[33] Believing the old-school fantasy of a Marxist revolution to have proved ineffective, and facing the reality that most victories in feminism had come about by reformist tactics instead, Wolf's prescription for action included organized political action that worked within the system. Her strategies stood out for their creativity, expansiveness, and specificity, yet they too depended less on the existence of an advocacy-based mass movement and more on the isolated behavior of generous women with capital. To old-school types, a feminist movement based on sororal charity seemed tame compared to the fiery structural demands of the radicals only two decades before.

Recasting feminism in a language intended to resonate with younger women—members of a more conservative generation who had come of age under Reagan and the first George Bush—other reclaimers offered a strictly individualistic portrait of feminism's future. Sisterhood was still powerful, but the fact that some sisters had more power than others seemed of less import now than in the past. Back in 1970, Carol Hanisch had claimed, "There are no personal solutions at this time . . . only collective action for a collective solution."[34] Twenty-some years later, some of feminism's daughters (and disgruntled aunts) were arguing that feminism should no longer be about communal solutions to communal problems but individual solutions to individual problems.

And herein lies one of the most profound ironies of contemporary feminism: At the century's end, the very women who rhetorically mimicked Betty Friedan's earlier oppositional stance in effect reversed the once-revolutionary premise of the New Left, the radicals, and *The Feminine Mystique*. Social problems were not social anymore. They were, to many, personal once again. Whereas the New Left logic of participatory democracy and the civil rights legacy of the beloved community had infused second-wave feminism with a utopian vision of a transformed social order based on the power of sisterhood, postfeminist feminism in the 1990s was permeated by a conservative zeitgeist that celebrated personal success and strength. For conservatives, it was about pulling oneself up by one's bootstraps. For the postfeminists, it was about propelling oneself forward in stiletto heels.

NEW FEMINIST MACHISMA?

By the late 1990s, the rhetorics of feminism and individualism had combined to create a new popular icon: the feminist badass. If second-wave feminism had promulgated a vision of individual women as vulnerable and sisterhood as strong, postfeminist feminism posited sisterhood as weak and celebrated instead a proud new female brawn.

Images of strong, sexy bad girls permeated late-1990s popular culture. Hip-hop and rap offered up new images of strong, powerful black women. The first all-female rap group, Salt-n-Pepa, won a Grammy for Best Rap Performance for their single, "None of Your Business" in 1995, while Missy "Misdemeanor" Elliott released *Supa Dupa Fly,* her first album, in 1997. Badass diva Queen Latifah joined Lisa Loeb and the Dixie Chicks (and softees Sarah McClaughlin and the Indigo Girls) at Lilith Fair. In Hollywood, Lori Petty and Naomi Watts raised hell and tore up the desert in a comic-book adaptation called *Tank Girl* (1995), while Hong Kong action diva Michelle Yeoh strutted her stuff to American audiences in the latest James Bond flick, *Tomorrow Never Dies* (1997). On television, actress Sarah Michelle Gellar battled demons as the buff, kick-boxing teenage demon killer known as Buffy the Vampire Slayer, while off-screen, thousands of women learned to kick box at the neighborhood gym. Svelte and powerfully sexy professional athletes—daughters of Title IX—were celebrated on the covers of women's magazines as real-world icons for female ambition, beauty, and strength. U.S. women won nineteen gold, ten silver, and nine bronze medals at the Summer Olympics in 1996, and, in 1999, the U.S. Women's Soccer Team made headlines not only for winning the Women's World Cup but because Brandi Chastain, after scoring the winning goal for the team, tore off her shirt.

Stars who embodied the new feminist machisma spoke out, encouraging "ordinary" women to follow suit. Said comedic actress—speaking quite seriously—Roseanne Barr, "The thing women have yet to learn is nobody gives you power. You just take it." In her book *Bitch: In Praise of Difficult Women* (1999), ex–rock critic/bad girl Elizabeth Wurtzel (of *Prozac Nation* fame) celebrated mythic and real women who flaunted their bitchiness, while Madonna celebrated her own: "I'm tough, I'm ambitious, and I know exactly what I want. If that makes me a bitch, okay."[35]

It was a confusing moment for feminist iconography. There were sports heroines like Mia Hamm and pro-woman politicians like Hillary Clinton. There was Anita Hill. There were singer/songwriters like Ani DiFranco, whose songs about contemporary social issues such as racism, sexism, sexual abuse, homophobia, reproductive rights, poverty, and war gained her a passionate following among politically active college students nationwide. And then there was Ally McBeal—the ditsy twenty-eight-year-old, Ivy League–educated Boston litigator on the hit FOX television series whose face appeared along with Susan B. Anthony's, Gloria Steinem's, and Betty Friedan's on a 1998 cover of *Time* magazine along with the headline "Is Feminism Dead?"

The *Time* cover was emblematic. It synthesized what many second-wavers perceived as a devolution in focus from the serious to the silly. Inside, an article by journalist Gina Bellafante ran with the juicy teaser "Want to know what today's chic young feminist thinkers care about? Their bodies! Themselves!" Ally's particular brand of "me-first" feminism was taken to be representative of her generation. Said her creator, David Kelley, "She's not a hard, strident feminist out of the '60s and '70s. She's all for women's rights, but she doesn't want to lead the charge at her own emotional expense." On one episode, as Bellafante pointed out, Ally characteristically answered the question "Why are your problems so much bigger than everyone else's?" with the honest response "Because they're mine."[36]

Raised in solidarity, this fictionalized daughter of feminism had seemingly internalized messages about women's progress only to become hyper-individualistic. Ally's dilemmas were fiction, but Katie Roiphe's were real.

What did this perceived turn toward individualism mean for feminism as a movement? On one level, it meant that a younger woman who had made it, like Roiphe, could believe that she—or her friends—were somehow invulnerable. It meant that many women who had been able to exercise their economic, social, and other freedoms no longer necessarily saw their connection, as women, to women who had been unable (for reasons that were not purely psychological) to access the same. It meant, perhaps, that the critique had swung too far in the other direction, that some of those who criticized second-wave feminism for harping on women's vulnerability dangerously believed that women were now invincible. The result? A feminism lacking in empathy and imagination—a brave new feminism that trafficked in selfishness, maybe, but more likely, in false bravado.

But perhaps the greatest irony of postfeminism 1990s-style was this: In falsely imagining that we were postpatriarchy, postfeminists had in effect redefined the enemy: other feminists. In the 1970s, feminists insisted on sexual difference between men and women and launched a targeted attack on male power, domination, androcentrism, sex discrimination, and sexual double standards. But in the early 1990s, as popular feminist writers like Roiphe and others turned their critical gaze on their predecessors and each other, the emphasis on patriarchal domination and control faded into the backdrop. Personal oppression became less about suppression under patriarchy and more about suppression under the sisters—meaning, for members of a younger generation, under the mothers.

CHAPTER 5

REBELS WITH A CAUSE

Mothers and daughters stand divided; how long until we are conquered?

—*Rebecca Dakin Quinn*

On a crisp, clear day in early 1992, academics and activists in New York City organized a conference, "Women Tell the Truth," at Hunter College. As the participants poured in, it felt a bit like a reunion. The older women all seemed to know each other, greeting each other with hugs, handshakes, and waves from across the room. Scores of younger women attended—bright-eyed, outraged, and awake. For older feminists, the recent Anita Hill affair was a fresh but sorry reminder of a situation they already understood all too well. For many of the younger ones—even those whose feminist mothers had regaled them with tales of the bad old days when male bosses called secretaries "toots"—it was still an episode as shocking as an unexpected pinch on the ass.

The conference was designed to capitalize on the anger many felt in the wake of the Senate Judiciary Committee hearings on Judge Thomas's nomination. Anger was in the air that day, echoing that of the newly elected Carol Mosely Braun and six of her Democratic women colleagues when they united in a march on the Senate to urge greater attention to Anita

Hill's charges. A famous *Washington Post* photograph published a week after the 1992 election captured the female legislators charging up the Capitol, which clearly was, their irate faces reminded us, still a bastion of male power.

Back in New York, the conference organizers promoted straightforward goals—how to get more women to run for Congress, how to make women's voices heard. But perhaps one of the most compelling issues underlying the day was the question of how to sustain the interest of the next generation. At day's end, twenty-something activists Shannon Liss and Rebecca Walker (daughter of Alice, the author of *The Color Purple* and an early contributing editor to *Ms.*) strode onto the stage to report back on a workshop on organizing younger feminists. Their presentation was brief. Taking the podium with the confidence of young women coming into their own, they leaned into the microphone and announced together in a single voice, *"We are not postfeminist feminists. We are the third wave!"* The audience gave them a standing ovation.

Rebecca Walker embodied the hope of a previous generation and was lighting the way for the next, giving younger women a banner under which they could join their mothers in the march through history—and an alternative to postfeminism. Walker had first used the term "third wave" in a *Ms.* magazine article published earlier that year.[1] In it she argued that Clarence Thomas's ascent to the Supreme Court was all but inevitable in today's society. In order for Hill's testimony to have derailed the nomination, a tectonic shift in the social order would have had to take place. "Can a woman's experience undermine a man's career?" she asked. "If Thomas had not been confirmed, every man in the United States would be at risk. For how many senators never told a sexist joke . . . ?" Sounding a lot like a radical feminist circa 1969, she continued, "For those whose sense of power is so obviously connected to the health and vigor of the penis, it would have been a metaphoric castration." Walker ended the article with a plea to women, especially young ones her age, not only to embrace feminism but to demand it of their men as well.

Walker's radical stance stood out among a generation becoming known alternatingly for its conservatism or perceived political apathy—a generation represented by television shows like *Beverly Hills 90210* and *Melrose Place* and movies like *Reality Bites*. But Walker was not alone. Renewed interest in feminism around the 1992 election had led to a rise in the memberships of existing women's organizations nationwide and to the development of new groups around the country—among them Bay Area Teenage Feminist Coalition, Campus Organizing Project, Feminists United to Represent Youth (FURY), National Abortion Rights Action League (NARAL), Students Organizing Students, Women's Action Coalition (WAC), Women's Health Action and Mobilization (WHAM), Women's Information Network (WIN), Women Express, Inc., Youth Education Life Line (YELL), Young Women's Action Network, the Young Women's Project, and, perhaps the one with the most telling name, Third Wave Direct Action Corporation (cofounded by Walker and Liss). Third Wave's first action, a voter registration drive modeled after an earlier era's "Freedom Summer," had successfully pulled 20,000 new voters into the election. Young feminist conferences proliferated. Twenty-five years after middle-age establishment ladies in suits and hats gathered at an Upper East Side brownstone for the founding of the New York NOW chapter, NOW held its first national Young Feminist Conference, for and by women under thirty, in Akron, Ohio. Seven hundred and fifty participants from forty-two states converged to attend issue hearings and sign up for campus action teams, internships, and field organizing work. Some organized "zap" actions to demonstrate their opposition to the Persian Gulf War. The issues were multifaceted and often global. Feminism was no longer just reproductive rights and equal pay. The swell of renewed action created a mood of intense—if tempered—optimism among those who had been pushing for progressive social change for years.

The early 1990s were not merely years of optimism for the women's movement but of results, in the United States and abroad. In the United States, battered women's shelters and sexual assault programs received increases in public funding. Planned Parenthood, long a key national player in women's reproductive and health issues, succeeded in getting Depo-Provera, an injectable, progestin-only contraceptive that works for three months, approved by the U.S. Food and Drug Administration. Women's nongovernmental organizations (NGOs) proliferated. An organized global movement strengthened and expanded, making its presence known through a number of important international conferences, culminating in the Fourth World Conference on Women in Beijing in September 1995—attended by First Lady Hillary and First Daughter Chelsea, who continued to set a very public feminist example. To many, it seemed like there was a movement once again—multiple movements, in fact, existing all at once and often interlocking toward greater effect.

All of which led to an interesting culture clash within U.S. feminism. At the same time that Katie Roiphe and Rene Denfeld were chronicling their disaffection and declaring themselves "post" feminist, a phalanx of self-declared third-wave feminists began recording their awakenings with a fervor reminiscent of yesterday's proto-radicals. Newly published magazines and journals by and about young women and their activism sprang forth, bearing galvanizing titles like *HUES*—Hear Us Sisters Emerging, a multicultural feminist magazine (or 'zine) written and produced by women in their twenties—and *GAYA: A Journal By and About Young Women.* Literary anthologies amassed essays by younger women, challenging the notion that younger feminists didn't exist with passionate explorations of what feminism still meant for a younger generation. In 1995 Barbara Findlen, a former editor of *Ms.,* came out with *Listen Up: Voices from the Next Feminist Generation,* and Rebecca Walker published *To Be Real: Telling the Truth and Changing the Face of Feminism*—two collections that announced the advent of and set the tone for the newly dubbed third wave. In heartfelt personal essays, contributors to both books chronicled their feminist awakenings, prompting Gloria Steinem to call *Listen Up* "a consciousness raising group between covers." Young professors Leslie Heywood and Jennifer Drake teamed up for *Third Wave Agenda: Doing Feminism, Being Feminist* and called on students to make feminism personal. Graduate students and newly minted professors wrote about popular culture, hip-hop, postmodernism, and social movements, updating feminist theory to fit their lives. Manifestos reappeared. Kristal Brent Zook published "A Manifesto of Sorts for a Black Feminist Movement" in *The New York Times Magazine,* while journalist Jennifer Baumgardner and writer/activist Amy Richards joined forces to write *ManifestA: Young Women, Feminism, and the Future*—a book that provided analysis and strategy for young women who believed in renewed commitment instead of postfeminist disaffection. Their book literally became a manifesto for a generation as the authors toured college campuses nationwide and provided a forum for young women to explore for themselves what it meant to be "third wave."

And what *did* it mean? It meant clash—not only with postfeminist peers, but also with second-wave mothers. The third wave was inextricably linked to the second, but third wavers' orientation to feminism was different because, among other reasons, they had grown up with it. For young women who came of age in the 1980s and 1990s, feminism was a curious thing. To those with feminist mothers, fathers, aunts, teachers, and role models, those who had grown up with sex education and Little League, feminism was as natural as cotton. But growing up, feminism had not felt like a *movement*. Or if it had, it was their mothers' movement—and, by association, not necessarily cool.

But now it was a movement that was theirs. Women just entering the workforce began to recognize patterns around men, women, and power on the job, proving true Gloria Steinem's statement that women grow more radical with age.[2] As younger women started to find each other, there was an excitement in learning that they were not merely isolated, empowered-feeling individuals but part of a rising surge—a new wave, as Walker put it.

Third wavers' branch of feminism was defined by continuity with their mothers', but also in large part by how it differed. When Walker declared "I am the Third Wave," the effect was both to link and to distinguish herself from her mother and her mother's politics. At the same time, her use of the phrase distinguished her from her alienated postfeminist sisters who had rejected older feminists' strategies, and especially the "dated" belief in women's oppression and second-class status in society. Simone de Beauvoir's *Second Sex* may have been a history book for the postfeminists, but for the third wave, it was still living text—as true in the 1990s as it had been in the 1960s.

Unlike the postfeminists, third wavers saw the war for women's social, political, and economic equality as far from won. In the mid-1990s, as the postfeminists were busy pronouncing the personal no longer political, the newly self-identifying third wavers proclaimed the opposite. Findlen declared that feminism was what helped women make sense of the unfairness of sexism by reminding them of the difference between political injustice and personal failure. Baumgardner and Richards agreed: "The personal is still political," they proclaimed. "To be sure, 'the personal is political' is the most used—and most abused—motto to come out of the Second Wave," they continued. "But as a concept it's too important to be allowed to languish in misunderstandings."[3]

The new wave of young feminist writers articulated very personal reasons why young women still needed a movement, and how feminism would help: Feminism was the frame that would help young women struggling with anorexia or HIV, rape survivors, and pregnant teens see their experiences in a broader and political light. Many of these problems were carry-overs—problems that had not gone away, despite the fact that they now had names. Others, however, were new, or at least newly inflected. Baumgardner and Richards offered a clear analysis of younger women's predicament and concerns, based on survey results: Young women cared about "sex discrimination (*and* harassment, the subject with which discrimination is frequently merged), pay inequities, custody and divorce laws, access to adoption and custody for lesbian parents, as well as the prevention of rape and incest."[4] They cared about "[r]elationships, marriage, bisexuality, STDs, abortion, having children . . . immigration problems, access to education, racism as manifest by white women befriending black women to get over their white guilt, taking care of an aging relative, credit-card debt, depression, and body image."[5] With still no ERA and no pro-woman female candidates running for president, the war, they reminded the newly amassed troops, was far from won.

But many third wavers agreed with the postfeminists that women in the 1990s were confused. Whereas postfeminists suggested that women were confused by feminism (which had become a crutch for individuals who were reluctant to take responsibility for their situation or status), third wavers felt women were confused by the illusion of progress. Taking Susan Faludi's premises to heart, third wavers feared that the assumption that women had "made it" in certain realms (they could now play on sports teams and be guaranteed an equal education) obscured the fact that other realms (such as the feminization of poverty and the lack of child care and good family policy at work) remained relatively unchanged— particularly for working-class women, immigrants, and women of color. And they believed that no degree of confidence or personal evolution would solve the inequities that many American women continued to face outside their heads.

Third wavers took up familiar questions: What is the root cause of women's continued oppression? How is feminist activism best expressed? What does it mean to be a feminist? Although second wavers had asked these questions as their cells and groups first started to form in the late 1960s, self-described third wavers often asked these questions as if they were the first to ponder them. Obviously, they were not.

Embracing aspects of second-wave legacies (consciously, or not), many third wavers distanced themselves from the movement that had enabled them to become who they were. Wrote Joan Morgan, author of *When Chickenheads Come Home to Roost: My Life as a Hip-Hop Feminist*, a young woman today is "going to have to push her foremothers' voices far enough away to discover her own."[6] While this was, perhaps, a natural progression, some older feminists were understandably peeved. They accused younger feminists—when they acknowledged that younger feminists existed—of reinventing the wheel. Others failed to recognize the questions third wavers asked as familiar (and once their own) and instead heard only the screeching sounds of dissent.

As the third wave defined itself against postfeminism and, increasingly, against—or at least as disparate from—their feminist mothers, an interesting public debate took shape across the generations. It was one of the rare times in history when exchanges between mothers and daughters played out in a public sphere. Although there exists an established male tradition of professional apprenticeship and generational transmission in and outside of the family (as Robert Bly sought to revive through his 1990 classic

Iron John), women were relative newcomers to this phenomenon outside the domestic sphere. In the 1990s, for the first time in history, we had two generations of feminists living side by side—the second wave still churning within and alongside the rising and boisterous third.

MAMA DRAMA

Feminist transmission generated new buzz in the world as feminists young and old began scribing intensely passionate, public letters to each other, their voices talking back and forth on the radio, on TV, at panels and forums, in magazines and over e-mail, addressing the issue of intergenerational conflict head on. This conversation took place in popular and academic spheres alike. In the fall of 1993, *Ms.* followed up on an earlier article, "Young Feminists Speak for Themselves," with an intergenerational dialogue among bell hooks, Gloria Steinem, Urvashi Vaid, and Naomi Wolf, titled "Let's Get Real about Feminism: The Backlash, the Myths, the Movement."[7] *Harper's Bazaar* jumped in with a celebration of the new generation titled "These Women Do Not Fear the Twenty-First Century" in September 1995, while Wendy Kaminer struck a slightly more skeptical note—"Feminism's Third Wave: What Do Young Women Want?"—in the *New York Times Book Review* in June that year.

More often than not, the tone of the mother generation, when addressing the daughters' complaints, was condescending. Gloria Steinem was one very gracious and notable exception. "Who could resist this bravery?" she asked in the foreword to Walker's *To Be Real.* "Not I."[8] Phyllis Chesler, author of the 1972 classic *Women and Madness,* struck a different tone in an extended, book-length series of epistles in 1997, *Letters to a Young Feminist,* in which she chastised younger women for being naively ungrateful. The book was intended to "correct" young women, who should presumably welcome the helpful instruction. Chesler's contemporary, Susan Brownmiller, naively applauded her tone: "The sweet, clear voice of these letters should reach across the generation gap like Joshua's trumpet," Brownmiller predicted.[9] Instead—perfectly capturing the generational disconnect of this time—it hit like a ton of bricks. Wrote *Spin* editor-at-large Kim France, *"Letters to a Young Feminist* reads like an object lesson in just how large the gap really is between second-wave feminists and the women who followed them. 'You are entitled to know our war stories,' Chesler writes. . . . But what she's failed to figure out is how to reach a generation that doesn't necessarily want to hear them."[10]

The tensions lasted into the new millennium. In 2002 Oprah herself joined the fray, airing a show called "What Younger Women Think about Older Women." The tone was alternatingly respectful and defiant. Younger women interviewed for the segment and identified only by their first names blamed Boomer women for creating new glass ceilings for the women coming up under them and for "ruining men." To make up for it, the cadre of young feminist spokeswomen on the show (Jennifer Baumgardner, Amy Richards, Rebecca Walker, Naomi Wolf) ended up thanking the older women (Suzanne Braun Levine, Faye Wattleton, Gloria Steinem) in a way that almost seemed forced.

The old-feminist–young-feminist drama was like any typical mother-daughter squabble, only writ large. Baumgardner and Richards wanted to absolve second wavers of their "mother guilt" and at the same time get them to back off. "You are not our mothers," they declared, though some of them, actually, were. Speaking, in effect, directly to Chesler (and sounding a bit like teenage girls demanding independence), Baumgardner and Richards continued: "You have to stop treating us like daughters. You don't have the authority to treat us like babies or acolytes who need to be molded."[11] Offered Rebecca Walker, "I think some of the older women have been a little threatened. It's a fear about being somehow displaced." Her words appeared, tellingly, in an article appearing in *Girlfriends* magazine titled "Don't Ask Alice: Rebecca Walker Steps Out."[12] English professor E. Ann Kaplan confirmed Walker's hunch, describing how women of her generation felt "shelved like a 'classic.'" In *Generations: Academic Feminists in Dialogue,* a book coedited by Kaplan (a senior feminist scholar) and Devoney Looser (a junior—that is, untenured—one at the time), Kaplan chronicled common second-wave feminist anxieties: "Worries include the idea of being left behind, of their day being over. . . . Many in this generation are located as 'pioneers' by younger academic feminists but no longer seen as forging new terrain." Steinem agreed. "[T]here are moments in [*To Be Real*] where I—and perhaps other readers older than thirty-five—feel like a sitting dog being told to sit."[13]

The exchanges were increasingly heartfelt, infused with competition, resentment, longings for prestige, and nostalgia for lost community. On both sides, egos, careers, and professional recognition were at stake. But ultimately it came down to a desire to be appreciated and understood. In a published exchange titled "Talking Across," senior feminist professor Jane Gallop confessed to graduate student Elizabeth Francis, "There's something about expecting to be appreciated and instead being criticized that is very, very painful."[14] Activist Robin Morgan gave voice to that pain in a poignant postscript to younger women with which she closed her latest anthology, *Sisterhood Is Forever:* "Speaking for myself, I'm hanging on to my torch, thank you. Get your own damned torch."[15]

Younger feminists felt not just unappreciated but ignored. Junior scholars wondered why some second-wave feminists have been so slow to see them. Mused Devoney Looser, "We are in their classrooms, their conferences. Haven't they also complained that we are occasionally too much in their faces?" Being unseen was like being at one's own funeral, the juniors explained, unable to tell one's mourners that one was still very much alive.[16] But nightmares about being passed over went both ways.

As much as they were about communication, these intergenerational exchanges were part of a family saga playing out—one that the warring parties often publicly denied. In a *Los Angeles Times* interview, Rebecca Walker said, "It's so easy for people to want to make it sexy and juicy by turning it into this kind of Greek tragedy of daughter against mother and matricide and all that. And that's not really what it is at all." Veteran journalist Katha Pollitt pondered, with distress, why it was that sisterhood had suddenly become mother-daughterhood.[17]

Inside academia, generational tension was extreme. Academics spent pages deconstructing the mother-daughter metaphor, trying to figure out what it all meant for the movement. Graduate student Rebecca Dakin Quinn even coined a new phrase to describe it: the "matrophor."[18] Ironically, the neologism was meant to convey the limitations and traps of this new metaphor; but instead, the fact that there was now a word merely underscored the metaphor's power. The matrophor, argued assistant professor Astrid Henry in a book devoted to the theme, had emboldened a younger generation—"Daughterhood Is Powerful!" this new generation had exclaimed. But Henry dutifully insisted that the matrophor too easily allowed younger women to reduce and dismiss previous generations and diminish their contributions. Others argued that the rhetoric of generational differences masked real political differences, while still others insisted that other differences were far more worth exploring.[19] No matter how much they theorized about it, dismissed it, or made it seem abstract, feminists across the generations were engaged in a power struggle. Like the radicals against themselves, and like Betty Friedan against the radicals, feminists across the generations were engaged in a power struggle not against patriarchy but among themselves.

At the dawn of the new millennium, it was no longer simply a battle between feminists but between older and younger women more broadly. The most common arena for conflict was work. Books with titles like *I Can't Believe She Did That!* updated the earlier analysis of "women's inhumanity to women" by exploring the themes of competition and betrayal—including generational—as they played out specifically in the workplace. *The Devil Wears Prada,* a 2003 bestselling novel by Lauren Weisberger about a young woman fresh out of college who works as a personal assistant to a powerful yet capricious fashion magazine editor, was widely seen as a roman à clef about *Vogue*'s iconic editor-in-chief Anna Wintour—though Weisberger, who interned at *Vogue,* denied it. *Devil* gave rise to a new subgenre within chick lit: tell-alls about the older and often female boss from hell as told by her young female assistant. Exposés of power abuse in Hollywood—with a particularly feminine tinge—followed suit, such as *Chore Whore: Adventures of a Celebrity Personal Assistant; The Second Assistant: A Tale from the Bottom of the Hollywood Ladder;* and *You'll Never Nanny in This Town Again: The True Adventures of a Hollywood Nanny.* But most searing, however, to the feminists was this: In 2004 Emma McLaughlin and Nicola Kraus (the duo behind the bestselling *Nanny Diaries*) came out with *Citizen Girl,* a spoof about a twenty-something women's studies major who goes to work for the founding mother of the Female Voice Movement and ends up having her work stolen by her evil boss's equally evil batik-wearing friend.

In women's organizations and women's studies departments, where things were supposed to have been different, older women's power sometimes felt like betrayal. Young women coming up within the ranks of women-run institutions accused older women of hypocrisy, charging them with hoarding—instead of sharing—power. Assistants were disillusioned to find that their bosses wielded power just like men. Hierarchies and power imbalances stimulated passionate reflection among women, young and old, who had expected a different set of rules. "Why Is There So Much Tension between Feminist Bosses and Their Assistants?" asked veteran feminist Phyllis Chesler's former assistant, the question capturing a dilemma increasingly widespread. Chesler responded by explaining the conflict in epic terms: "Like the mythic Electra, who helped kill her mother Clytemnestra, [older feminists] may be especially wary of daughters and daughter-figures as potentially matricidal. Which, traditionally, many younger women are toward older women. Feminists included."[20] On a less epic note, Chesler also charged younger women with being dreamy, hyper, and too impatient to follow instructions.[21]

Sisterhood in the workplace was apparently failing. In the modern workplace, including feminist institutions that now had multiple departments and staff, hierarchy was necessary in order to get things done. But within feminism, "power" was still often considered anathema and "hierarchy" a dirty word. Senior women who knew how to negotiate office politics with men, where rules of exchange were familiar and recognized—even if often sexist—had a difficult time, it seemed, negotiating power differentials with junior women, whom they accused of being slackers unwilling to earn their stripes. Meanwhile, junior women who experienced a lack of mentoring by senior women felt demoralized and let down.

The idea that second-wave women held power while third-wave women didn't was, to many, an ironic perversion—a case of using the master's tools (that is, the tools of patriarchy and power) to re-create the master's house (that is, to oppress younger women). Older feminists agreed that feminism was supposed to have been more than "patriarchy with a face-lift" and seemed surprised that some of their peers were capable of misusing it.[22] One senior feminist who agreed that feminists should be different wrote on the subject of feminists and power with language that some might read as a Freudian slip: "It was never our goal to challenge the patriarchal fathers, simply to take their place."[23]

Feminism's third wave thus began in a swirl of intense, ironic, and often painful contradictions around issues of progress, promotion, and power. But the greatest contradiction of all, perhaps, was this: If second-wave feminism had succeeded, that is, if second-wave feminists had won all their battles, there would have been no third wave. Indeed, there would have been no need. By definition, third-wave daughters embraced a movement that had yet to succeed. In that sense, the third wave was the ironic embodiment of their mothers' failure.

In contrast, postfeminists had believed in and internalized feminism's success. Women's equality and liberation was, to them, not a goal but a reality. In this regard, they implicitly paid the second wave greatest respect. In the postfeminist rubric, one could no longer cry "patriarchy" to excuse one's personal failures and disappointments, nor claim "victim" status when wronged by the system because, they felt, women were no longer victims—no longer the "second sex." Postfeminists existed on the presumption that feminists had effectively changed the world.

What is so striking about this profound difference in the way younger women viewed feminism's progress was how it shaped the way they related to their foremothers—and to the second wave. If you believed that traditional feminism was still needed, as third wavers firmly believed, the question then became: Where did the mothers go wrong?

Third wavers acknowledged that the culture was hostile, in many ways, to feminist goals and ideals. But at the same time, they felt their mothers had made plenty of mistakes. Third wavers' criticisms of feminism hit second wavers hard, because they hit close to home. Second-wavers could dismiss postfeminists as deluded or misguided offspring who both were more conservative and felt more entitled than their mothers. Postfeminists were the daughters who had achieved a certain level of success only to bite the hand that had fed them. But third wavers were the daughters who were following more closely in their mothers' footsteps. They were the eager students in their women's studies classrooms and the willing assistants in their organizations. They were the mirrors into which second-wave feminists peered, expecting to see themselves.

Rebecca Walker felt these contradictions, dramas, and expectations more, perhaps, than most. As the only child of a famous feminist author and a psychoanalyst father, Rebecca had grown up in a liberal feminist community (her godmother was Gloria Steinem) and had her share of generational drama. And what a lot of it boiled down to, she wrote in *To Be Real*, was a desire to oblige.

Walker was aware of her significance as a symbol—and of her expected role in preserving feminism's legacy. She was also keenly aware of the need to differentiate her feminism without rupturing her relationship with her mother—and her mother's movement. "[We] change the face of feminism as each new generation will, bringing a different set of experiences to draw from, an entirely different set of reference points, and a whole new set of questions," she declared, longing to build a bridge between the generations—and, at the same time, burning it.[24]

And therein lies the central drama of the third wave: wanting to belong but being inherently different. Empowered by second-wave feminists and yet wanting to carry their own torch. Embodying a dream—and its failure. Needing to stand independent but also, as Walker said, wanting, still, to please.

THE POLITICS OF AMBIGUITY

So what did empowerment mean for these more dutiful daughters of women's liberation? It meant a triangulated rebellion: Third wavers sought to be more classically feminist than the postfeminists and more accepting of difference—and contradiction—than the second wave.

For starters, third-wave empowerment first meant freeing oneself of, to borrow Oprah's phrase, the disease to please. If postfeminists thought of older feminists as victim mongerers, third wavers thought of them as identity police. Blaming their bosses and professors for mandating "politically correct" behavior, for scripting feminist identity, for hoarding power, and for legislating personal life in ways that seemed overly rigid and suffocating to the young, third wavers joined the postfeminists in creating a bogey: the Second-Wave Feminist. She was rigid, uninviting, dowdy, and, again, plain old no fun—a close cousin of conservative commentator Rush Limbaugh's "feminazi," and equally unappealing. As in the postfeminists' version, Second-Wave Feminism was asexual, or worse: antisex. Merri Lisa Johnson, editor of the third-wave anthology *Jane Sexes It Up*, no doubt shocked some readers when she publicly articulated her desire to "force feminism's legs apart like a rude lover, liberating her from the beige suit of political correctness."[25] Although Johnson explicitly framed this desire as the naive outlook of a young feminist who had not yet understood the complexity of feminist history, and although she went on to explain that she immediately realized on learning more about history that this view was inaccurate, many second-wave readers heard only the inflammatory rhetoric and not the rest of the paragraph, which was about aligning the third wavers of her collection with the radical, and marginalized, sex-positive theorists of the second wave.

Still, shock tactics were intentional, if not exemplary—part of an effort to rouse and arouse women of a new generation to discover and reinvent feminism for themselves. The metaphorical mothers soon countered with an unflattering caricature of daughterhood of their own: third wavers fast became known as navel-gazing, self-indulgent, undisciplined, apolitical, overly empowered, and spoiled.

But to young women, the third wave stood for something different: freedom, tolerance, sexual exploration, and the embrace of contradictions inherent in late-millennium women's lives, in all their diversity. Since Second Wave Feminism (their view of it) was overly confining, the new generation feminists would be defined by their individuality. And since Second Wave Feminism (their understanding of it) was by and for middle-class white women, third wavers insisted that theirs would be multicultural—and multi-issue—from the start.

Women of color played a central role in defining the third wave and setting its course. Invoking Gloria Anzaldúa, Audre Lorde, Cherríe Moraga, Barbara Smith, and other feminists of color as the chosen mothers to emulate, third wavers looked back to and reclaimed a tradition of what they called "U.S. third-world feminism." Calling attention to the whiteness and the academic elitism of Second-Wave Feminism, third wavers like Joan Morgan heralded new strains that embraced the "delicious complexities inherent in being black girls now—sistas of the post–civil rights, post-feminist, post soul, hip-hop generation."[26] Yet Morgan was not alone in wanting to distinguish and distance herself from a mythic black Mother Feminism, too—a demanding ideal that the daughters found too rigid to live up to, and impossibly unreal.

Looking to women of color writing in the 1970s and early 1980s as their guides, third wavers wrote prolifically about their multiple and multiplied selves. Race, class, and sexuality in all their updated and "outed" permutations—bisexuality, queerness, biraciality, transgenderism—figured prominently in their musings, but this time, multiculturalism became a jumping-off point for exploring modern multiplicities in all their myriad forms. For example, in the anthology *Listen Up,* Lisa Bowleg explored being Bahamian and feminist; Sonia Shah described being Indian and feminist; Robin Neidorf explored being feminist and Jewish; and Sonja D. Curry-Johnson examined what it meant to be an "educated, married, monogamous, feminist, Christian, African American [and a] mother."[27] *To Be Real'*s Anna Bondoc delved into her Filipina American feminist identity, while Jeannine Delombard explored what it meant to be feminist and femme. Joan Morgan spoke for many when she explained that she sought a feminism that went beyond black or white and was "brave enough to fuck with the grays."[28]

Third-wave multiplicity also went beyond skin color and embraced ideological gray zones. Rejecting the black-and-white binaristic thinking of Second-Wave Feminism, the new model claimed to better because it was an amalgam, building on everything that came before. Wrote Rebecca Walker, "[W]e find ourselves seeking to create identities that accommodate ambiguity and our multiple positionalities: including more than excluding, exploring more than defining, searching more than arriving."[29] Walker's open-ended description sounded good to members of a generation known for their rejection of labels and rigid identity categories or ideologies. But what exactly, questioned skeptical second wavers, did it mean?[30]

For those who were writing about and living it, "accommodating ambiguity" meant holding opposing ideas in tension—and living comfortably with paradox. It was no longer about being part of the problem or part of the solution, being with "us" or with "them." It was no longer a matter of either/or. In the third-wave paradigm, you could be a feminist aerobics instructor, a feminist exhibitionist, or a feminist supermodel. Third-wave feminism contained "elements of second wave critique of beauty culture, sexual abuse, and power structures while it also acknowledges and makes use of the pleasure, danger, and defining power of those structures."[31] In other words, third-wave feminism meant that you could be a champion of the downtrodden, a critic of oppression, a dominatrix, and a wearer of hot pink lip gloss all at once. You could be a feminist without believing in the Goddess or in the essential goodness of women's culture. If you wanted to be spanked before sex, get married, own a BMW, or listen to misogynist hip-hop music, third wavers claimed, you weren't automatically a traitor to the cause. You could even be unintentionally feminist—and outrageous— like punk rocker Courtney Love, wife of the late rock icon Kurt Cobain. To Heywood and Drake, Love personified third wave: She was "[g]lamorous and grunge, girl and boy, mothering and selfish, put together and taken apart, beautiful and ugly, strong and weak, responsible and rebellious"—combinations of traits that defied the alleged Second-Wave Feminist identity straightjacket and defined daughterly flexibility. Because she was "a highly visible lightning rod for third wave issues," Heywood and Drake suggested that Love may even be the "the Gloria Steinem" of the new wave.[32] Love may not have had quite as much intention behind her actions as did Steinem, but it didn't matter. She could be a lighting rod nonetheless.

Third-wave magazines pushed forth these new principles—tolerance, ambiguity, individuality, fun, and an embrace of sexuality, irony, and contradiction—in print. Much as *Ms.* had a generation back, these publications spread word about the new movement—and new culture?—sweeping the land. The once-neologistic "Ms." was an apt title for a magazine intended to galvanize the newly awakened former housewives of an earlier time. But in a world where the target audience—younger women—was known for failing to identify with labels and causes, the editors of the newly founded *BUST* magazine decided to engage prospective readers through a shockingly retro common denominator: their breasts.

Not so long ago, an unassuming consumer passing by the neighborhood newsstand would assume that a magazine named *BUST* was a girlie magazine, rife with pin-up spreads and airbrushed images of jiggling flesh. Instead of the old objectification, however, identifying women by female parts—or reclaiming words like "slut" and "cunt"—signaled to younger women of the 1990s a hip new feminist machismo. Some of these nouns were powerful verbs: "bust" meant busting out, and "bitch" (the name of a magazine that launched slightly later) meant speaking out. Unacceptable to older women as means by which to identify women, words like "bust" and "bitch" ironically now drew younger ones in.

BUST's editors claimed the name was parodic and that much of what appeared inside the magazine hailed a new kind of feminine celebration, or conscious performance. *BUST: The Magazine for Women with Something to Get Off Their Chests* debuted as a twenty-nine-page Xeroxed-and-stapled 'zine in 1993 pieced together by two self-described "overeducated, underpaid, late-twenty-something cubicle slaves working side-by-side at a Giant Media Conglomerate": Debbie Stoller (who held a doctorate from Yale) and Marcelle Karp (a television producer). Aimed at an audience of women in their late twenties and early thirties—women who had grown up reading *Sassy,* chafed at the old-school stodginess of *Ms.,* and were grossed out by the retro dating advice dished out in *Cosmo—BUST* heralded a new kind of sexy. The editors described it as "brazen," a "magazine for broads who weren't afraid of any f-words—from feminism to fucking to fashion—where we could work out the kinks of our ideology while trying to figure everything else out."[33]

The magazine's name came to the founders in a flash: "*BUST* was at once sexy and aggressive, a joke that would be instantly recognizable by the girls we wanted to reach—it was a mystery wrapped up inside an enigma."[34] Following suit, Stoller and Karp adopted jokey enigmatic pseudonyms for themselves—"Betty Boob" and "Celina Hex"—and so would their writers, many of whom had their own cut-and-paste 'zines or were part of the cyberfeminist explosion then bursting out on the World Wide Web. Drawing on iconic female influences as different as Patti Smith, Excene Cervenka, Barbara Kruger, Cindy Sherman, bell hooks, Debbie Harry, Chrissie Hynde, Kim Gordon, Pam Grier, Susie Bright, Cynthia Heimel, Salt-N-Pepa, and Madonna, the editors wanted *BUST* to be a magazine that, unlike *Ms.*, was both serious and silly, both feminist and frilly. Parody, irony, and an embrace of contradiction and f-words were recurring tropes, giving the magazine a unified feel, much as the trope of awakening had in the early issues of *Ms. BUST*, like early *Ms.*, immediately hit a nerve. In the first five years, *BUST* grew from a homemade 'zine with a circulation of 1,000 to a professionally designed glossy with a circulation of 32,000. It had developed, as its editors declared, from an AA cup to a C. (Today it has surely surpassed a D with a circulation of over 100,000.)

BUST's images spoke volumes, visually capturing the contradictions the editors sought to celebrate and explore. On the cover of the inaugural issue was a black-and-white cut-out of a woman, lips accentuated (in stark white) with what appeared to be lipstick, her hair presumably bleached blond. Hands perched on her hips, the letter "B" overlaid suggestively across her chest in the shape of two semicircular boobs, she aggressively dared the reader to take her on. Under the image of this assertive new woman ran a tagline that played on the well-known ad campaign for Secret deodorant: "*BUST*. The zine that's strong enough for a man, but made for a woman." The *BUST* woman, though fully feminine, the editors suggested, sweated. She did not perspire.

In *BUST*, new configurations of femininity were not merely a statement but a mission. For *BUST* readers and writers, revolution took place through representation. The "problem" facing women as *BUST* defined it—much as Friedan had back in *The Feminine Mystique*—was that mass culture created, circulated, and perpetuated false and constraining ideas about what it meant to be female. Creatively reimagining femininity was therefore a revolutionary act. Turning stereotypes on their head, early *BUST* writers and artists subsequently offered images and word pictures that were alternately or simultaneously girlish and assertive, slutty and wholesome or pure. Through first-person narratives, *BUST* sought to capture, in the words of its editors, "the voice of a brave new girl"—one critical of the way culture imagined her and one who busted back with fiery self-representations of her own.[35] On the heels of a girlish punk rebellion that had recently captured the popular imagination, this woman was also known within young feminist circles as a "grrl."

"Grrl" was "girl" with a healthy dose of youthful female rage, minus the sugar and spice. The word entered the lexicon sometime around 1991, along with the Riot Grrl movement—a loosely connected network of all-girl punk bands and their fans that started in Olympia, Washington, and Washington, D.C. [36] It was coined and initially popularized by Kathleen Hanna, lead singer of a band called Bikini Kill and a woman who cited Shulamith Firestone's *Dialectic of Sex* as a critical piece of work. Described by the *New York Times'* Ann Japenga as girl "with an angry 'grrrowl,'" "grrl" was also a derivation and a repossession of "girl" (when used to refer to a grown or young woman in a pejorative or infantilizing sense), its self-affirming undertones akin to the reclamation of the words "queer" by the gay and lesbian community and "nigger" by some African Americans.[37] Most often invoked as a supportive term of affection, the word's celebratory emphasis was appropriated, in part, from an African American expression of affirmation, "You go, girl!"[38] Not to be confused with the girls' empowerment movement (the Carol Gilligan–inspired initiative to remedy girls' failing self-esteem) or "Girl Power" (a marketing ploy that deployed empowerment rhetoric to sell products), grrl was a grassroots popular expression engendered and disseminated by girls and young women themselves.

As Riot Grrrl bands dispersed and the musical movement died down, followers turned their cut-and-paste 'zines into Web sites, and the "grrl" spirit lived on—online. By 1996, what some were calling "modem post-feminist grrl culture" had so permeated the Web that guide books began to appear, such as Laurel Gilbert and Crystal Kile's *Surfergrrls: Look, Ethel!*

An Internet Guide for Us! Culture—or at least virtual culture—was in the process of being transformed.

In 1996—the year female rapper Lil' Kim released her first album, *Hard Core*—a second magazine rose up alongside *BUST,* one that similarly took popular culture as its primary stage for action. Founding editor Lisa Jervis called it a magazine "about theorizing and fostering a transformation of pop culture."[39] *Bitch: Feminist Response to Pop Culture,* took a more directly activist stance than did its sister magazine—though still its pursuits were mainly in the realm of representation. In *Bitch* perhaps more prominently than in *BUST,* feminist "revolution" meant actively monitoring and challenging popular representations of women and girls, finding independent meanings, and creating new ones to counter the old. The "about" page of *Bitch's* Web site—"it's a noun, it's a verb, it's a magazine!"—defended the title and laid out the mission: "Where are the female-friendly places in the mass media? Where are the things we can see and read and listen to that don't insult our intelligence? How can we get more of them? *Bitch* is about saying, We can make them."

The "New Girl Order," as advocates of the new feminist culture called their vision of the future, was just as much a revolution in representation as it was a continuation of sexual revolution. In early *BUST* issues, articles with titles like "Power to the Pussy" and "Boobs Are Power" recalled older pro-sex lines of feminist thinking—updated with an edgy frankness characteristic of the younger generation. In *BUST* issue number four, "The Sex Issue," the editors demanded the right to be whomever they want to be sexually, with a bravura that defined the daughters of women's liberation: "We want the freedom to be a top, a bottom, or a middle. The freedom to say 'maybe' and mean it. The freedom to wear spike heels one day and Birkenstocks the next."[40] Like Rebecca Walker, Barbara Findlen, and the writers in their anthologies, grrl feminists refused to live by the limitations that came with thinking in terms of either/or. Their demand for sexual freedom was vintage radical feminist. But their hallmark call for multiplicity was third wave—as was the embrace of the Internet as a forum through which to explore it.

This new feminist culture's ties to the past were occasionally acknowledged by its adherents. In *BUST's* tenth issue, for instance, Celena Hex and Betty Boob situated their rebellion in the context of earlier ones: "While women have won a good number of battles, we can't come out of the trenches just yet. . . . So we, the women of the New Girl Order, are going back out onto the sexual battlefield to try and get what's cumming to us."[41] Reaching back to the lexicon of an earlier era, these new feminists abstracted the language of freedom, rights, and liberation to describe the experience of expressing themselves sexually and achieving sexual pleasure. Their revolution had little to do with the politics of City Hall. In this respect, they playfully, passionately, and utterly unselfconsciously revived the very sexual politics that Betty Friedan had once so vehemently deplored.

BUT IS IT *FEMINISM?*

And what did members of the mother generation think of it all? Apparently, not much. Germaine Greer lumped together all the emerging images of femininity in pop culture—from feisty Riot Grrrl to fluffy Ginger Spice—together and dismissively labeled the resulting mishmosh "post-post-feminism," which basically boiled down to "ostentatious sluttishness and disorderly behavior."[42] Seventies icon Erica Jong—the woman who popularized the liberating potential of no-strings-attached sex—told *New York* magazine writer Ariel Levy that she'd be happier if her daughter and her friends were crashing through the glass ceiling instead of the sexual ceiling. Being able to have an orgasm with a man you don't love was not liberation. "Sexual freedom can be a smokescreen for how far we *haven't* come," said Jong.[43] Some third wavers actually agreed. Wrote "Babe Queen" in a *BUST* article called "Don't Call Me (a Do-Me Feminist)": "[S]peaking up and speaking out, doing what and who you want when and how you want to does not a feminist make. It may be novel, shocking, and titillating, and give you the self-confidence of Madonna, but it has jack to do with the grunt work of feminism."[44] Second-wave feminist founders— women more familiar with the brass tacks tactics of protest, organizing, and legislation—couldn't agree more.

While veterans wished that women of the younger generation would focus more on wage gaps rather than orgasm gaps, most early third wavers defended their focus with fervor of the newly awakened. Turned on to sexual revolution and tuned in to MTV and HBO, younger women insisted that critiquing pop culture and liberating themselves sexually was their generation's way of resisting patriarchal culture. But were multiple orgasms and new representations enough? And were the third wave's new politics around identity any more externally engaged than the "PC" identity politics straitjacket against which they rebelled? Perhaps they were merely creating a new identity—the Third-Wave Feminist—against which future fourth wavers would rebel. These questions fanned the flames of disagreement across generations. And once again, as with the radicals, as with Betty Friedan, the question came down to how you defined your terms.

Third wavers defended their politics of gray, their revolution in images and words, and their workshops on vibrator usage as legitimate forms of activism. Echoing, unconsciously perhaps, the radical feminists who expanded on the New Left definitions, early third wavers talked about "learn[ing] to negotiate ourselves" in a postmodern landscape as a novel and effective form of political activity, updating the lifestyle revolution for the postmodern age. Writers like Danzy Senna refuted second wavers' charge that they were politically apathetic and insisted that negotiating identity was political: "Breaking free of identity politics has not resulted in political apathy," she insisted, "but rather it has given me an awareness of the complexity and ambiguity of the world we have inherited—and the very real power relations we must transform."[45] Second wavers, however, weren't so sure.

Once again, much came down to a slogan. The mothers claimed the daughters—postfeminists and third wavers alike—were twisting feminism's foundational catchphrase and that this was a huge mistake. "'The personal is political' did not mean that personal testimony, impressions, and feelings are all you need to make a political argument," Katha Pollitt chided in a critique of postfeminist writing that appeared in the *New York Times* in April 1999 aptly titled "The Solipsisters."[46] Young feminists—channeling younger versions of their mothers?—countered such critiques by claiming that their personal writing was, in effect, their consciousness raising. Or were they perhaps merely following the mandate of founding mother Gloria Steinem, who, in 1992, had published a book titled *Revolution from Within: A Book of Self-Esteem?* Drawing on her own experience as a movement leader and spokeswoman during the 1970s, Steinem had explained that this book emerged out of the recognition that "even I, who had spent the previous dozen years working on external barriers to women's equality, had to admit there were internal ones, too."[47] Reflecting on her own psychic exhaustion and need for self-restoration, Steinem offered a conclusion pertaining to the movement as a whole. In "A Personal Preface," she argued it's time to turn the feminist adage around. "*The political is personal*," she said.[48]

History was repeating itself in odd ways. Mirroring the dilemmas of the foremothers, third-wave feminists struggled with the relationship between a slogan's central terms. As in the writings of their predecessors, tensions and competing impulses were acknowledged but not resolved. Barbara Findlen defended the correlation between personal truth-telling and political change by declaring that the voicing of young women's personal experiences was "just the beginning." Her hope was that *Listen Up,* "along with all the other platforms we are creating," would "serve as a catalyst for consciousness, action, and, ultimately, change in the lives of young women and those whose lives we touch."[49] Walker had voiced a similar dream for *To Be Real.* Her hope was that "these voices can help us continue to shape a political force . . . concerned with mandating and cultivating freedom. . . ."[50] Although the personal essays in these early collections were rich in inspiration, they were light on the details for a program for external change; the organizational shape of Walker's "political force" remained conspicuously unclear.

Why were some of feminism's more progressive daughters so focused (early on, at least) on themselves? Although early third-wave essays were no doubt helpful to others experiencing similar struggles for authenticity and craving political engagement, their authors chronicled their journeys of self-exploration not merely in the context of a wished-for mass movement but as participants in a memoiristic literary trend. Third wavers entered feminism during a cultural moment awash in personal truth-telling. Raised on *Oprah,* coming into adulthood at the height of the memoir boom, they

were finding their voices at a time when recovery-movement memoirs—
many of which sounded remarkably like television talk show confessions
and Alcoholics Anonymous testimonials—occupied the front tables at
Barnes & Noble. Young memoirists were making headlines with intimate
tales of survivorship, journeys, and personal transformations. Confessional
culture had so permeated consciousness that it was easy, perhaps, to mistake personal epiphany and radical acceptance for social change.

Yet another reason may be that third wavers came to feminist consciousness in a different climate. Younger women who grew up in the cynical 1970s, came of age in the conservative 1980s, and came to activism
under Clinton may have felt less hopeful than their foremothers about
their ability to effect lasting, outside change. They may have felt empowered, but their sense of personal empowerment had not yet translated into
confidence that they could effectively transform the outer world. Easier,
perhaps—or at least more practical—to work on oneself.

If early second-wave activism was about strikes, guerrilla theater,
protest, legislation, and consciousness raising, for the nascent third wave,
the arena for activism remained sex, culture, and identity. Second wavers
skeptically raised their eyebrows—forgetting, perhaps, their own earlier
forays into self-discovery along these very lines. But one thing was beginning to seem clear: With both *Bitch* and *BUST* advertising those T-shirts,
sold by *Ms.,* that bore the words "This Is What A Feminist Looks Like"
blazoned across the chest, the "f" word was becoming a word that many
younger women, once again, were increasingly willing to wear.

FORTY YEARS AND FIGHTING

"**F**eminism" in the new millennium is not so much dead or an anachronism as it is a former seedling that took root and is now so grown, its DNA so mutated by forces it has encountered along the way, that it has branched out into the culture at large. Like an organism in evolution, a single word, identity, slogan, or catchphrase can never hope to capture the sum totality again. To attempt to sum it all up at the end of this book, therefore, would be like trying to push a tree back into a seed.

Returning for a moment to the image of Gloria Steinem in the bunny suit, the image that opened this book, I am struck by the way certain iconic moments and scenes of the early women's movement presage the battles that characterize debates about feminism today. Steinem's exposé of Hugh Hefner's testosterone-infused Playboy Club signaled the launch of what would be a famous feminist career. Yet looking back at photos of her from this underground assignment, it's hard to see the feminist icon in the picture. Instead, it's the legs that leap out—so to speak. In the *Show* article of 1963, Steinem herself reports looking in the mirror and seeing not herself but a bunny. While we know full well that Steinem traded on her sex appeal in the service of a larger cause, looking at the photo today, one can't help but be a bit distracted by the tail. It's difficult to look at Steinem in this photo and not, on some level, in some respect, see her as a sex object. In that gray area, between bunny and radical, sexually objectified and sexually liberated, is a key to a legacy of feminist conflict—and continuity.

Elements of third-wave feminism circulate freely now in our culture at large. Women's attitudes toward their own sexuality have today become flashpoints for controversy about what it means to be liberated, empowered, and in power. And in that photo of Steinem so early in her career, we see an unbroken chain between that ambiguous identity—emerging feminist activist posing as Playboy bunny—and the politics of ambiguity that define so much of younger women's feminism now.

What *does* popular feminism look like today? In the early 1970s, on the surface and in the eyes of the media, "women's lib" stereotypically meant long hair, no makeup, no bra, and jeans. Today, in the urban center historically associated with manufacturing feminism's public image, New York City, feminism has superficially come to be associated with sexually aggressive behavior, provocative posturing, and glam. In the runaway hit HBO series *Sex and the City*, now in reruns, four female friends living in New York glamorously tool around town on a half-empowered, half-desperate quest for love and sex, not always in that order. The *Sex and the City* four have been hailed as prototypes for the new sexually empowered woman. The show tapped a nerve. Showtime followed with *The "L" Word*, which chronicles the sexual exploits of a close-knit group of lesbians and bisexual women in L.A., while over on mythical suburban Wisteria Lane, the trapped housewives of ABC's *Desperate Housewives* are "desperate" for sex. In the seemingly inexhaustible genre of fiction known as chick lit, a commercial outpouring of popular women's fiction set off by novelist Helen Fieldings' *Bridget Jones' Diary* back in 1996, mostly straight modern-day Elizabeth Bennetts seek their Mr. Darcys while chronicling in messy detail their sexual exploits, foibles, and the dissolution of romantic ideals. The audience for such books—and shows—is huge. In 2002, a single *Sex and the City* episode brought in 7.3 million viewers, while the new pop literature of manners raked in $71 million for its publishers, prompting many publishers to create new imprints specifically devoted to this genre.

The *Sex and the City*/chick lit vibe and philosophy is replicated off-screen in fashion and in advertising, and especially in magazines targeted at teenage girls. Instead of "Just Say No," girls and women today are encouraged to say yes. An ad for *CosmoGirl!* features a pouty fresh-skinned beauty in a short red dress threatening the ostensibly male gazer with the words "What part of 'Yes, I Can,' don't you understand?" This brave new "yes" merges sexual empowerment and satisfaction with general empowerment and satisfaction with life. Female sexual bravado similarly fuels the entrepreneurial venture known as CAKE, a forward-looking enterprise complete with events, a Web site, a membership program, a newsletter, a manifesto, and followers, which launched in 2000. CAKE's founders, Emily Scarlet Kramer and Melinda Gallagher, two Ivy-educated (and women's studies–educated) twenty-somethings, recently published a book called *A Piece of CAKE: Recipes for Female Sexual Pleasure* in which they declare, "We believe that the next wave of feminism will be our generation of women demanding that sexual empowerment leads to gender equality." At CAKE parties, hundreds of younger women dress like Playboy bunnies (minus the tail), posing, some might say, as feminists, flaunting their hot pants and peek-a-boo thongs as proof of their empowerment, French kissing other women while male "guests" watch. An outside observer might ask whether this new empowerment is any different from the old objectification. Why call such sexed-up behavior "liberated" and "feminist" and not what it looks like: false consciousness or even, to use an even more outdated-sounding term, "oppression?"

The question points to a larger dilemma. To my mind, slinking around a pole or writing about it is not the pinnacle of real-world empowerment, but nor are the women who do so and feel empowered being duped. I have no doubt that the women at CAKE parties feel powerful. Perhaps they are ahead of their time. More likely, I fear, they are out of touch with it. In many ways, they epitomize the dilemma of a generation: caught between the hope of a world that no longer degrades women and the reality of a culture that is still, nevertheless, degrading.

In a world that has changed, yes, but not enough, empowered young women can easily experience confusion around the question "What is power?" Sexual power is not the only variety of power, and alone, it is far from enough. Feminism has yet to make a meaningful difference in many lives, but for many with resources and access, this reality is often masked by the gains that *have* been won. For poor women, especially poor women of color and poor immigrant women, the classic problems feminism was meant to address still exist. To a woman who has yet to see a modicum of power in economic and political realms, rather than empower her, the notion that more sexual freedom will lead to gender equity (instead of the other way around) is a reversal of logic and an argument that seems disempowering—even demeaning.

But younger women who equate sex with power are hardly operating in a vacuum. Images of power babes bear tremendous currency in a culture more obsessed with who does what (or who) in bed then who does what in the House. As young girls are encouraged to emulate celebrity hotties like Christina Aguelira and Jessica Simpson, the proportion of female legislators, to use but one example, remains impossibly low. Some pop idols, aware of their influence, speak out against current popular standards for female ambition. In a satire called "Stupid Girls," singer/songwriter P!nk reminds fans that there is more to power than lifting weights. In a biting critique of Paris Hilton types with their "itsy bitsy doggies and their teeny-weeny tees," P!nk asks: "What happened to the dreams of a girl president?"[1]

The question of whether the new sexual bravado is feminism has sparked hot debate in all the places young feminists gather—most notably, online. On popular blogs like Salon.com's Broadsheet or feministing.com (which, according to the site's recent data, gets more than 50,000 actual hits a day), younger women spar over whether the new forms of public sexual expression—radical bravery or bimbo feminism?—represent progress or regression. Attitudes vary and, following in the footsteps of their mothers, younger women's public stances are often diametrically opposed. In her anthology of personal essays, *Jane Sexes It Up,* for instance, Merri Lisa Johnson suggests that the new sexual bravado *is* part of the new feminism—part of what she calls the "Jane generation's" revamping. "Jane generation" is Johnson's shorthand for a generation of women who are "lodged between the idea of liberation and its incomplete execution," who consciously *want* to reconnect with their movement, and for whom sexuality has become a kind of lightning rod for hopes and discontents in the same way that civil rights and Vietnam galvanized a generation during in the 1960s.[2] Johnson's title anchors this new feminism in its past. ("Jane" was the code name for the underground abortion collective—"Pregnant? Don't want to be? Call Jane at 643–3844," read leaflets passed around in Chicago in the early 1970s. "Jane" was also the name of a putative early feminist magazine envisioned by Susan Brownmiller and Sally Kempton—years before Jane Pratt's *Jane*—that, in the shadow of *Ms.*, never made it off the ground.) In Johnson's view, the women writing for her anthology—modern-day Janes—demonstrate a studied awareness of the pleasure and danger of sex. Their attitudes toward sex and power, Johnson argues, are not merely irresponsible, privileged postfeminist play, but bravery: "Our writing *is* play, but it is play *despite* and *in resistance to* a context of danger and prohibition, *not* a result of imagining there is none."[3] Her work is convincing.

Speaking from the other side of the debate, Ariel Levy, author of *Female Chauvinist Pigs,* disagrees that sexed-up play is the bold new face of feminist courage. According to Levy, what some are calling "the new feminism" is really the old patriarchy thinly disguised in stilettos and a thong. Younger women who consider actual exhibitionism and other forms of sexually promiscuous public play to be radical or revolutionary only think they are in control of the rules. In Levy's view—perhaps a more classically second-wave stance—there are darker forces at work, namely, patriarchy. According to Levy, the enemy has once again staked down outposts in women's heads. Specifically, Levy blames a phenomenon she dubs "raunch culture"—a rising trend that causes women to take up cardio striptease classes at the local gym, install stripping poles in their bedrooms, flash the cameras for the program *Girls Gone Wild,* and go topless at CAKE—for surreptitiously co-opting the ideals of sex radicalism and feminism by equating sexually provocative or promiscuous behavior with freedom. Under the guise of liberation, raunch culture mingles and garbles the vocabularies of sexual revolution and feminist radicalism, parading regressive throwback postures as innovatory and avant-garde. The women who buy it, who enact it, Levy argues, are being sold a bill of goods. She is persuasive.

But not completely convincing.

Many of the women Levy writes about join those anthologized in Johnson's collection, the women of CAKE, fans of *Sex and the City*, chick lit readers, and other moderately privileged members of the so-called Jane generation in an unprecedented experiment with newfound freedoms in a world that has not yet fully progressed. It is not a failure of feminism that is leading to the confusion of these empowered young women about the contours of real power. They are a generation wedged between old definitions of feminism that no longer work and new ones that have yet to be fully lived out. But it would indeed be a failure of feminism if younger women failed to recognize that the sexual arena is not the only platform on which women must stage their feminist rebellion. And it will be a failure of feminism if veteran feminists cannot find a way to understand that these very conversations are offshoots of their own.

GENERATION DISCONNECT

Thirty-five years ago, feminists began debating the definitions of political action, the form of revolution, and whether change began outside or within. Today, many younger women—known for their abhorrence of "–isms"—probe the meaning, form, and the extent of their power, in the bedroom, yes, but elsewhere as well. If the 1990s was a decade of young feminist manifestos focused on personal identity and individual power, in the 2000s, the accent has shifted once more to incorporate collective and systemic change. "Power feminism" has turned out to be about more than individualism. Fueled by this philosophy, growing organizations like the Woodhull Institute for Ethical Leadership (now entering its tenth year) urge younger women to both empower themselves *and* engage in the world, reminding us that younger feminist expressions, like those that preceded them, still orbit among the age-old dual pulls of internal transformation and external change.

Feminist writing and activism has intensified with the turn of the millennium, and a second flurry of self-styled "third-wave" books and activist projects offer models for engagement with the world outside and in venues beyond the bedroom, the strip club, the bar.[4] In 2001—the year of the September 11 attacks and the U.S. invasion of Afghanistan—the American public learned of the plight of Afghan women under the Islamic fundamentalist Taliban regime (which feminists in the United States and Europe had been advocating about for quite some time) and activist Medea Benjamin cofounded CODEPINK, a women's grassroots peace and social justice activist group named in response to the Bush Administration's color-coded "terror alert" system. When, after much was made over the fact that 22 million single women did not vote in the 2000 election, single young women were courted in the next presidential election by both George W. Bush and John Kerry, and White House Project president Marie Wilson asked Mattel to complement her organization's efforts to get more girls to aspire to be president. Mattel agreed and introduced "Barbie for President" (but refused to remove the doll's high heels or the wording on the box that read, "Doll cannot stand alone").[5]

Ten years into the so-called third wave, and in line with the movement's cyclical nature, the emphasis has shifted, once again, to external change. In 2003, the year the United States declared war on Iraq, more young feminist action-oriented anthologies appeared. In 2005, Baumgardner and Richards followed their still-popular *ManifestA,* which itself offered concrete strategies for making change, with a book called *Grassroots,* a field guide to activism intended for young people who want to make real-world change but do not always know where to go or what to do. In 2006, the editors of *Bitch* came out with an anniversary collection of the magazine's best articles that wraps up with an advocacy guide on how to reclaim, reframe, and reform the media. While *BUST* editor Debbie Stoller has since published a series of books about knitting, both she and the magazine continue to emphasize the community-building and culture-changing activism of "grrl."

Younger women's activism in the new millennium is no longer easily categorized. Instead, it is all over the map. It has become about protesting U.S. imperialism abroad, violence in rap music, police brutality, and global warming. "Feminist" issues now include enforced sterilization, female genital mutilation, sex trafficking policies, immigrant rights, prison reform, health care, and the working conditions of women who labor in sweat-shops, at home and abroad. Feminist "actions" range from the hugely popular campus stagings of the *Vagina Monologues* (to raise money to fight violence against women), to the new Mothers Movement, to the creation of New Girls Networks and affinity groups within the corporate sphere.

Yesterday's radical feminists argued over whether "telling it like it is" was a political action or wallowing. Today, a new generation of feminist bloggers debate whether sexually provocative behavior liberates or en-slaves, where and how the antiglobalization movement and feminism intersect, whether the psychology of power can merge with the psychology of abundance and replace the psychology of the oppressed—and more. Some question whether the new all-encompassing feminism is still feminism. If feminism is everything, is it anything? Others debate the viability of the latest popular campaigns and arguments to advance women: Dove soap's "Real Beauty" campaign—good or bad for women? Linda Hirshman's thesis in her book *Get to Work* that women who stay at home with their kids are holding women back—feminist mistake or continuation of Betty Friedan's *The Feminine Mystique?* Laura Kipnis's *The Female Thing*—trenchant new analysis or an updated return to looking at women's own psyche as an internal block to equality? UrbanBaby.com—virtual bitch session or ground zero for a radical mothers' rights movement? The venues and the subject matter have changed, updated to fit the times. Older women don't always recognize these conversations as familiar; many don't even know that they are taking place. Younger women who live these debates don't always embrace the feminist label or see their conversations as having much to do with feminist history. But they are, and they do.

Contemporary feminism is about nothing if not irony. Early third-wave feminist writers claimed parody, irony, and an embrace of contradiction as the hallmarks of their feminism. But the most profound ironies of modern feminism in general are not the ones the pundits and spokeswomen I've identified here have written about but those they've overlooked—specifically, that members of a younger generation who think they are rebelling are instead treading well-worn ground and that older women don't recognize their own progeny. The result is nothing short of tragic: Instead of making tidal waves together, we splash about in separate pools.

Not all points of contention within popular feminism today, of course, are generational. White feminists' lack of sensitivity to issues of race and class turned many women off and undermined second-wave feminism's broad-scale mission. Self-described third-wave feminists, anxious not to replicate their mothers' mistakes, have taken great strides to brand their feminism as a more inclusive model, and indeed, their rhetoric and commitments reflect a far broader diversity. Still, racial tensions remain, as do tensions between heterosexual women and lesbians—and now the transgendered too. Compared to the days of the Lavender Menace, however, younger feminists seem more adept at bridging the sexuality divide.

The age gap, however, only seems to be widening. The generational disconnect within feminism disturbs and muddies the waters of "sisterhood" like never before. With fingers wagging, movement mothers alienate themselves from their successors, while younger women slam the door. I've written about self-described third-wave feminism in these pages with genuine sympathy. The women I identify as the third wave's early articulators inspire me deeply. I laud their impulse to take the best of what second-wave feminism has to offer, lose the rest, forge a feminism truly their own. The term "third wave" itself has been historically important. But 15 years after the term's debut, my sympathy is marred by my fear that women across generations who are intrinsically joined by a shared struggle have forgotten that we are allies, not opponents, in a cause. Not all younger women are slackers. Not all older feminists are killjoys. In blaming each other for feminism's failures, we have lost sight of common ground.

Like it or not, women (and men—but that's the subject of another book) still need feminism. Feminists of different ages still need each other. The original mission—social, economic, and political equality for women—remains relevant, because so much of it remains unfulfilled. Although younger women, peers and allies of men in their careers and all other realms, may not always want to acknowledge it in their bold efforts to forge ahead, most women sense the lag. Deep down, we know. The awareness that women are not yet the equals of men in the eyes of society transcends age. According to a March 2006 Lifetime poll, women across three generations—Boomer, Gen X, and Gen Y—agreed that while it has never been a better time to be a woman, women still face discrimination, and men have more advantages in society. According to Lifetime, the women interviewed in 2006 felt more strongly that men had more advantages than did women who were asked this same question in 1974.[6] In spite of the articles now pouring forth about how women outperform men in college, there is still the nagging reality that as soon as these men and women of so-called equal standing graduate and get jobs, the men will still, immediately, be earning more.

In many realms, gains have been made from which there can be no retreat. In contrast to the days when women couldn't get credit in their names, today there are more than 7.7 million women-owned businesses in the United States. Women are now earning more than half of all bachelor's and master's degrees, and 40 percent of doctoral degrees as well. We now have our own radio network (launched in 2006 by none other than Gloria Steinem). There are more female Muppets. Young girls flipping through channels will now see that women can be heads of state in Chile, Liberia, and Germany—even if they still aren't here in their own country, though the speculation about a potential run by Hillary Clinton no doubt sends a positive message. In urban centers, among the upper and middle class, and for white women in particular, the changes feminism has wrought are profound.

Younger women who *have* experienced a degree of empowerment feel acutely the effects of living in a world not fully transformed. But they have no real language—other than journalist Peggy Orenstein's apt word "flux"—for this growing sense of living between the aspiration and the reality of equality.[7] Today, for a young woman living in flux, the awareness that she is not as equal as she thinks might crystallize on the job, when a boss treats a male coworker differently or pays a man she supervises more. More often, and more prolifically, such realizations come at home, when a working woman (and statistically that means most) who marries and becomes pregnant soon realizes that her husband, who believes in egalitarian marriage, expects her to quit her job and raise the kids full time. Anthologies beginning with *The Bitch in the House* chronicle a new generation of angst-ridden epiphany, but the epiphanies come without catharsis. Friedan's wished-for second stage—where men and women work together to revolutionize the division of labor in the home—seems only slightly more visible on the distant horizon. Men do more housework today but still, in comparison to their working wives, not much. External supports are slow in coming. The United States is one of the only industrialized democracies in the world without a national system of child care. Our family leave policies leave much to be desired.

Raised with "Take Our Daughters to Work Day" and told that they are valued for their talent and brains, younger women are nevertheless more obsessed than ever with the way they look—as Gen Y writer Courtney Martin makes clear in *Perfect Girls, Starving Daughters: The Frightening New Normalcy of Hating Your Body.* Standards for female beauty remain impossible to meet. The Miss America Pageant has morphed into a weekly reality series known as *America's Next Top Model,* where the winner not only has to be physically flawless and skinny, but able to outfox her fellow beauty queens by preying on their weaknesses. Although younger women now have the morning-after pill, they will still have to fight for their reproductive rights, equal pay, and access to top jobs in fields such as science, engineering, and politics. Women who accuse men of sexual harassment or rape are still publicly humiliated and disbelieved. More women still live in poverty than men. No one growing up with the assumption and promise of equality likes to be reminded, but the unsexy reality is that we are not fully equal. Yet.

Antifeminist attitudes—among women as well as men—abound. The postfeminist ethos of the 1990s has morphed into a populist conservatism with stars like Dr. Laura and conservative poster girl Ann Coulter— women with call-in radio shows, columns, book deals, and Rush Limbaugh–caliber zingers. ("I think [women] should be armed but should not [be allowed to] vote," taunts Coulter on *Politically Incorrect* in February 2001.) New networks and organizations continue to spring forth on campus, with names like the Network of Enlightened Women. New critics update the old stereotypes to fit the times. A recent book by young conservative Carrie Lukas, vice president for policy at the Independent Women's Forum, provocatively titled *The Politically Incorrect Guide to Women, Sex, and Feminism,* claims, "Modern feminism has strayed far from [its] original mission. It is now associated with radical liberal politics, including support for an ever larger federal government, a European-style welfare state, and a general hostility to traditional families."[8] Breathing new life into old fears, Lukas warns her followers that feminists' greatest desire is to usher in an androgynous age. A few decades back, feminism's opponents held up the specter of unisex bathrooms. New bogeys, layered on top of the old.

Cultural and political trends toward conservatism in America that consolidated in the 1980s have reached new heights. Social and religious conservatives today are much more activist than they were in the past. There are more of them. They have a lot more power than they have ever had. While conservatives young and old continue to demonize feminism, many of the gains second-wave feminists fought for and won in the legislative arena have been methodically chipped away. In recent years, government information agencies and councils that monitored governmental efforts on behalf of women and girls have disappeared. These include the President's Interagency Council on Women, which was mandated to develop policies for the advancement of women and girls under the UN Platform for Action adopted by the nations of the world in 1995 at Beijing, and the Office of Women's Initiatives and Outreach in the White House, mandated with ensuring that the concerns of women are addressed in policy development.[9]

Under George W. Bush's administration, information routinely posted on government Web sites, such as critical health data for women, has been withdrawn or altered, and, instead, such sites broadcast conservative or religious beliefs about sex and sexuality. A 2004 report found that over 80 percent of federally funded abstinence-only curricula taught in sex education courses at schools contained false, misleading, or distorted information about reproductive health.[10] The Department of Labor's Women's Bureau, an agency charged by Congress with providing information on women's economic status and rights, has become nearly silent on those issues. Government publications that focused specifically on job rights as well as fact sheets that analyzed women's status and rights are no longer available. Title IX is under attack. Due to war expenditures and tax cuts, funding for the recently reauthorized Violence against Women Act (legislation that improves community-based and criminal justice responses to domestic violence, dating violence, sexual assault, and stalking) was in danger of being cut. Basic rights many thought secure are proving frail. Ours is an unfinished revolution.

There are many women, young and old and in between, who still see feminism as a social movement that aims to rally the masses, work collectively to better all women's lives, and effect irreversible structural change. It's no longer about Betty versus Gloria, though the divide between heartland and coast remains largely intact. We are a nation increasingly polarized—Right versus Left, those who support old-fashioned gender arrangements versus those who support gender equality, red states versus blue states (although the Democratic sweep during the 2006 midterm elections suggests that Americans across divides are fed up with the current administration's status quo). Against this backdrop, the Internet has become the great uniter, exponentially amplifying—and multiplying—the feminist megaphone. Feminism today comes in countless flavors, brands, and styles. Within the organized women's movement—a wide yet at the same time insular network of nonprofits, NGOs, lobbyists, academics, and campus organizations—the pointed debate between Betty and the radicals lives on in the form of heated internal conversations about whether to use language and jargon that appeals to the "already converted" or whether to pitch to the mainstream (and to both sides of the political aisle) by muting the radical edge. Younger women within the organized movement push for attention-grabbing, sexy, and playful language that speaks to their own generation: "We Do It for Money: Young Feminists for Economic Equity" reads a tight-fitting baby-doll T-shirt designed by women working at NOW.

Although they may disagree about ways to do it, arguing internally over wording, message, and tone, populists and mainstreamers continue to try valiantly, in Betty Friedan's legacy, to make the old, original principles edgy, relevant, and fashionable. Again. Some of the older models of activism still have shelf life or, as advocates call it, legs. The Guerrilla Girls ("Fighting discrimination with facts, humor and fake fur!") celebrated their twentieth anniversary in 2005, with no plans of stopping. In 2006, the Boston Women's Health Collective published *Our Bodies, Ourselves: Menopause*—and continues to come out with updated versions of the original book, now in its twelfth edition, published in seventeen languages and Braille—and *Ms.* recently launched its second "I had an abortion" campaign and petition, albeit to mixed reviews. (The first petition appeared in the 1972 debut issue of the magazine when over fifty well-known women declared that they had abortions, illegal at the time.)

For the most part, nonprofits, think tanks, advocacy organizations, and women's magazines spend a great deal of energy thinking about what kinds of words will successfully play with a new public in a new era, nurturing women's sense of their own growing and, in some realms, receding power. "Vote! Run! Lead!" urges the White House Project, an organization dedicated to increasing the representation of women at all levels of politics, including the presidency, teaming up with *CosmoGirl!* in an effort to encourage young girls to shoot for the nation's top job. Promoting women to leadership positions is good for the bottom line, argues Catalyst, an organization dedicated to helping women in business advance their careers.

Times have changed and feminist rhetoric has adapted. Within organized feminism, phrases like "women's movement" and "women's issues" are often cast aside in favor of more politically neutral and red-state friendly phrases, such as "women's priorities and values." The f-word is frequently discarded as well. If women's organizations themselves are dumping the f-word to avoid alienating the mainstream and safeguard their public image, one might argue that the word, so fatally tainted, is not worth reclaiming.

But it is.

Words give us common ground. To drop "feminist" wholesale is to let those who have trashed the word win. Some think it is time for a new word, but why reinvent yet another wheel? The one we have can still do the trick. Yet whether we call it "feminist" or something else, without some word to call ourselves collectively and in public, it becomes increasingly difficult to invest with focused intention in women's collective future. Without such a word, it is difficult to unite in common cause. Words are more than a matter of semantics, or labels. They not only express but shape the way we think.

Over the past twenty years, right-wing commentators and communications strategists have become masters at manipulating language to influence policy. In recent political elections, they have seized the language and terms of debate. It matters whether you call something an "estate tax" or a "death tax"—who in their right mind wants a tax on death? Or whether something is called "late-term" or "partial birth" abortion—who wants to give partial birth? Who in their right mind wants to call themselves "anti-life?" Words continue to change minds and influence policy, and thereby the course of history. Words have the power not just to name but to change.

It is time, no doubt, to retire some words. Many younger women are wary, for example, of "sisterhood." To many, the term feels obsolete. Recently I asked *ManifestA* coauthor Amy Richards, cofounder of the Third Wave Foundation, how her own thinking about the meaning of "sisterhood" has evolved. Said Richards, "When Third Wave [the organization] incorporated, Rebecca [Walker] was adamant that we *not* be an organization that works by consensus. I was like, 'Hey, it's sisterhood—of course it should all be consensus.' But now I realize that sisterhood is phony. Even when there's consensus, there isn't. I think younger women have a better sense that it is a big facade."[11]

In contrast to the days when women in consciousness-raising groups experienced collective relief in realizing that they were not alone, younger women lambast false unity with sass and wit. Richads notes that the absence of consensus does not undermine the work. Sisterhood is not the answer, but neither is the unqualified embrace of difference—the principle that seems to have replaced it. "Difference is Powerful" has achieved the status of an unspoken mantra in many feminist circles. But difference, as an organizing principle, has its limitations. We can respect differences without fragmenting ourselves to the extent that we no longer see that some of our greatest disappointments and frustrations are still shared.

Women—those of us who call ourselves feminists and those of us who don't—need to find the common ground, the space between where we can work in coalition, fighting together and not merely against ourselves. Although sisterhood is interrupted, feminism remains compelling. And the time has come to regain control of our terms.

So what might feminists agree on? When we back off far enough to see the larger picture, women might be able to agree on some basic tenets: What is a "feminist?" Anyone (regardless of whether she or he embraces the label) who believes that women and girls should be on par—politically, economically, socially with boys and men. And "feminism?" At its most basic level, and historically speaking, it is still an individual and collective fight for personal empowerment and social change. Back in 1971, the editors of *Notes from the Third Year* reminded early followers of the movement's dual emphasis: "The women's movement is . . . not only an organized political force but a state of mind as well." Although the popular image of feminism today may be that of a sexed-up push for personal empowerment rather than an organized political force focused on reforming or transforming structures, it is clear that in the hearts and minds of women across generations, the dual impulse beats on.

WHAT ARE WE FIGHTING FOR?

Although this has been a book about feminist infighting, I end on a note of truce: Younger women need older feminists to understand that for a women's movement to continue to move forward, it will require updating and reinvention. At the same time, younger women need to stop blaming older ones and ditch old stereotypes about the second wave that preclude them from rallying around common themes.[12] Older generations need to take an active role in passing down what they have learned and mentor with an eye toward letting go.

This work will not be easy, nor will it be popular. There are many for whom the feminist catfight remains the ultimate spectator sport, and, like all good sports fans, they will not take the loss of the spectacle lightly.

Feminists will continue to fight, and well they should. Feminism is about passion; the strength of conviction among women fighting for change is often extreme. It is retro to think that women—who are as different from each other as they are from men—should always agree. But in the battle for power and parity, feminists have historically been, and continue to become, each other's easiest target.

Why do feminists fight? Perhaps there is something about the personalities of well-known feminist spokeswomen—regardless of generation—that gives rise to rhetorically aggressive face-offs. Visionaries are difficult, impatient people by nature, suggests Susan Brownmiller in *In Our Time,* her juicy memoir of those early days. But perhaps it is something more. Have women young and old so internalized sexism that it remains far easier for us to lash out each other than external targets? If so, then it is time, borrowing an old phrase from the New Left, to "change our heads" once more.

Feminist conflict has, in the past, been productive. Early second-wave feminism actually thrived on dispersion and dissent. Although frequently at odds, *both* Betty Friedan and radical feminists played a key role in making feminism a widespread movement within the United States. The thoughts and writings of divergent feminist thinkers played an essential role in bringing feminism and feminist issues to the forefront of national attention in a remarkably short period of time. Different arenas of feminist activism and debate have had their distinct effects on different sectors of society. Radical feminism had a major influence, for example, on the intellectual formation of faculty who would go on to develop women's studies, which, in turn, had a major impact on mainstreaming core principles of second-wave feminism within the nation's colleges and universities. Radical feminism also spawned, for instance, the antirape and anti–domestic violence movements, touching the lives of countless women through hotlines, shelters, and other community supports. Friedan's *McCall's* columns, side by side with *Ms.* magazine, played a crucial role in making the women's movement attractive to women in America's heartland. Without the contribution of either of these forces, feminism and its philosophies would have failed to achieve the far-reaching influence across American culture that it did, so fast, and so early on.

But now, when so few of us seem to recognize the commonalities of our dreams, when women are fragmented and more likely to see problems as strictly personal once again, when the overall climate is conservative and collective mass actions are scarce, the cost of feminist infighting is more than most women can afford.

Almost everyone talks about the so-called death of feminism, while few talk about its actual life.[13] In 2007 feminism is not a self-contained phenomenon with a beginning, middle, and end. Nor has it been a straightforward transmission of tactics and values across time. Rather, it is an ongoing, breathing legacy, a lived experience that, in order to remain effective, must constantly be refashioned, revamped, and reexplored. As we forge a feminism for the future, we should honor generational and other differences but keep our eyes on the prize. If those who support gender parity in this country can't talk to each other or get along, then feminism's grandchildren may pay the ultimate price.

NOTES

INTRODUCTION

1. In San Francisco, the flyers denounced "mass media images of the pretty, sexy, passive, childlike vacuous woman." See Ruth Rosen, *The World Split Open: How the Modern Women's Movement Changed America*, 205.
2. For an account and criticism of the decline of civic participation and its consequences for politics, see Robert D. Putnam's *Bowling Alone: The Collapse and Revival of American Community*.
3. Fewer single women than married women vote (52 percent as compared to 68 percent in the 2000 election), and more young women today are likely to be single. See "Women's Voices, Women Vote: National Survey Polling Memo," Lake, Snell, and Perry Associates, October 19, 2004.
4. Nancy Cott, *The Grounding of Modern Feminism*, 365, quoting *Judy* 1:1 (June 1919): 2:3.
5. Academics Deborah Rosenfelt and Judith Stacey are also credited for reintroducing the term "postfeminist" during this time. See their "Second Thoughts on the Second Wave," 341–361.
6. Summers's remarks were made at the NBER Conference on Diversifying the Science & Engineering Workforce in Cambridge, Massachusetts on January 14, 2005. At an industry conference in Toronto on October 21, 2005, French said, "Women don't make it to the top because they don't deserve to. They're crap." He added that women inevitably "wimp out and go suckle something." See Tom Leonard, "Advertising Chief Loses Job over French Maid and Sexist Insults."
7. See The White House Project, *Who's Talking Now: A Follow-Up Analysis of Guest Appearances by Women on the Sunday Morning Talk Shows*.
8. For more on the current status of women worldwide, see the National Council for Research on Women, *Gains and Gaps: A Look at the World's Women*.
9. Jennifer Baumgardner and Amy Richards, *ManifestA: Young Women, Feminism, and the Future*, 62.
10. In August 1992, television evangelist Pat Robertson wrote a letter to help raise money to defeat Amendment 1, an Iowa ballot initiative that would extend the protections of the state constitution to women. In it, he wrote, "The feminist agenda is not about equal rights for women. It is about a socialist, anti-family political movement that encourages women to leave their husbands, kill their children, practice

witchcraft, destroy capitalism and become lesbians." See Maralee Schwartz and Kenneth J. Cooper, "Equal Rights Initiative in Iowa Attacked."

11. Helen Fielding, *Bridget Jones' Diary*, 20; Julie Bosman, "Glamour's Hollywood Side: Films by and About Women"; Akiba Solomon, "Boss Lady," 69.

12. According to the May 2–5, 2005, poll: "College students said 9/11 jolted them out of their complacency about life in general and made them more serious about making a contribution to society through their work." See Celinda Lake and Kellyanne Conway, *What Women Really Want: How American Women Are Quietly Erasing Political, Racial, Class, and Religious Lines to Change the Way We Live*, 163.

13. See Lifetime Women's Pulse Poll, "Generation Why?" March 2006. Generation Y was defined as those aged eighteen to twenty-nine. Generation X, ages thirty to forty-four, and Baby Boomers, age forty-five to fifty-nine. The poll, conducted by Kellyanne Conway and Celinda Lake, looked at women's attitudes regarding sex, men, marriage and career. Center for the Advancement of Women, *Progress and Perils: New Agenda for Women*. Lorraine Dusky, "*Ms.* Poll: Feminist Tide Sweeps in as the 21st Century Begins," 56–61. Young women are most appreciative of the impact of the women's movement on their careers, with 84 percent of those under twenty-five and 85 percent of working women ages twenty-six to thirty reporting a positive effect, according to Business and Professional Women and the Institute for Women's Policy Research, "Working Women Speak Out."

14. See Lyn Mikel Brown and Carol Gilligan, *Meeting at the Crossroads: Women's Psychology and Girls' Development* and Jill McLean Taylor, Carol Gilligan, and Amy M. Sullivan, *Between Voice and Silence: Women and Girls, Race and Relationships*.

15. See, for instance, Beth Brykman, *The Wall Between Women*; Leslie Morgan Steiner, *Mommy Wars*; and Nan Mooney, *I Can't Believe She Did That! Women Sabotaging Women at Work*.

16. Sheelah Kolhatkar, "Les Ms.-erables Bust Cover."

17. Susan Douglas, *Where the Girls Are: Growing Up Female with the Mass Media*, 244.

18. See Joan Cassell, *A Group Called Women: Sisterhood and Symbolism in the Feminist Movement*; Jo Freeman, "The Origins of the Women's Liberation Movement," and *The Politics of Women's Liberation*; J. Rothschild-Whitt, "The Collectivist Organization: An Alternative to Rational-Bureaucratic Models"; and Myra Marx Ferree and Beth B. Hess, *Controversy and Coalition: The New Feminist Movement Across Four Decades of Change*, esp. 58–59.

19. See Rachel Fudge's analysis of feminist celebrity in "Celebrity Jeopardy: The Perils of Feminist Fame."

20. To date, little has been written about the traffic between waves. Sara Evans's *Tidal Wave: How Women Changed America at Century's End* expertly tracks the personal as political, but dedicates only one chapter to the emergence of the third wave. For an academic treatment of recent traffic between waves from a psychoanalytic perspective, see Astrid Henry, *Not My Mother's Sister: Generational Conflict in Third Wave Feminism*.

CHAPTER 1

1. Steinem's exposé, "I Was a Playboy Bunny," was reprinted in her later collection, *Outrageous Acts and Everyday Rebellions*, 33–78. It originally appeared as a two-part article, "A Bunny's Tale," in *Show* magazine in 1963.

2. Gloria Steinem, "The City Politic: 'After Black Power, Women's Liberation,'" 8–10. The article won a Penney-Missouri Journalism Award in 1970 as one of the first aboveground reports on second-wave feminism.

3. Ibid., 8.

4. Dana Densmore, "A Year of Living Dangerously: 1968," *The Feminist Memoir Project*, 71.

5. Amy Kesselman, with Heather Booth, Vivian Rothstein, and Naomi Weisstein, "Our Gang of Four: Friendship and Women's Liberation," 38. See also Bonnie Watkins and Nina Tothchild, eds., *In the Company of Women: Voices from the Women's Movement*.

6. Vivian Gornick, "What Feminism Means to Me," 372. Gloria Steinem, "Sisterhood," 128. Originally published in 1972.

7. See www.contactmusic.com, "Shakira: 'I'm No Feminist'" February 16, 2006, www.contactmusic.com/new/xmlfeed.nsf/mndwebpages/shakira%20im%20no%20feminist_16_02_2006.

8. Louis Harris, "The Harris Survey," May 20, 1971.

9. Betty Friedan, *It Changed My Life: Writings on the Women's Movement*, 76.

10. See Carol Hanisch, "The Personal Is Political." Before making its way there, the slogan was brandished about by women in the Redstockings and New York Radical Women as they theorized an emerging revolution. See Kesselman et al., "Our Gang of Four," 42.

11. The social and political landscape of the late 1960s and early 1970s has been well documented by historians of the civil rights movement, chroniclers of the student protest movements, and feminist historians alike. See, for instance, Clayborne Carson, *In Struggle: SNCC and the Black Awakening of the 1960s;* James Miller, *Democracy Is in the Streets: From Port Huron to the Siege of Chicago;* Todd Gitlin, *The Whole World Is Watching: Mass Media in the Making and Unmaking of the New Left;* Richard Flacks, *Making History: The American Left and the American Mind;* Ronald Fraser et al., *1968: Student Generation in Revolt;* and, especially, Sara Evans, *Personal Politics: The Roots of Women's Liberation in the Civil Rights Movement.*

12. See Abe Peck, *Uncovering the Sixties: The Life and Times of the Underground Press* for an account of frustrations that led some radicals to drop out or to try, quite literally, to "bring the war home." For additional accounts of disillusionment among radicals in the 1960s, see Todd Gitlin, *The Sixties: Years of Hope, Days of Rage* and Sohnya Sayres et al., eds., *The '60s Without Apology.*

13. Valerie Solanas, "Excerpts from the S.C.U.M. Manifesto," 518.

14. The early SDS Jobs or Income Now (JOIN) and Newark Projects, the Southern Conference Educational Fund projects in Kentucky and Appalachia, and the Mississippi Voter Registration Project, among others, were based on this new concept of a "revolutionary class." For further accounts of differences between the Old and New Left in the United States, see Maurice Isserman, *If I Had a Hammer . . . The Death of the Old Left and the Birth of the New Left;* Alan Wald, *The New York Intellectuals: The Rise and Decline of the Anti-Stalinist Left from the 1930's to the 1980's;* Ellen Kay Trimberger, "Women in the Old and New Left: The Evolution of a Politics of Personal Life"; and Wini Breines, *Community and Organization in the New Left, 1962–1968.*

15. For more on how early radical feminists borrowed from organizing philosophies of the civil rights movement, see Sara Evans, *Personal Politics,* and Casey Hayden, "A Nurturing Movement: Nonviolence, SNCC, and Feminism." For a discussion of Ella Baker's influence on radical feminists, see Myra Marx Ferree and Beth B. Hess, *Controversy and Coalition: The New Feminist Movement Across Four Decades of Change,* 58.

16. Densmore, "A Year of Living Dangerously: 1968," 73

17. Barbara Winslow, "Primary and Secondary Contradictions in Seattle," 244.

18. Jo Freeman, "On the Origins of the Women's Liberation Movement from a Strictly Personal Perspective," 176.

19. For famous exposés of sexism in the New Left, see Robin Morgan, "Goodbye to All That," first published in *Rat* earlier in 1970; New York Radical Women, "A Letter to the Editor of *Ramparts* Magazine" in *Notes from the First Year* (1969); Rita Mae Brown, "Say It Isn't So"; and Marge Piercy, "The Grand Coolie Damn."

20. Freeman, "On the Origins," 180. At an SDS convention in June 1968, women were thrown out for demanding that women's liberation become a plank of the national platform.

21. There are different interpretations of this comment. According to one account, after an intense SNCC meeting at a location near a lake, a number of participants had strolled out to a wooden dock to lie in the sun. When some began to talk about "the position of women," Carmichael made his crack, intended as a joke. As the lore goes, Eldridge Cleaver is also alleged to have mocked the fledgling women's liberation movement by referring to it, condescendingly, as "pussy power."

22. Kesselman et al., "Our Gang of Four," 38–39.

23. The article, titled "Women Unite for Revolution," was later reprinted in the widely circulated anthology *Voices from Women's Liberation* edited by Leslie Tanner in 1970 (131).

24. In "The Politics of Housework," first published as a satirical broadside in mimeograph form and later published in *Notes from the Second Year* and *Sisterhood Is Powerful* in 1970, Redstockings member Pat Mainardi wittily detailed her mate's ploys for avoiding housework. Also that year, Alix Kates Shulman wrote "A Marriage Agreement," first published in the second issue of the new feminist journal *Up from Under* in August 1970 and later reprinted *New York* magazine and in *Redbook* magazine, where it elicited 2,000 letters in response.

25. Steinem, "Words and Change," 174. Italics in original.

26. Anselma Dell'Olio, "Home Before Sundown," 158.

27. Steinem, "Words and Change," 170.

28. Naomi Weisstein, "Days of Celebration and Resistance: The Chicago Women's Liberation Rock Band, 1970–1973," 354.

29. Steinem, "Sisterhood," 132–133.

30. Vivian Gornick, "Consciousness (Female Symbol)."

31. See Alice Echols, *Daring to Be Bad: Radical Feminism in America 1967–1975;* Winifred Wandersee, *On the Move: American Women in the 1970s;* and Flora Davis, *Moving the Mountain: The Women's Movement in America Since 1960.*

32. Marxist-feminist groups formed around the country, and study groups emerged primarily on the coasts. The journal *Quest: A Feminist Quarterly,* founded in 1974, gathered socialist feminist theorizing. Theorists examined traditionalist socialist

ideas from a feminist perspective. For examples of influential socialist feminist scholarship, see Linda Gordon, *Woman's Body, Woman's Right: A Social History of Birth Control in America* and Alice Kessler-Harris, *Out to Work: A History of Wage-Earning Women in the United States.*

33. For a more detailed who's who of the radical feminist movement, see Echols, *Daring to Be Bad,* Appendix 1.

34. See Rosalyn Baxandall and Linda Gordon, *Dear Sisters: Dispatches from the Women's Liberation Movement.* See also Shirley Geok-lin Lim, "'Ain't I a Feminist?': Re-forming the Circle"; Barbara Smith, "'Feisty Characters' and 'Other People's Causes': Memories of White Racism and U.S. Feminism"; Beverly Guy-Sheftall, "Sisters in Struggle: A Belated Response"; and Michele Wallace, "To Hell and Back: On the Road with Black Feminism in the 1960s & 1970s."

35. Elizabeth (Betita) Martinez, "History Makes Us, We Make History," 118.

36. Baxandall and Gordon, *Dear Sisters,* 14.

37. See Benita Roth, *Separate Roads to Feminism: Black, Chicana, and White Feminist Movements in America's Second Wave* and Kimberly Springer, *Living for the Revolution: Black Feminist Organizations, 1968–1980.*

38. Eleanor Holmes Norton, "For Sadie and Maude," 398. See also Catherine Stimpson, "'Thy Neighbor's Wife, Thy Neighbor's Servants': Women's Liberation and Black Civil Rights," and the early writings of Barbara Smith.

39. See, for example, Toni Morrison, *The Bluest Eye* and *Sula;* Alice Walker, *Revolutionary Petunias and Other Poems;* Audre Lorde, *Chosen Poems—Old and New;* and Shange's *for colored girls who have considered suicide/ when the rainbow is not enough.*

40. Echols, the radical movement's key chronicler, notes that, with few exceptions, these were the groups that made significant theoretical contributions. Although often these groups were quite small, they had an influence far beyond their numbers. A number of localized studies focused on other important regions are currently under way. See Barbara Winslow, "Primary and Secondary Contradictions in Seattle," and Amy Kesselman, "Women's Liberation and the Left in New Haven, Connecticut 1968–1972." For an account of groups active in Columbus, Ohio, see Nancy Whittier, *Feminist Generations: The Persistence of the Radical Women's Movement.*

41. Dell'Olio, "Home Before Sundown," 150

42. Hanisch, "The Personal Is Political," 76.

43. Pamela Allen, "The Small Group Process," 277.

44. Steinem, *Outrageous Acts,* 181.

45. Gloria Steinem, *Moving Beyond Words: Age, Rage, Sex, Power, Money, Muscles: Breaking the Boundaries of Gender,* 270. Italics in original.

46. R. Z. S., "Up Against the Men's Room Wall," *Time* 31 Aug. 1970.

47. Kate Millett, *Sexual Politics,* 43.

48. Ibid., 22.

49. Ibid., 23.

50. Ibid. Millett also acknowledged that her understanding of power relations was influenced by Ronald V. Samson's *The Psychology of Power.* In a footnote she acknowledged Samson "for his intelligent investigation of the connection between formal power structures and the family and for his analysis of how power corrupts basic human relationships" (24).

51. Frances Beal, "Double Jeopardy," 395.
52. Shulamith Firestone, *The Dialectic of Sex: The Case for Feminist Revolution,* 38.
53. Germaine Greer, *The Female Eunuch,* 347.

CHAPTER 2

1. Qtd. in Sara Evans, *Tidal Wave: How Women Changed America at Century's End,* 214.
2. Qtd. in Ruth Rosen, *The World Split Open: How the Modern Women's Movement Changed America,* 159.
3. See New York Radical Women, "No More Miss America! Ten Points of Protest" circulated in August 1968. Women's Movement General Files, Tamiment Library, New York University.
4. See Alice Echols, *Daring to Be Bad,* 94.
5. Qtd. in Susan Douglas, *Where the Girls Are: Growing Up Female with the Mass Media,* 159.
6. Barbara Winslow, "Primary and Secondary Contradictions in Seattle," 238.
7. Qtd. in Carol Hanisch, "Two Letters from the Women's Liberation Movement," 198.
8. Carol Hanisch, "A Critique of the Miss America Protest," *Notes from the Second Year,* 87.
9. See Echols, *Daring to Be Bad,* 94.
10. Ibid., 96.
11. Hanisch, "The Personal Is Political," 76. For positions parallel to Hanisch's, see Redstockings, "Taking Politics Out of the Analysis"; and Brooke Williams, "The Retreat to Cultural Feminism." See also Elizabeth Fox-Genovese, "Personal Is Not Political Enough."
12. Partial sponsors included Representative Shirley Chisholm, Robin Morgan, Kate Millett, Helen Southard (YWCA), Beulah Sanders (National Welfare Rights Organization), New York Radical Feminists, National Organization for Women, and Columbia Women's Network.
13. Linda Charlton, "Women March Down Fifth in Equality Drive," *New York Times,* August 27, 1970. "Women Rally to Publicize Grievances," *Newsweek,* August 5, 1970. Grace Lichtenstein, "For Most Women, 'Strike' Day Was Just a Topic of Conversation," *New York Times,* August 27, 1970. For more detailed accounts of the press coverage, see Douglas, *Where the Girls Are,* 180–181 and Rosen, *The World Split Open,* 358 n63.
14. The poll was conducted on September 4–5, 1970. See Rosen 92–93.
15. Qtd. in Rosen, *The World Split Open,* 173. The pro-lesbian line was promoted in additional radical feminist publications including "Women Rap About Sex"; Anne Koedt, "The Myth of the Vaginal Orgasm"; Dana Densmore, "On Celibacy"; Martha Shelley, "Notes of a Radical Lesbian."
16. Radicalesbians, "The Woman-Identified Woman," 243, 245.
17. Qtd. in Echols, *Daring to Be Bad,* 264.
18. Robin Morgan, "Forum: Rights of Passage."
19. Kathie Sarachild, "A Program for Feminist Consciousness Raising," 274.
20. Roxanne Dunbar, "Outlaw Woman: Chapters from a Feminist Memoir in Progress," 112.

21. Amy Kesselman et al., "Our Gang of Four," 40.

22. Monique Wittig's *Les Guérillères* was important to the development of this line, as was Adrienne Rich's *Of Woman Born: Motherhood as Experience and Institution* and her poems that appeared separately before appearing in *The Dream of a Common Language.*

23. Qtd. in Echols, *Daring to Be Bad,* 155.

24. Brooke Williams, "The Retreat to Cultural Feminism," 66.

25. Gail Paradise Kelly, "Women's Liberation and the New Left," 42.

26. Naomi Weisstein and Heather Booth, "Will the Women's Movement Survive?" 5.

27. Ibid. 4.

28. "Redstockings Manifesto," 224.

29. Jennifer Gardner, "False Consciousness," 231.

30. Qtd. in Echols, *Daring to Be Bad,* 145.

31. Celestine Ware's *Woman Power: The Movement for Women's Liberation* (1970) was the earliest book to challenge the new feminist movement to address racism, including its own. Ware, a member of the Stanton-Anthony Brigade of New York Radical Feminists, was among the few black women who were active in "women's liberation." For contemporaneous critiques of the white, middle-class bias of the movement, see Charlayne Hunter, "Many Blacks Wary of 'Women's Liberation Movement'"; T. Morrison, "What the Black Woman Thinks About Women's Lib"; Toni Cade, ed., *The Black Woman: An Anthology;* and Pauli Murray, "The Liberation of Black Women"—all appearing in 1970. For later analyses of the racial bias perpetuated by the early women's liberation movement, see Gloria T. Hull, Patricia Bell Scott, and Barbara Smith, eds., *All the Women Are White, All the Blacks Are Men, But Some of Us Are Brave: Black Women's Studies;* Gloria Anzaldúa and Cherríe Moraga, eds., *This Bridge Called My Back: Writings by Radical Women of Color;* and Combahee River Collective, *Combahee River Collective Statement:* Kimberly Springer, *Living for the Revolution: Black Feminist Organizations, 1968–1980.*

32. Brooke Williams, "Retreat to Cultural Feminism," 66. Rosalind Delmar and Juliet Mitchell, writing from Britain, agreed: "The effects of oppression do not become the manifestations of liberation by changing values, or, for that matter, by changing oneself—but only by challenging the social structure that gives rise to those values in the first place." See Rosalind Delmar and Juliet Mitchell, "Women's Liberation in Britain," *Leviathan* 38. See also Weisstein and Booth, "Will the Women's Movement Survive?" 4.

33. Qtd. in Mary Thom, *Inside Ms.: 25 Years of the Magazine and the Feminist Movement,* 206. For many, the magazine was a lifeline, a way out of rural or suburban isolation. A fourteen-year-old girl wrote in to tell the editors how important the magazine had become, in spite of her father, who urged her that women's lib was just a fad and not to be spending money on that "junk." "I have kept every issue (hidden in my dresser under my padded bras)," she wrote. "Please print my letter to assure me there is a world outside of Milburn!" "Letter," *Ms.* (July 1973).

34. Qtd. in Amy Farrell, "'Like a Tarantula on a Banana Boat': *Ms.* Magazine, 1972–1989," 53–54.

35. Qtd. in Thom, *Inside Ms.,* 25.

36. Ibid., 26.

37. Qtd. in Farrell, "'Like a Tarantula on a Banana Boat': *Ms.* Magazine, 1972–1989," 53.

38. Qtd. in Thom, *Inside Ms.*, 46.

39. Jane O'Reilly, "The Housewife's Moment of Truth," *Ms.* 55.

40. Amy Farrell, *Yours in Sisterhood: Ms. Magazine and the Promise of Popular Feminism,* 61

41. Carolyn Heilbrun, *The Education of a Woman: The Life of Gloria Steinem,* 223.

42. Ibid., 286.

43. Ibid., 281.

44. See Echols, *Daring to Be Bad,* 265–266.

45. Ibid., 267.

46. Qtd. in Echols, 267.

47. See Heilbrun, *The Education of a Woman,* 286.

48. Ellen Willis, "The Conservativism of *Ms.*"

49. Ibid., 173.

50. Ibid. 173–174.

51. Qtd. in Echols, *Daring to Be Bad,* 267.

52. See Rosen, *The World Split Open.*

53. Qtd. in Heilbrun, *The Education of a Woman,* 291.

54. Ibid., 287.

55. Susan Brownmiller, *In Our Time: Memoir of a Revolution,* 165. For a savvy discussion of the early women's movement's disdain of feminist celebrity, see Rachel Fudge, "Celebrity Jeopardy: The Perils of Feminist Fame."

56. Qtd. in Heilbrun, *The Education of a Woman,* 286.

57. For a discussion of the "structureless" approach, see Jo Freeman, "The Tyranny of Structurelessness."

58. Carol Williams Payne, "Consciousness-Raising: A Dead End?" 283.

59. Brooke Williams, "Retreat to Cultural Feminism," 65.

60. Carol Hanisch, Editorial, 27–28.

61. New York Radical Women, *Notes from the Third Year,* 300.

62. Kathie Sarachild, "The Power of History," 8.

CHAPTER 3

1. Roxanne Dunbar, "Outlaw Woman: Chapters from a Feminist Memoir-in-Progress," 103. Solanas was ultimately freed. She later disappeared, only to turn up dead in a welfare hotel in San Francisco on April 26, 1988, broke and alone.

2. Atkinson had smuggled Solanas's S.C.U.M. Manifesto out of the mental institution where she was subsequently confined. In a public show of support, Atkinson had appeared at Solanas's trial. Atkinson later resigned from NOW to form her own organization, the October 17th Movement (named for the day she left), which later became The Feminists.

3. Dunbar, "Outlaw Woman," 105.

4. Ibid. 105.

5. Betty Friedan, *The Feminine Mystique,* 69. Like Virginia Woolf before her, who wrote of killing "the angel in the house," Friedan exhorted women to confront their own internalized sense of limitation. See Woolf's "Professions for Women."

6. Friedan, *It Changed My Life: Writings on the Women's Movement,* 174.

7. Qtd. in Ruth Rosen, *The World Split Open: How the Modern Women's Movement Changed America,* 161.

8. Though, as the previous chapter argues, radical feminism was a highly multivocal movement, Friedan, like many outside its circles, tended to regard it as monolithic discourse. Friedan invokes the term "ideology" throughout her writings in its colloquial sense, a usage that reinforces her impression of the power that radical feminists had over the movement. The term "ideology," as developed within Marxism and used in neomarxist discourse, generally refers to a coherent system of ideas about social, political, and economic organization produced and disseminated by those in power and containing a view that obscures the real workings of power relations in a society. In its colloquial usage, the term refers more loosely to any system of ideas about politics and is often applied equally to groups in power and groups resisting that power.

9. With few exceptions, scholarly criticism on Friedan is scarce, generally beginning and ending with *The Feminine Mystique.* Four studies of note are Rachel Bowlby, "'The Problem with No Name': Rereading Friedan's *The Feminine Mystique*"; Sandra Dijkstra, "Simone de Beauvoir and Betty Friedan's *The Feminine Mystique*"; Joanne Meyerowitz, "Beyond the Feminine Mystique: A Reassessment of Postwar Mass Culture, 1949–1958"; and Eva Moskowitz, "It's Good to Blow Your Top: Women's Magazines and a Discourse of Discontent, 1945–1965." Two recent biographies pay close attention to Friedan's development as a feminist thinker. See Judith Hennessee, *Betty Friedan: Her Life;* and Daniel Horowitz, *Betty Friedan and the Making of the Feminine Mystique: The American Left, the Cold War, and Modern Feminism.* For an extended account of Friedan's Left background as a foundation for her feminism, see Horowitz.

10. Qtd. in Hennessee, *Betty Friedan,* 82.

11. Friedan, *The Feminine Mystique,* 378.

12. Betty Friedan, "Violence and NOW."

13. Betty Friedan, "Introduction to The National Women's Political Caucus," in *It Changed,* 166–67.

14. Friedan, *It Changed My Life,* 84.

15. Friedan, "The Crisis in Women's Identity," 65.

16. See Barbara Kantrowitz, "When Women Lead." See also Betsy Morris, "Trophy Husbands Arm Candy? Are You Kidding?"

17. Pauli Murray, *The Autobiography of a Black Activist, Feminist, Lawyer, Priest and Poet* and *Proud Shoes.*

18. See Rosen, *The World Split Open,* 69.

19. Betty Friedan, "An Open Letter to the Women's Movement," 384.

20. "NOW Statement of Purpose," *It Changed My Life,* 87.

21. Ibid. 163.

22. Betty Friedan, "'The First Year': President's Report to NOW, Washington, D.C., 1967," 98.

23. See Myra Marx Ferree and Beth B. Hess, *Controversy and Coalition: The New Feminist Movement Across Four Decades of Change,* 66. Regarding the withdrawal of labor union women's support, historian Ruth Rosen notes: "When 1967 NOW convention voted to endorse ERA, Caroline Davis, respecting the UAW's wishes, resigned

as NOW's secretary-treasurer. But a year later, the UAW reversed its position and came out in favor of ERA. Soon after, the entire AFL/CIO changed its position and also supported the amendment" (82).

24. NOW won a victory in the Colgate-Palmolive case in September 1969. See http://law.enotes.com/american-court-cases/bowe-v-colgate-palmolive.

25. Jo Freeman, "On the Origins of the Women's Liberation Movement from a Strictly Personal Perspective," *Feminist Memoir Project,* 190–191.

26. Kathie Sarachild, "The Power of History," 10.

27. Qtd. in Hennessee, *Betty Friedan: Her Life,* 124. When NOW eventually adopted the practice of CR in the early 1970s, its "Guidelines for CR Groups" made clear that CR was by no means a substitute for action: "Consciousness-raising is a process of making ourselves aware of society's role for us and where we personally are. It is not action. From time to time your CR group, after it has discussed a topic, say employment, may wish to know what action is taking place to change the situations. [NOW] has many committees actively working on changing things. Your CR group might like to hear what is taking place. So at any point after the first month or so, feel free to call your guide and ask for someone to discuss the action" (NOW New York Chapter, "Guidelines for CR Groups").

28. See Rosen, *The World Split Open,* 86.

29. Friedan, *It Changed My Life.*

30. Friedan, "Introduction to Call to Women's Strike for Equality," 138.

31. Qtd. in Susan Douglas, *Where the Girls Are: Growing Up Female in the Mass Media,* 168.

32. Qtd. in Rosen, *The World Split Open,* 86.

33. In Friedan's archived papers, a copy of Millett's talk lies in the folder with drafts of Friedan's own address. Betty Friedan Papers, Schlesinger Library, Radcliffe Institute, Series III.

34. Betty Friedan, "Introduction to Critique of Sexual Politics," 157.

35. Betty Friedan, "Critique of Sexual Politics," 162.

36. Betty Friedan, "Some Days in the Life of One of the Most Influential Women of Our Time," 36.

37. The resulting interview between *Social Policy*'s reporter and Friedan, a searing critique of the general "ideology" informing sexual politics, never directly mentioned Kate Millett. As Friedan noted later, "It was unwritten law that we not publicly disagree with each other" ("Introduction to Critique of Sexual Politics," 157).

38. Friedan, "Critique of Sexual Politics," 163.

39. The "New Right" refers to the well-funded network of scholars, think-tanks, and politicians that coalesced in the years preceding the 1964 presidential campaign of conservative icon Barry Goldwater, attacked the liberalism of JFK's brief tenure, and succeeded in propelling Reagan into the White House in 1980.

40. Qtd. in Alice Echols, *Daring to Be Bad: Radical Feminism in America 1967–1975,* 213.

41. Rosen, *The World Split Open,* 83.

42. Anselma Dell'Olio, "Home Before Sundown," 161.

43. Friedan, "Introduction to Critique of Sexual Politics," 159. Friedan herself was convinced that the FBI had intentionally manipulated the gay/straight split. As she explained, "I think it is possible that the CIA or FBI manipulated some of the lesbians. . . . The agents deepened the divisions and I think that agents used ambi-

tions and other issues like the lesbian thing and so on" (qtd. in Rosen, *The World Split Open*, 253). Activists old and young often imagined that FBI agents were everywhere and that the FBI viewed the women's movement as a serious threat to national security. Given her years in and around the Left labor movement, Friedan never doubted that the FBI would eventually infiltrate any women's movement—especially an organization as large and visible as NOW. While in retrospect her fear appears motivated by her own well-documented homophobia, there is evidence that there was truth behind Friedan's concern.

44. As Friedan's biographer Judith Hennessee documents, Dolores Alexander convinced Friedan to speak on behalf of the sexual preference plank (also known as the lesbian plank), which stated that homosexuals were entitled to the same civil rights as heterosexuals. Friedan consented and delivered the following statement: "I am considered to be violently opposed to the lesbian issue in the women's movement, and I have been. This issue has been used to divide us and disrupt us and has been seized on by our enemies to try and turn back the whole women's movement to equality, and alienate our support. As a woman of middle age who grew up in middle America—in Peoria, Illinois—and who has loved men maybe too well I have my personal hang-ups on this issue. I have made mistakes, we have all made mistakes in our focus on this issue. But now we must all transcend our previous differences to devote our full energies to get the Equal Rights Amendment ratified, or we will lose all we have gained. Since, contrary to the lies of the John Birchers, we know that the Equal Rights Amendment will do nothing whatsoever for homosexuals, we must support the separate civil rights of our lesbian sisters" (qtd. in Hennessee, *Betty Friedan*, 233–234).

45. Friedan, "Introduction to Critique of Sexual Politics," 159.
46. Betty Friedan, *Life So Far: A Memoir*, 232.
47. Betty Friedan, "Introduction to Strike Day," 146, 153.
48. Ibid., 151.
49. "Up from the Kitchen," *New York Times Magazine*, 4 March 1973, 8.
50. It was not the first time this popular writer would use women's magazines as a forum to promote her feminist message. Excerpts from *The Feminine Mystique* had appeared in *Ladies' Home Journal*, *McCall's*, *Mademoiselle*, and *Good Housekeeping*.
51. Betty Friedan, "Postscript to the National Women's Political Caucus," 183.
52. Betty Friedan, "Introduction to Betty Friedan's Notebook," 188. Friedan described the circumstances of her *McCall's* engagement as follows: "It was during the brief period in *McCall's* history that it was headed by women—Shana Alexander and Pat Carbine—that I was asked to write a column for it, on the assumption that the women's movement was now part of every woman's experience in America, and thus that the Middle-American readers of *McCall's* would identify with my words." (Ibid., 189.)
53. Betty Friedan, "Everything I Know Has Come from My Own Experience," 191.
54. Ibid.
55. Betty Friedan, *The Second Stage*, 15. Italics in the original.

CHAPTER 4

1. Susan Brownmiller, *Against Our Will*, 5. Italics in original.

2. The U.S. rape conviction rate rose sharply, from .099 (per 1,000 population) in 1981 to .212 in 1995. http://www.ojp.usdoj.gov/bjs/pub/html/cjusew96/cpp.htm.

3. Katie Roiphe, "Date Rape Hysteria," *New York Times* 20 Nov 1991: 27.

4. Katie Roiphe, "Date Rape's Other Victim."

5. Barbara Presley Noble, "At Lunch with Katie and Anne Roiphe."

6. Naomi Wolf, *Fire with Fire: The New Female Power and How It Will Change the 21st Century*, xvii.

7. A number were funded by right-wing think tanks and other conservative institutions. (With ecstatic support from conservative media mogul Rush Limbaugh, Sommers's *Who Stole Feminism? How Women Have Betrayed Women* became one of the most discussed titles of the year.) Fellow academics expressed their outrage at the apparent hypocrisy of colleagues who made their fame by attacking academic feminism from their perches within the academy. In fall 1994 the editors of the journal *Democratic Culture* devoted an entire issue to an analysis of Sommers' popular success. See *Democratic Culture* 3.2 (Fall 1994).

8. Camille Paglia, *Sexual Personae: Art and Decadence from Nefertiti to Emily Dickinson,* 13, 2.

9. Katie Roiphe, *The Morning After: Sex, Fear, and Feminism,* 112.

10. Karen Lehrman, *The Lipstick Proviso: Women, Sex, and Power in the Real World,* 5.

11. I use the term in this chapter in the sense commonly adopted by the mainstream press: after or beyond feminism. In academic circles, "postfeminism" also began to refer to a feminism influenced by multiculturalist, poststructuralist, and postmodern theorizing. See, for instance, Ann Brooks, *Postfeminisms: Feminism, Cultural Theory, and Cultural Forms* and Deborah Siegel, "The Legacy of the Personal."

12. Mona Charen, "The Feminist Mistake."

13. See Michele Wallace, "To Hell and Back: On the Road with Black Feminism in the 1960s and 1970s," 440.

14. Not all antipornography feminists saw men as violent by nature. Many were against violent pornography because of its tendency to encourage violence against women through objectification. For a detailed discussion of the pornography wars within feminism, see Susan Brownmiller's chapter, "The Pornography Wars," in *In Our Time.*

15. http://bushlibrary.tamu.edu/research/papers/1991/91050401.html.

16. http://www.rotten.com/library/bio/entertainers/pundits/rush-limbaugh/.

17. Cited as an editor's note in Anita Hill, "The Nature of the Beast: Sexual Harassment," 296.

18. Sarah Crichton, "Sexual Correctness: Has It Gone Too Far?" and Hellman, "Crying Rape: The Politics of Date Rape on Campus." *New York Magazine,* March 8, 1993.

19. Reported in *Time,* March 9, 1992, 54. The poll was a telephone poll of 625 American women taken on February 20 by Yankelovich Clancy Shulman.

20. Wolf, *Fire with Fire,* 53.

21. Ibid., 17.

22. EMILY's List was founded in 1985.

23. http://www.emilyslist.org/about/where-from.html.

24. http://en.wikipedia.org/wiki/Year_of_the_Woman.

25. Center for American Women in Politics, "Gender Gap: Voting Choices in Presidential Elections," http://www.cawp.rutgers.edu/Facts5.html. In 1992, more women than ever before filed as candidates for U.S. Senate elections (22D, 7R), and

a record number won major-party nominations for the U.S. Senate (10D, 1R). Center for American Women in Politics, http://www.cawp.rutgers.edu/fac-toidarchive.html.

26. See "The Feminist Chronicles, Epilogue," http://www.feminist.org/research/chron-icles/fc1993.html.

27. Elizabeth Fox-Genovese, *Feminism Is Not the Story of My Life*, 29; Lehrman, *The Lipstick Proviso*,154.

28. Lehrman, *The Lipstick Proviso*, 20; Sommers, *Who Stole Feminism?* 23; Roiphe, *The Morning After*, 165.

29. Wolf, *Fire with Fire*, 121.

30. Rene Denfeld, *The New Victorians: A Young Woman's Challenge to the Old Feminist Order*, 27.

31. Daphne Patai, *Heterophobia: Sexual Harassment and the Future of Feminism*, 196, 21.

32. Patai called liberal feminism "a threat to civil liberties, to personal autonomy, to the dignity of women and men." See Lehrman, *The Lipstick Proviso*, 20; Patai, *Heterophobia*, 4; Denfeld, *The New Victorians*, 264. For a similar argument by British journalist Natasha Walter, see *The New Feminism*.

33. Wolf, *Fire with Fire*, xviii-xix.

34. Carol Hanisch, "The Personal Is Political," *Notes from the Second Year*, ed. Shulamith Firestone.

35. See Quote Garden, http://www.quotegarden.com/feminism.html.

36. *Time*, June 29, 1998.

CHAPTER 5

1. Rebecca Walker, "Becoming the Third Wave," 41. In *Not My Mother's Sister*, Astrid Henry offers a helpful chronology for the coining of the term. Previous usages include the title of an anthology that never materialized, titled "The Third Wave: Feminist Perspectives on Racism." Here the term referred not to generation but to a new wave of feminism led by women of color with an explicitly anti-racist approach. In a 1987 essay, "Second Thoughts on the Second Wave" by Deborah Rosenfelt and Judith Stacey, the authors reflect on the ebbs and flows of feminism throughout the late 1970s and 1980s and write, "what some are calling a third wave of feminism [is] al-ready taking shape." As Henry points out, in *The Beauty Myth*, Naomi Wolf first im-bued the term with an explicitly generational meaning. There Wolf referred to the "feminist third wave" as women in their twenties circa the early 1990s (See Henry 23).

2. See Gloria Steinem, "Why Young Women Are More Conservative," *Outrageous Acts*, 238–246.

3. Jennifer Baumgardner and Amy Richards, *ManifestA: Young Women, Feminism, and the Future*, 18–19.

4. Ibid., 33.

5. Ibid., 47.

6. Joan Morgan, *When Chickenheads Come Home to Roost: My Life as a Hip-Hop Fem-inist*, 26.

7. See Jenice, Ambey, Barbara Findlen, et al., "Young Feminists Speak for Themselves" and Urvashi Vaid, Naomi Wolf, Gloria Steinem, and bell hooks, "Let's Get Real about Feminism: The Backlash, the Myths, the Movement."

8. Gloria Steinem, "Foreword," in *To Be Real*, xxvii.

9. Quote appears on the back cover of Chesler's book.

10. Kim France, "Passing the Torch," *New York Times*. http://www.nytimes.com/books/98/04/26/reviews/980426.26francet.html

11. Baumgardner and Richards, *ManifestA*, 233.

12. Retha Powers, "Don't Ask Alice: Rebecca Walker Steps Out."

13. E. Ann Kaplan, "Introduction 2," 22; Gloria Steinem, "Foreword," xxvii.

14. Gallop in Looser, 126.

15. Robin Morgan, "To Younger Women," *Sisterhood Is Forever: The Women's Anthology for a New Millennium*, 579.

16. Looser, "Introduction 2: Gen X Feminists? Youthism, Careerism, and the Third Wave," 42–43.

17. Quoted in Meri Nana-Ama Danquah, Review of *To Be Real*; Katha Pollitt, *Letters of Intent*, 31.

18. Rebecca Dakin Quinn, "An Open Letter to Institutional Mothers," 174–182.

19. I am grateful to Astrid Henry for identifying such conversations—and many others that will be helpful for future scholars of the waves—in *Not My Mother's Sister*, 187, 189.

20. Liza Featherstone and Dr. Phyllis Chesler, "Why Is There So Much Tension Between Feminist Bosses and Their Female Assistants?" 119.

21. Ibid., 116.

22. The phrase "patriarchy with a face-life" is scholar Diane Elam's. See Diane Elam, "Sisters Are Doing It to Themselves," 64.

23. Qtd. in Looser, "Introduction 2," 36.

24. Walker, "being real," xxxiv.

25. Merri Lisa Johnson, *Jane Sexes It Up*, 2.

26. Qtd. in Henry, *Not My Mother's Sister*, 156.

27. Sonja D. Curry-Johnson, "Weaving an Identity Tapestry," 222. Such explorations expanded and deepened in later anthologies, like *YELL-Oh Girls! Emerging Voices Explore Culture, Identity, and Growing Up Asian American* published in 2001, and *Colonize This! Young Women of Color on Today's Feminism* in 2002. Kimberly Springer went on to question the very relevance of the concept "third wave" for young black women in her article "Third Wave Black Feminism?" in the summer 2002 issue of *Signs*.

28. Quoted in Henry, *Not My Mother's Sister*, 158.

29. Walker, "being real," xxxiii.

30. Steinem again insisted that second-wave feminists had been equally interested in exploring these themes.

31. Leslie Heywood and Jennifer Drake, eds., *Third Wave Agenda: Being Feminist, Doing Feminism*, 3.

32. Ibid., 5.

33. Ibid., xiii.

34. Marcelle Karp and Debbie Stoller, eds., *The BUST Guide to the New Girl Order*, xiii, xiv.

35. Ibid., xiv. Articles covered topics like sex, girlhood, female friendships, and female bodies. Of the twenty-eight articles appearing in the first two issues of *BUST*, twenty focused on a celebration of female sexual desire. Other early issues also featured clusters of stories on travel, "Men We Love," and money.

36. For feminist discussions of Riot Grrrl, see Ednie Kaeh Garrison, "U.S. Feminism-Grrrl Style! Youth (Sub)cultures and the Technologics of the Third Wave"; Melissa Klein, "Duality and Redefinition: Young Feminism and the Alternative Music Community"; Jessica Rosenberg and Gitana Garafalo, "Riot Grrrl: Revolutions from Within"; Gayle Wald, "Just a Girl? Rock Music, Feminism, and the Cultural Construction of Female Youth"; Joanne Gottlieb and Gayle Wald. "Spells Like Teen Spirit: Riot Grrrls, Revolution, and Women in Independent Rock"; and Karen Green and Tristan Taormino, eds. *A Girl's Guide to Taking Over the World: Writings from the Girl Zine Revolution.*

37. Ann Japenga "Punk's Girl Groups Are Putting the Self Back in Self-Esteem."

38. This brand of white grrl feminism unconsciously borrowed from black culture. The word "girl," for example, was never given up by black women; nor was the word "lady." Both words were heavily attacked in second-wave feminism in favor of the use of "woman," yet black women retained these terms as part of their discourse. Such a borrowing draws on a long legacy; as Gayle Wald suggests in "Just a Girl? Rock Music, Feminism, and the Cultural Construction of Female Youth," black culture has often been a primary inspiration for white popular cultural innovation.

39. *Bitch* mission statement, *Bitch* 1, No. 1 (Spring 1996).

40. "Editors' Letter," *BUST* issue no. 4 (1992): 2.

41. "Editor's Letter," *BUST* issue no. 10 (1998): 4.

42. Qtd. in Lisa Johnson 360.

43. Jong qtd. in Ariel Levy, *Female Chauvinist Pigs: Women and the Rise of Raunch Culture,* 195.

44. Babe Queen, "Don't Call Me (a Do-Me Feminist)," *BUST* 50.

45. Danzy Senna, "To Be Real," *To Be Real,* 20.

46. Katha Pollitt, "The Solipsisters," 5.

47. Gloria Steinem, *Revolution from Within: A Book of Self-Esteem,* 3.

48. Ibid., 17. Italics in original.

49. Findlen, "Introduction," *Listen Up,* xvi.

50. Walker, "being real," xxxv.

CONCLUSION

1. P!nk, "Stupid Girls," *I'm Not Dead,* La Face, 2006.

2. Merri Lisa Johnson, "Jane Hocus, Jane Focus: An Introduction," 1, quoting Nan Bauer Maglin and Donna Perry, *"Bad Girls/Good Girls": Women, Sex, and Power in the Nineties.*

3. Lisa Johnson, "Jane Hocus, Jane Focus: An Introduction," 2.

4. See Rory Dicker and Alison Piepmeier, eds., *Catching a Wave: Reclaiming Feminism for the 21st Century;* Vivien Labaton and Dawn Lundy Martin, eds., *The Fire This Time: Young Activists and the New Feminism;* Jennifer Baumgardner and Amy Richards, *Grassroots: A Field Guide for Feminist Activism;* Lisa Jervis and Andi Zeisler, eds., *Bitchfest: Ten Years of Cultural Criticism from the Pages of Bitch Magazine;* and Melody Berger, ed., *We Don't Need Another Wave: Dispatches from the Next Generation of Feminists.*

5. See Leslie Heywood, *The Women's Movement Today: An Encyclopedia of Third-Wave Feminism,* Vol. 1, xxvii.

6. Lifetime Women's Pulse Poll, "Generation Why?" March 2006.

7. See Peggy Orenstein, *Flux: Women on Sex, Work, Love, Kids, and Life in a Half-Changed World.*

8. Carrie L. Lukas, *The Politically Incorrect Guide to Women, Sex, and Feminism,* xiv.

9. See National Council for Research on Women, *MISSING: Information on Women's Lives.*

10. See U.S. House of Representatives Committee on Government Reform/Minority Staff Special Investigations Division, *The Content of Federally Funded Abstinence-Only Education Programs.* http://www.democrats.reform.house.gov/Documents/20041201102153–50247.pdf.

11. Author interview with Amy Richards, May 22, 2006.

12. Lisa Jervis also makes this point in "The End of Feminism's Third Wave."

13. See Katha Pollitt, *Virginity or Death! And Other Social and Political Issues of Our Time.*

REFERENCES

Allen, Pamela. "Free Space: A Perspective on the Small Group in Women's Liberation." 1970. Koedt et al., 271–279.

———. "The Small Group Process." 1970. *Radical Feminism: A Documentary Reader*. Ed. Barbara A. Crow. New York: New York University Press, 2000. 277–281.

Altbach, Edith Hoshino, ed. *From Feminism to Liberation*. Cambridge: Schenkman Publishing Co., 1971.

———. "Notes on a Movement." Altbach, *From Feminism*. 1–18.

Ambey, Jenice, Barbara Findlen, et al. "Young Feminists Speak for Themselves." *Ms.* (Mar./Apr. 1991): 28–34.

American Association of University Women Educational Foundation. *How Schools Shortchange Girls:* The AAUW Report. Washington, DC: AAUW Educational Foundation, 1992.

Anzaldúa, Gloria and Cherríe Moraga, eds. *This Bridge Called My Back: Writings by Radical Women of Color.* Watertown, MA: Persephone Press, 1981.

Atkinson, Ti-Grace. *Amazon Odyssey.* New York: Links Books, 1974.

Baumgardner, Jennifer, and Amy Richards. *Grassroots: A Field Guide for Feminist Activism.* New York: Farrar Straus and Giroux, 2005.

———. *ManifestA: Young Women, Feminism, and the Future.* New York: Farrar Straus Giroux, 2000.

Baxandall, Rosalyn Fraad. "Catching the Fire." DuPlessis and Snitow, 208–224.

Baxandall, Rosalyn, and Linda Gordon, eds. *Dear Sisters: Dispatches from the Women's Liberation Movement.* New York: Basic Books, 2000.

Beal, Frances. "Double Jeopardy: To Be Black and Female." Morgan, *Sisterhood* 382–404.

Berger, Melody ed. *We Don't Need Another Wave: Dispatches from the Next Generation of Feminists.* Emeryville, CA: Seal Press, 2006.

Black Women's Liberation. "Statement on Birth Control." Morgan, *Sisterhood* 404–406.

Bolotin, Susan. "Views from the Post-feminist Generation." *The New York Times Magazine* 17 Oct. 1982: 103–116.

Bondoc, Anna. "Close, But No Banana." R. Walker, *To Be Real* 167–184.

Bosman, Julie. "Glamour's Hollywood Side: Films by and About Women," *The New York Times* 31 July 2006.

Bowlby, Rachel. "'The Problem with No Name': Rereading Friedan's *The Feminine Mystique*." *Feminist Review* 27 (Fall 1987): 61–75.

Bowleg, Lisa. "Better in the Bahamas? Not If You're a Feminist." Findlen, 45–53.

Breines, Wini. *Community and Organization in the New Left 1962–1968*. New Brunswick, NJ: Rutgers University Press, 1982.

———. "Retreat to Cultural Feminism." *Feminist Revolution*. Ed. Redstockings. New York: Random House, 1975. 65–68.

Brooks, Ann. *Postfeminisms: Feminism, Cultural Theory, and Cultural Forms*. New York: Routledge, 1997.

Brown, Lyn Mikel. *Raising Their Voices: The Politics of Girls' Anger*. Cambridge, MA: Harvard University Press, 1998.

Brown, Rita Mae. *Rita Will: Memoir of a Literary Rabble-Rouser*. New York: Bantam Doubleday Dell, 1999.

———. "Say It Isn't So." *Rat* 7–21 (Mar. 1969).

Brownmiller, Susan. *Against Our Will: Men, Women, and Rape*. New York: Simon & Schuster, 1975.

———. *In Our Time: Memoir of a Revolution*. New York: Dial Press, 1999.

Bulkin, Elly, Minnie Bruce Pratt, and Barbara Smith, eds. *Yours in Struggle: Three Feminist Perspectives on Anti-Semitism and Racism*. Brooklyn, NY: Long Haul Press, 1984.

Business and Professional Women and the Institute for Women's Policy Research. "Working Women Speak Out." Washington DC: BPW Foundation, 2004.

Butler, Judith. *Gender Trouble: Feminism and the Subversion of Identity*. New York: Routledge, 1990.

Butler, Judith and Joan W. Scott, eds. *Feminists Theorize the Political*. New York: Routledge, 1992.

Cade, Toni. *The Black Woman: An Anthology*. New York: New American Library, 1970.

"Can Feminism Survive the ERA Defeat?" *Majority Report* 15–29 Nov. 1975: 4, 10.

Carabillo, Toni, Judith Meuli, and June Bundy Csida, eds. *Feminist Chronicles, 1953–1993*. Los Angeles: Women's Graphics, 1993.

Carlip, Hilary, ed. *Girl Power: Young Women Speak Out! Personal Writings from Teenage Girls*. New York: Warner, 1995.

Carroll, Peter N. *It Seemed Like Nothing Happened: America in the 1970s*. New Brunswick, NJ: Rutgers University Press, 1990.

Carson, Clayborne. *In Struggle: SNCC and the Black Awakening of the 1960s*. Cambridge, MA: Harvard University Press, 1981.

Cassell, Joan. *A Group Called Women: Sisterhood and Symbolism in the Feminist Movement*. New York: McKay, 1977.

Center for the Advancement of Women. *Progress and Perils: New Agenda for Women*. Princeton, NJ: Princeton Survey Research Associates, 2003.

Chafe, William. *The American Woman: Her Changing Social, Economic, and Political Roles 1920–1970*. New York: Oxford University Press, 1972.

Chambers, Veronica. "Betrayal Feminism." Findlen, 21–28.

Charen, Mona. "The Feminist Mistake." *National Review*, 21 Sept. 1984.

Chastain, Sherry. "Exactly What to Say to Get the Salary You Want." *Ms.* (Sept. 1979): 12.

Chelser, Phyllis. *Letters to a Young Feminist*. New York: Four Walls Eight Windows, 1997.

Chernik, Abra Fortune. "The Body Politic." Findlen, 75–84.

Christian, Barbara. "The Race for Theory." *Gender and Theory: Dialogues on Feminist Criticism*. Ed. Linda Kauffman. Cambridge: Blackwell, 1989.

Cixous, Hélène. "The Laugh of the Medusa." 1975. *New French Feminisms: An Anthology*. Eds. Elaine Marks and Isabelle de Courtivron. Amherst: University of Massachusetts Press, 1980. 245–264.

Coburn, Judith. "Is NOW on the Brink of Then?" *The Village Voice*, 17 Nov. 1975: 24.

Combahee River Collective. *A Black Feminist Statement: Combahee River Collective Statement.* New York: Kitchen Table: Women of Color Press, 1985. 210–218.

"Consciousness Raising." Koedt et al., 280–281.

Costain, A., and W. D. Costain. "Strategy and Tactics of the Women's Movement in the United States: The Role of Political Parties." *The Women's Movements of the United States and Western Europe.* Eds. M. F. Katzenstein and C. M. Mueller. Philadelphia: Temple University Press, 1987. 196–214.

Cott, Nancy. *The Grounding of Modern Feminism.* New Haven, CT: Yale University Press, 1987.

Crow, Barbara A., ed. *Radical Feminism: A Documentary Reader.* New York: New York University Press, 2000.

"Crying Rape: The Politics of Date Rape on Campus." *New York* 8 Mar. 1993: 32.

Curry-Johnson, Sonja D. "Weaving an Identity Tapestry." Findlen, 221–229.

Curtis, Charlotte, "Miss America Pageant Is Picketed by 100 Women." *New York Times,* 8 Sept. 1968: 81.

D'Souza, Dinesh. *Illiberal Education.* New York: Free Press, 1998.

Daly, Steven, and Nathaniel Wice. *alt.culture: an a-z guide to the 90s—underground, online and over-the-counter.* New York: HarperPerennial, 1995.

Danquah, Meri Nana-Ama. Rev. of *To Be Real,* by Rebecca Walker. *Los Angeles Times* 6 Dec. 1995: 1.

Davis, Eisa. "Sexism and the Art of Feminist Hip-Hop Maintenance." R. Walker. *To Be Real* 127–142.

Davis, Flora. *Moving the Mountain: The Women's Movement in America Since 1960.* New York: Simon & Schuster, 1991.

Davis, Susan. "Organizing from Within: Justice on the Job." *Ms.* (Aug. 1972): 92–98.

Dean, Jodi. "Coming Out as Alien: Feminists, UFOs, and the 'Oprah Effect.'" *"Bad Girls"/"Good Girls": Women, Sex, and Power in the Nineties.* Eds. Nan Bauer Maglin and Donna Perry. New Brunswick: Rutgers University Press, 1996. 90–105.

Dell'Olio, Anselma. "Home Before Sundown." DuPlessis and Snitow, 149–170.

Delmar, Rosalind and Juliet Mitchell. "Women's Liberation in Britain." *Leviathan* 1970: 38.

DeLombard, Jeannine. "Femmenism." R. Walker, *To Be Real* 21–34.

Denfeld, Rene. *The New Victorians: A Young Woman's Challenge to the Old Feminist Order.* New York: Warner Books, 1995.

Densmore, Dana. "A Year of Living Dangerously: 1968." DuPlessis and Snitow, 71–89.

———. "On Celibacy." Tanner, 264–268.

Dent, Gina. "Missionary Position." R. Walker, *To Be Real* 61–76.

Dicker, Rory, and Alison Piepmeier, eds., *Catching a Wave: Reclaiming Feminism for the 21st Century.* Boston: Northeastern University Press, 2003.

Dijkstra, Sandra. "Simone de Beauvoir and Betty Friedan's *The Feminine Mystique*." *Feminist Studies* 6 (1980): 290–303.

Dixon, Marlene. "On Women's Liberation." *Radical America* (Feb. 1970).

Douglas, Susan. *Where the Girls Are: Growing Up Female with the Mass Media.* New York: Times Books, 1994.

Dowd, Maureen. *Are Men Necessary?: When Sexes Collide.* New York: G. P. Putnam's Sons, 2005

Duffett, Judith. "Atlantic City Is a Town with Class—They Raise Your Morals While They Judge Your Ass," *Voice of Women's Liberation Movement* 1, no. 3 (Oct. 1968).

Duffy, Martha. "The Bête Noire of Feminism." *Time* (Jan. 1992): 62.

Dunbar, Roxanne. "Outlaw Woman: Chapters from a Feminist Memoir-in-Progress." DuPlessis and Snitow, 90–114.

Duncombe, Stephen. *Notes from Underground: Zines and the Politics of Alternative Culture.* London: Verso, 1997.

DuPlessis, Rachel Blau and Ann Snitow, eds. *The Feminist Memoir Project: Voices from Women's Liberation.* New York: Three Rivers Press, 1998.

Dusky, Lorraine. "*Ms.* Poll: Feminist Tide Sweeps in as the 21st Century Begins" (Spring 2003): 56–61.

Dworkin, Andrea. *Intercourse.* New York: Free Press, 1987.

Echols, Alice. *Daring to Be Bad: Radical Feminism in America 1967–1975.* Minneapolis: University of Minnesota Press, 1989.

———. "The Taming of the Id: Feminism, Sex, Politics 1965–81." Paper presented at "Toward a Politics of Sexuality," Barnard College, 1982.

Edmiston, S. "How to Write Your Own Marriage Contract." *Ms.* (Spring 1972).

Edmiston, Susan. "How to Write Your Own Marriage Contract." *Ms.* (Spring 1972).

Elam, Diane. "Sisters Are Doing It To Themselves." Looser and Kaplan, 55–68.

Elam, Diane, and Robyn Wiegman, eds. *Feminism Beside Itself.* New York: Routledge, 1995.

Ellerbe, Linda. "The Feminist Mistake." *Seventeen* March 1990: 274–275.

Embree, Alice. "Media Images 1: Madison Avenue Brainwashing—The Facts." Koedt et al. 175–191.

Estrich, Susan. *Sex and Power.* New York: Riverhead Books, 2000.

Evans, Sara. *Personal Politics: The Roots of Women's Liberation in the Civil Rights Movement.* New York: Random House, 1980.

———. *Tidal Wave: How Women Changed America at Century's End.* New York: Free Press, 2003.

Faludi, Susan. *Backlash: The Undeclared War Against American Women.* New York: Crown, 1991.

Farrant, Patricia. "Chutzpah Isn't Enough: Some Thoughts on Reading *Who Stole Feminism?*" *Democratic Culture* 3.2 (Fall 1994): 29–30.

Farrell, Amy. *Yours in Sisterhood: Ms. Magazine and the Promise of Popular Feminism.* Chapel Hill: University of North Carolina Press, 1998.

———. "'Like a Tarantula on a Banana Boat': *Ms.* Magazine, 1972–1989," *Feminist Organizations: Harvest of the New Women's Movement.* Eds. Myra Marx Ferree and Patricia Yancey Martin. Philadelphia: Temple University Press, 1995. 53–68.

Fay, Elizabeth. "Composing Feminism." *Democratic Culture* 3.2 (Fall 1994): 25–26.

Featherstone, Liza, and Dr. Phyllis Chesler. "Why Is There So Much Tension Between Feminist Bosses and Their Female Assistants?" *Letters of Intent: Women Cross the Generations to Talk about Family, Work, Sex, Love and the Future of Feminism.* Eds. Anna Bondoc and Meg Daly. New York: Free Press, 1999. 109–120.

Ferree, Myra Marx, and Beth B. Hess. *Controversy and Coalition: The New Feminist Movement Across Four Decades of Change.* New York: Routledge, 2000.

Fielding, Helen. *Bridget Jones' Diary.* New York: Penguin, 1996.

Findlen, Barbara, ed. *Listen Up: Voices from the Next Feminist Generation.* Seattle: Seal Press, 1995.

Firestone, Shulamith. *The Dialectic of Sex: The Case for Feminist Revolution.* New York: William Morrow & Co., 1970.

Flacks, Richard. *Making History: The American Left and the American Mind.* New York: Columbia University Press, 1989.

Florika, "Media Images 2: Body Odor and Social Order." Koedt et al. 191–196.

Fox-Genovese, Elizabeth. *Feminism Is Not the Story of My Life: How Today's Feminist Elite Has Lost Touch with the Real Concerns of Women.* New York: Doubleday, 1996.

———. "Personal Is Not Political Enough." *Marxist Perspectives* (Winter 1979–80): 94–113.

France, Kim. "Gurls' Greatest Hits." *Harper's Bazaar* (Aug. 1997): 98–104.

———. "Passing the Torch," *New York Times Book Review* 26 April 1998.

Fraser, Ronald et al. *1968: Student Generation in Revolt.* New York: Pantheon, 1988.

Freeman, Jo. "The Origins of the Women's Liberation Movement." *American Journal of Sociology* 78 (Jan. 1973): 792–811.

———."On the Origins of the Women's Liberation Movement from a Strictly Personal Perspective." DuPlessis and Snitow, 171–96.

———. *The Politics of Women's Liberation.* New York: David McKay, 1975.

———. "The Tyranny of Structurelessness." *The Second Wave* 2.1 (1972): 20.

Friedan, Betty. "The Anti-Man Extremists Are Not the True Radicals—They Are the Enemy of Change." *McCall's* (May 1972): 47–52.

———. "Beyond Women's Liberation." *McCall's* (August 1972): 52–53, 134–136.

———. "Call to Women's Strike for Equality." Friedan, *It Changed* 143–145.

———. "The Crisis in Women's Identity." Friedan, *It Changed* 62–71.

———. "Critique of Sexual Politics." Friedan, *It Changed* 161–164.

———. "Everything I Know Has Come from My Own Experience." Friedan, *It Changed* 190–196.

———. *The Feminine Mystique.* 1963. New York: Bantam Doubleday Dell, 1983.

———. "'The First Year': President's Report to NOW, Washington, D.C., 1967." Friedan, *It Changed* 97–103.

———. "Introduction to Abortion: A Woman's Civil Right." Friedan, *It Changed* 120–122.

———. "Introduction to Betty Friedan's Notebook." Friedan, *It Changed* 187–189.

———. "Introduction to Call to Women's Strike for Equality." Friedan, *It Changed* 137–142.

———. "Introduction to Critique of Sexual Politics." Friedan, *It Changed* 155–160.

———. "Introduction to Strike Day." Friedan, *It Changed* 146–151.

———. "Introduction to The National Women's Political Caucus." Friedan, *It Changed* 165–169.

———. *It Changed My Life: Writings on the Women's Movement.* New York: Random House, 1976.

———. *Life So Far: A Memoir.* New York: Simon & Schuster, 2000.

———. "The Need for Love." *McCall's* (June 1972): 24–28, 138.

———. "An Open Letter to the Women's Movement." Friedan, *It Changed* 370–388.

———. "Postscript to The National Women's Political Caucus." Friedan, *It Changed* 175–183.

———. "Some Days in the Life of One of the Most Influential Women of Our Time." *McCall's* (June 1971): 32–36.

———. "Strike Day." Friedan, *It Changed* 152–154.

———. The Second Stage. 1981. Cambridge: Harvard University Press, 1998.

———. "Tokenism and the Pseudo-Radical Cop Out: Ideological Traps for New Feminists to Avoid." Address. Cornell University Intersession on Women. Jan. 1969. Betty Friedan Papers. Schlesinger Library, Radcliffe Institute, Cambridge.

———. "Up from the Kitchen." *The New York Times Magazine* 4 Mar 1973: 8.

———. "Violence and NOW." Editorial. *NOW Acts* (Fall 1968): 6.

———. "We Don't Have to Be That Independent." *McCall's* (Jan. 1973): 18–21, 147.

Friedman, R. Seth, ed. *The Factsheet Five Zine Reader: The Best Writing from the Underground World of Zines.* New York: Three Rivers Press, 1997.

Friedman, Susan Stanford. *Mappings: Feminism and the Cultural Geographies of Encounter.* Princeton, NJ: Princeton University Press, 1998.

———. "The Politics of Feminist Epistemology: The Sommers Debate." *Democratic Culture* 3.2 (Fall 1994): 20–21.

Friend, Tad. "Yes." *Esquire Magazine for Men* (Feb. 1994): 48–57.

Fudge, Rachel. "Celebrity Jeopardy: The Perils of Feminist Fame," *Bitch* (Winter 2002).

Gabin, Nancy. *Feminism in the Labor Movement: Women and the United Auto Workers 1925–1975.* Ithaca, NY: Cornell University Press.

Gallop, Jane. *Around 1981.* New York: Routledge, 1992.

Gallop, Jane and Elizabeth Francis. "Talking Across." Looser and Kaplan, 103–131.

Gamble, Sarah. "Postfeminism." *Routledge Critical Dictionary of Feminism and Postfeminism.* Ed. Sarah Gamble. New York: Routledge, 2000. 43–54.

Gardner, Jennifer. 1969. "False Consciousness." Tanner, 231–233.

———."The Small Group: Prison Guards at Work." *The Women's Page,* no. 4, 18 Feb. 1971, 7.

Garrison, Ednie Kaeh. "U.S. Feminism—Grrrl Style! Youth (Sub)cultures and the Technologics of the Third Wave." *Feminist Studies* 26.1 (Spring 2000): 141–170.

Gibian, Peter, ed. *Mass Culture and Everyday Life.* New York: Routledge, 1997.

Gilbert, Laurel. "You're Not the Type." Findlen, 102–112.

Gilbert, Laurel, and Crystal Kile. *SurferGrrls: Look, Ethel! an Internet Guide for Us.* Seattle: Seal Press, 1996.

Gilligan, Carol. *In a Different Voice: Psychological Theory and Women's Development.* Cambridge, MA: Harvard University Press, 1982.

Gilligan, Carol, Nona Lyons, and Trudy J. Hanmer. *Making Connections: The Relational Worlds of Adolescent Girls at Emma Willard School.* Cambridge: Harvard University Press, 1990.

Gitlin, Todd. *The Sixties: Years of Hope, Days of Rage.* New York: Bantam, 1987.

———. *The Whole World is Watching: Mass Media in the Making and Unmaking of the New Left.* Berkeley: University of California Press, 1980.

Gordon, Linda. *Woman's Body, Woman's Right: A Social History of Birth Control in America.* New York: Grossman, 1976.

Gornick, Vivian. "Consciousness." 1971. *Radical Feminism: A Documentary Reader.* Ed. Barbara A. Crow. New York: New York University Press, 2000. 287–300.

———. "Consciousness (Female Symbol)." *New York Times Magazine,* Jan. 10, 1971, 22–23, 77–82.

———. "What Feminism Means to Me." DuPlessis and Snitow, 372–76.

Gornick, Vivian, and Barbara Moran, eds. *Woman in Sexist Society: Studies in Power and Powerlessness.* New York: Basic Books, 1971.

Gottlieb, Joanne, and Gayle Wald. "Spells Like Teen Spirit: Riot Grrrls, Revolution, and Women in Independent Rock." *Critical Matrix* 7.2 (1992): 11–43.

Green, Karen, and Tristan Taormino, eds. *A Girl's Guide to Taking Over the World: Writings from the Girl Zine Revolution.* New York: St. Martin's Griffin, 1997.

Greene, Gayle, and Coppelia Kahn, eds. *Changing Subjects: The Making of Feminist Literary Criticism.* New York: Routledge, 1993.

Greer, Germaine. *The Female Eunich.* London: MacGibbon and Kee Limited, 1970.

Gunderloy, Mike, and Cari Goldberg Janice. *The World of Zines: A Guide to the Independent Magazine Revolution.* New York: Penguin Books, 1992.

Guy-Sheftall, Beverly. "Sisters in Struggle: A Belated Response." DuPlessis and Snitow, 485–492.

Hamil, Peter. "Does the Women's Movement Still Have Clout?" *The Village Voice* 17 Nov. 1975: 13.

Hanisch, Carol. "A Critique of the Miss America Protest." 1969. *Notes from the Second Year.* Ed. New York Radical Women. New York: Ace, 1970. 86–88.

———. Editorial. *Meeting Ground* 1 (1977): 27–28.

———. "The Personal Is Political." *Notes from the Second Year.* Ed. Shulamith Firestone. New York: New York Radical Feminists, 1970. 76–78.

———. "Two Letters from the Women's Liberation Movement." DuPlessis and Snitow, 197–207.

Haraway, Donna. "A Cyborg Manifesto: Science, Technology, and Socialist Feminism in the Late Twentieth Century." *Simians, Cyborgs, and Women: The Reinvention of Nature.* New York: Routledge, 1991. 149–181.

Harris, Louis. "The Harris Survey," May 20, 1971; December 11, 1975, December 8, 1975.

Hartmann, Susan. *The Other Feminists: Activists in the Liberal Establishment.* New Haven, CT: Yale University Press, 1997.

Hayden, Casey. "A Nurturing Movement: Nonviolence, SNCC, and Feminism." *Southern Exposure* (Summer 1988): 48–50.

Hebdige, Dick. *Subculture: The Meaning of Style.* London: Methuen, 1979.

Heilbrun, Carolyn. *The Education of a Woman: The Life of Gloria Steinem.* New York: Ballantine Books, 1995

Hennessee, Judith. *Betty Friedan: Her Life.* New York: Random House, 1999.

Henry, Astrid. *Not My Mother's Sister: Generational Conflict in The Third Wave Feminism.* Bloomington: University of Indiana Press, 2004.

Hernández, Daisy, and Bushra Rehman, eds. *Colonize This! Young Women of Color on Today's Feminism.* Seattle: Seal Press, 2002.

Herrup, Mocha Jean. "Virtual Identity." R. Walker, *To Be Real* 239–252.

Hewett, Heather. "Tightrope Walker." *Time Out* 11–18 Jan. 2001: 66.

Hewlett, Sylvia Ann. *Creating a Life: Professional Women and the Quest for Children.* New York: Talk Miramax Books, 2002.

Hex, Celina. "Editors' Letter." *BUST* 4 (Summer-Fall 1994): 2.

———. "Editor's Letter: The Second Sex." *BUST* 10 (Winter-Spring 1998): 4.

Heywood, Leslie, ed. *The Women's Movement Today: An Encyclopedia of Third-Wave Feminism.* Vol. 1, 2. Westport, CT: Greenwood Press, 2006.

Heywood, Leslie and Jennifer Drake, eds. *Third Wave Agenda: Doing Feminism, Being Feminist.* Minneapolis: University of Minnesota Press, 1997.

Higginbotham, Anastasia. "Chicks Goin' At It." Findlen, 3–11.

Hill, Anita. "The Nature of the Beast: Sexual Harassment." Morgan, *Sisterhood is Forever* 296–305.

Hirsch, Marianne and Evelyn Fox Keller, eds. *Conflicts in Feminism.* New York: Routledge, 1990.

Hogeland, Lisa Maria. "Fear of Feminism: Why Young Women Get the Willies." *Ms.* (Nov.-Dec. 1994): 18–21.

Hollibaugh, Amber. "Desire for the Future." Paper presented at Toward a Politics of Sexuality, Barnard College, 1982.

hooks, bell. *Black Looks: Race and Representation.* Boston: South End Press, 1992.

Horowitz, Daniel. *Betty Friedan and the Making of the Feminine Mystique: The American Left, the Cold War, and Modern Feminism.* Amherst: University of Massachusetts Press, 1998.

Hull, Gloria T., Patricia Bell Scott, and Barbara Smith, eds. *All the Women Are White, All the Blacks Are Men, But Some of Us Are Brave: Black Women's Studies.* Old Westbury, CT: Feminist Press, 1982.

Hunter, Charlayne. "Many Blacks Wary of 'Women's Liberation Movement.'" *New York Times* 17 Nov. 1970: 60.

Isserman, Maurice. *If I Had a Hammer . . . The Death of the Old Left and the Birth of the New Left.* New York: Basic Books, 1987.

"It Was A Great Day for Women On the March." 30 Aug. 1970. Women's Movement General Files. Tamiment Library, New York University.

James, Stanlie M. and Abena P. A. Busia, eds. *Theorizing Black Feminisms: The Visionary Pragmatism of Black Women.* New York: Routledge, 1993.

Japenga, Ann. "Grunge 'R Us: Exploiting, Co-opting, and Neutralizing the Counter Culture." *Los Angeles Times* 14 Nov. 1993: 26+.

———. "Punk's Girl Groups Are Putting the Self Back in Self-Esteem." *New York Times* 15 Nov. 1992: 30.

Jay, Karla. *Tales of the Lavender Menace: A Memoir of Liberation.* New York: Basic Books, 2000.

Jervis, Lisa. "The End of Feminism's Third Wave." *Ms.* (Winter 2004): 56.

Jervis, Lisa and Andi Zeisler, eds., *Bitchfest: Ten Years of Cultural Criticism from the Pages of Bitch Magazine.* New York: Farrar Straus and Giroux, 2006.

Johnson, Merri Lisa. "Jane Hocus, Jane Focus: An Introduction." Johnson, 1–11.

———, ed. *Jane Sexes It Up: True Confessions of Feminist Desire.* New York: Four Walls Eight Windows, 2002.

Johnston, Jill. *Lesbian Nation: The Feminist Solution.* New York: Simon & Schuster, 1973.

Jong, Erica. *Fear of Flying.* New York: Signet 1973.

Kamen, Paula. *Feminist Fatale: Women of the Twentysomething Generation Explore the Future of the Women's Movement.* New York: Donald I. Fine, 1991.

Kaminer, Wendy. "What Do Young Women Want?" *New York Times Book Review* 4 June 1995: 3.

Kantrowitz, Barbara. "Men, Women, and Computers." *Newsweek* 16 May 1994: 48–53.

———. "When Women Lead," *Newsweek* 25 Oct. 2005. 46.

Kaplan, E. Ann. "Introduction 2: Feminism, Aging, and Changing Paradigms." *Generations,* 13–29.

Karp, Marcelle, and Debbie Stoller eds. *The BUST Guide to the New Girl Order.* New York: Penguin Books, 1999.

Kauffman, Linda, ed. *Feminism and Institutions.* Oxford: Blackwell, 1989.

Kelly, Gail Paradise. "Women's Liberation and the New Left." Altbach, *From Feminism.* 39–49.

Keniston, Kenneth. *Young Radicals: Notes on Committed Youth.* New York: Harcourt, Brace, & World, 1968.

Kesselman, Amy. "Women's Liberation and the Left in New Haven, Connecticut 1968–1972." *Radical History Review.* Issue 81 (Fall 2001): 15–33.

Kesselman, Amy, with Heather Booth, Vivian Rothstein, and Naomi Weisstein. "Our Gang of Four: Friendship and Women's Liberation." DuPlessis and Snitow, 25–52.

Kessler-Harris, Alice. *Out to Work: A History of Wage-Earning Women in the United States.* New York: Oxford University Press, 1982.

Kilbourne, Jean. *Killing Us Softly: Advertising's Image of Women.* Cambridge Documentary Films, 1979.

Kipnis, Laura. *The Female Thing: Dirt, Sex, Envy, Vulnerability.* New York: Pantheon Books, 2006.

Klein, Melissa. "Duality and Redefinition: Young Feminism and the Alternative Music Community." *Third Wave Agenda: Being Feminist, Doing Feminism.* Eds. Leslie Heywood and Jennifer Drake. Minneapolis: University of Minnesota Press, 1997. 207–225.

Koedt, Anne. "The Myth of the Vaginal Orgasm." 1969. *Notes from the Second Year.* Ed. New York Radical Women. New York: Ace, 1970. 37–41.

Koedt, Anne, Ellen Levine, and Anita Rapone, eds. *Radical Feminism.* New York: Quadrangle Books, 1973.

Koertge, Noretta, and Daphne Patai. *Professing Feminism: Cautionary Tales from the Strange World of Women's Studies.* New York: Harper Collins, 1994.

Kolhatkar, Sheelah. "Les Ms.-erables Bust Cover." *New York Observer* 4 April 2005.

Komisar, Lucy. "The Image of Woman in Advertising." *Woman in Sexist Society: Studies in Power and Powerlessness.* Eds. Vivian Gornick and Barbara Moran. New York: Basic Books, 1971. 207–217.

Kristeva, Julia. *The Revolution in Poetic Language.* 1974. Trans. Margaret Waller. New York: Columbia University Press, 1984.

Kuczynski, Alex. "The New Feminist Mystique." *New York Times* 10 Sept. 2001.

Labaton Vivien, and Dawn Lundy Martin, eds., *The Fire This Time: Young Activists and the New Feminism.* New York: Anchor, 2004.

Lake, Celinda, and Kellyanne Conway. *What Women Really Want: How American Women Are Quietly Erasing Political, Racial, Class, and Religious Lines to Change the Way We Live.* New York: Free Press, 2005.

Lee, JeunYuen. "Beyond Bean Counting." Findlen, 205–211.

Lehrman, Karen. *The Lipstick Proviso: Women, Sex and Power in the Real World.* New York: Doubleday, 1997.

Leonard, Tom. "Advertising Chief Loses Job Over French Maid and Sexist Insults" *Telegraph.co.uk,* 22 Oct. 2005. http://www.telegraph.co.uk/news/main.jhtml? xml=/news/2005/10/22/ncrap22.xml.

Leon, Barbara. "Consequences of the Conditioning Line." *Feminist Revolution.* Ed. Redstockings. New York: Random House, 1975. 54–59.

Lerner, Gerda. *The Majority Finds Its Past: Placing Women in History.* New York: Oxford University Press, 1979.

"Letter," *Ms.* (July 1973).

Levy, Ariel. *Female Chauvinist Pigs: Women and the Rise of Raunch Culture.* New York: Free Press, 2005.

Lim, Shirley Geok-lin. "'Ain't I a Feminist?': Re-forming the Circle." DuPlessis and Snitow, 450–466.

Ling, Amy. "I'm Here." *New Literary History* 19 (1987): 151–160.

Looser, Devoney, and E. Ann Kaplan, eds. *Generations: Academic Feminists in Dialogue*. Minneapolis: University of Minneapolis Press, 1997.

———. "Introduction 2: Gen X Feminists? Youthism, Careerism, and the Third Wave." *Generations*, 42–43.

Lorde, Audre. *Chosen Poems—Old and New*. New York: W. W. Norton, 1982.

Lukas, Carrie L. *The Politically Incorrect Guide to Women, Sex, and Feminism*. Washington, DC: Regnery Publishing, Inc., 2006.

Lydon, Susan. "The Politics of Orgasm." Koedt et al., 197–205.

MacKinnon, Catherine. *Feminism Unmodified: Discourses on Life and Law*. Cambridge, MA: Harvard University Press, 1986.

Macko, Lia, and Kerry Rubin. *Midlife Crisis at 30: How the Stakes Have Changed for a Generation—And What to Do About It*. New York: Rodale, 2004.

Maglin, Nan Bauer and Donna Perry, eds. *"Bad Girls"/"Good Girls": Women, Sex, and Power in the Nineties*. New Brunswick: Rutgers University Press, 1996.

Mainardi, Pat. "The Politics of Housework." *Notes from the Second Year*. Ed. New York Radical Women. New York: Author, 1970. 28–31.

Mansbridge, Jane. "What Is the Feminist Movement?" *Feminist Organizations: Harvest of the New Women's Movement*. Eds. Myra Marx Ferree and Patricia Yancey Martin. Philadelphia: Temple University Press, 1995. 27–34.

Maran, Meredith. *Notes from an Incomplete Revolution: Real Life Since Feminism*. New York: Bantam, 1997.

Marks, Elaine, and Isabelle de Courtivron. "Introduction." *New French Feminisms: An Anthology*. Amherst: University of Massachusetts Press, 1980.

Martinez, Elizabeth (Betita). "History Makes Us, We Make History." DuPlessis and Snitow, 115–123.

Meyerowitz, Joanne. "Beyond the Feminine Mystique: A Reassessment of Postwar Mass Culture, 1949–1958." *Journal of American History* 79.4 (March 1993): 1455–1482.

Miller, James. *Democracy Is in the Streets: From Port Huron to the Siege of Chicago*. Cambridge, MA: Harvard University Press, 1987.

Miller, Nancy K. *Getting Personal: Feminist Occasions and Other Autobiographical Acts*. New York: Routledge, 1991.

Miller, Stephen Paul. *The Seventies Now: Culture as Surveillance*. Durham, NC: Duke University Press, 1999.

Millett, Kate. "Sex, Politics, and the New Feminism." Address. Cornell University. Nov. 1969. Betty Friedan Papers. Schlesinger Library, Radcliffe Institute, Cambridge.

———. *Sexual Politics*. Garden City, NY: Doubleday, 1970.

———. "Sexual Politics: A Manifesto for Revolution." 1969. *Notes from the Second Year*. Ed. New York Radical Women. New York: Ace, 1970, 111.

Mitchell, Juliet. *Woman's Estate*. New York: Random House, 1973.

Modleski, Tania. *Feminism without Women: Culture and Criticism in a "Postfeminist" Age*. New York: Routledge, 1991.

Morgan, Emilie. "Don't Call Me a Survivor." Findlen, 177–184.

Morgan, Joan. *When Chickenheads Come Home to Roost: My Life as a Hip-Hop Feminist*. New York: Simon & Schuster, 1999.

Morgan, Robin. *Going Too Far: The Personal Chronicle of a Feminist*. New York: Random House, 1977.

———. "Goodbye to All That." Tanner, 268–276.

————. "Forum: Rights of Passage." *Ms.* (Sept. 1975): 77.

————. *Saturday's Child: A Memoir.* New York: W. W. Norton, 2000.

Morgan, Robin, ed. *Sisterhood Is Powerful.* New York: Random House, 1970.

————. *Sisterhood Is Forever: The Women's Anthology for a New Millennium.* New York: Washington Square Press, 2003.

Morris, Betsy. "Trophy Husbands Arm Candy? Are You Kidding?" *Fortune* 27 Sept. 2002. 79.

Morrison, T. "What the Black Woman Thinks About Women's Lib." *New York Times Magazine,* 22 Aug. 1971: 14.

Morrison, Toni. *The Bluest Eye.* New York: Holt, Rinehart and Winston, 1970.

————. *Sula.* New York: New American Library, 1973.

Moskowitz, Eva. "It's Good to Blow Your Top: Women's Magazines and a Discourse of Discontent, 1945–1965." *Journal of Women's History* 8.3 (1996): 66–98.

"*Ms.* Poll: Feminist Tide Sweeps in as the 21st Century Begins," *Ms. Magazine* 8:1 (1988): 56–61.

Murray, Pauli. *The Autobiography of a Black Activist, Feminist, Lawyer, Priest and Poet.* Knoxville: University of Tennessee Press, 1989.

————. "The Liberation of Black Women." *Voices of the New Feminism.* Ed. Mary Lou Thompson. Boston: Beacon, 1970. 87–102.

————. *Proud Shoes.* Boston: Beacon Press, 1999.

Muscio, Inga. "Abortion, Vacuum Cleaners, and the Power Within." Findlen, 160–166.

Nam, Vickie, ed. *YELL-Oh Girls! Emerging Voices Explore Culture, Identity, and Growing Up Asian American.* New York: HarperCollins, 2001.

National Council for Research on Women. *Gains and Gaps: A Look at the World's Women.* New York: Author, Spring 2006.

————. *MISSING: Information on Women's Lives.* New York: Author, 2004.

National Organization for Women. "An Invitation to Join." Carabillo et al., 164.

————. New York Chapter. "Guidelines for CR Groups." ca. 1971–1973. Women's Movement General Files. Tamiment Library, New York University.

————. "NOW Bill of Rights." Carabillo et al., 214.

————. "NOW Statement of Purpose." Carabillo et al. 159–163.

Needleman, Jacob, and George Baker. *Understanding the New Religions.* New York: 1978.

Neidorf, Robin M. "Two Jews, Three Opinions." Findlen, 212–220.

Nelson, Cary, Paula Treichler, and Lawrence Grossberg. "Introduction." *Cultural Studies.* Eds. Cary Nelson, Paula Treichler, and Lawrence Grossberg. New York: Routledge, 1992. 1–22.

Neuborne, Ellen. "Imagine My Surprise." Findlen, 29–35.

New York Radical Feminists. "Introduction to Consciousness Raising." nd. Women's Movement General Files. Tamiment Library, New York University.

————. "Politics of the Ego: A Manifesto for New York Radical Feminists." 1969. Koedt et al., 124.

————. "Principles." Morgan, *Sisterhood* 583–584.

New York Radical Women. "A Letter to the Editor of Ramparts Magazine." *Notes from the First Year.* Ed. New York Radical Women. New York: Author, 1968.

————. Editorial. *Notes from the Third Year.* New York: Author, 1971. 300

————. "No More Miss America! Ten Points of Protest." 1968. Women's Movement General Files. Tamiment Library, New York University.

————. "Principles." Morgan, *Sisterhood* 520.

New York Radical Women, eds. *Notes from the First Year*. New York: Author, 1968.

——. *Notes from the Second Year*. New York: Ace, 1970.

——, ed. *Notes from the Third Year*. New York: Author, 1971.

Nicholson, Linda J., ed. *Feminism/Postmodernism*. New York: Routledge, 1990.

Noble, Barbara Presley. "At Lunch with Katie and Anne Roiphe: One Daughter's Rebellion or Her Mother's Imprint?" *New York Times* 10 Nov. 1993: C1.

Norton, Eleanor Holmes. "For Sadie and Maude." Morgan, *Sisterhood* 397–404.

O'Reilly, Jane. "The Housewife's Moment of Truth," *Ms.* (Spring 1972): 54–55, 57–59.

Orenstein, Peggy. *Flux: Women on Sex, Work, Love, Kids, and Life in a Half-Changed World*. New York: Anchor Books, 2000.

Oxford English Dictionary. Vol. 2. Oxford: Oxford University Press, 1971.

Paglia, Camille. *Sexual Personae: Art and Decadence from Nefertiti to Emily Dickinson*. New Haven, CT: Yale University Press, 1990.

Patai, Daphne. *Heterophobia: Sexual Harassment and the Future of Feminism*. Lanham, MD: Rowman and Littlefield, 1998.

Payne, Carol Williams. "Consciousness-Raising: A Dead End?" Koedt et al., 282–284.

Peck, Abe. *Uncovering the Sixties: The Life and Times of the Underground Press*. New York: Pantheon, 1985.

Perry, Ruth. "A Short History of the Term *Politically Correct*." *Beyond PC: Towards a Politics of Understanding*. Ed. Patricia Aufderheide. St. Paul, MN: Graywolf Press, 1992. 71–79.

Piercy, Marge. "The Grand Coolie Damn." Morgan, *Sisterhood*. 473–492.

P!nk. "Stupid Girls." *I'm Not Dead*. La Face: 2006.

Pipher, Mary. Reviving Ophelia: Saving the Selves of Adolescent Girls. New York: Putnam, 1994.

Pogrebin, Letty Cottin. "Down with Sexist Upbringing!" *Ms.* (Spring 1972).

Poll. *Time* 9 March 1992: 54.

Pollitt, Katha. "The Solipsisters." *New York Times Book Review* 18 April 1999: 5.

——. *Virginity or Death! And Other Social and Political Issues of Our Time*. New York: Random House Trade Paperbacks, 2006.

Pollitt, Katha, and Emily Gordon. "Does Your Generation Resent Up-and-Coming Women?" Bondoc and Daly, eds. *Letters of Intent*, 321–332.

Powers, Retha. "Don't Ask Alice: Rebecca Walker Steps Out," *Girlfriends* (May/ June 1996): 21.

Putnam, Robert D. *Bowling Alone: The Collapse and Revival of American Community*. New York: Simon & Schuster, 2000.

Queen, Babe. "Don't Call Me (a Do-Me Feminist)." *BUST* 4 (Summer-Fall 1994): 50.

Quinn, Rebecca Dakin. "An Open Letter to Institutional Mothers." Looser and Kaplan, 174–182.

Radicalesbians. "The Woman-Identified Woman." Koedt et al., 240–245.

Raphael, Amy. *Grrls: Viva Rock Divas*. New York: St. Martin's Griffith, 1994.

Redstockings. "Feminist Consciousness Raising and 'Organizing.'" Tanner, 154–157.

——. Press Release. May 9, 1975. In Redstockings, *Feminist Revolution*.

——. "Redstockings Manifesto." 1969. *Radical Feminism: A Documentary Reader*. Ed. Barbara A. Crow. New York: New York University Press, 2000. 223–225.

——. "Taking Politics Out of the Analysis." *Feminist Revolution*. Ed. Redstockings. New York: Random House, 1975. 69.

Redstockings, ed. *Feminist Revolution*. New York: Random House, 1975.

Rich, Adrienne. *Of Woman Born: Motherhood as Experience and Institution.* New York: W. W. Norton, 1976.

———. *The Dream of a Common Language.* W. W. Norton, 1978.

———. "When We Dead Awaken: Writing as Re-Vision (1971)." *On Lies, Secrets, and Silence: Selected Prose 1966–1978.* New York: W. W. Norton, 1979.

Ridder, Kathleen. *Shaping My Feminist Life: A Memoir.* Minneapolis: Minnesota Historical Society Press, 1998.

Riesman, Frank. Letter to Betty Friedan. 8 Sept. 1970. Betty Friedan Papers. Schlesinger Library, Radcliffe Institute, Cambridge.

Roiphe, Anne. *1185 Park Avenue: A Memoir.* New York: Free Press, 1999.

Roiphe, Katie. "Date Rape Hysteria." *New York Times* 20 Nov. 1991: 27.

———. "Date Rape's Other Victim," *New York Times Magazine,* 13 June 1993.

———. *The Morning After: Sex, Fear, and Feminism.* Boston: Little, Brown, 1993.

Rosen, Ruth. *The World Split Open: How the Modern Women's Movement Changed America.* New York: Viking, 2000.

Rosenberg, Jessica, and Gitana Garafalo. "Riot Grrrl: Revolutions from Within." *SIGNS* 23.3 (Spring 1998): 809–841.

Rosenberg, Norman. "The Sixties." *Oxford Companion to United States History.* Ed. Paul S. Boyer. New York: Oxford University Press, 2001. 710–712.

Rosenfelt, Deborah, and Judith Stacey. "Second Thoughts on the Second Wave." *Feminist Studies* 13, no. 2 (Summer 1987): 341–361.

Roth, Benita. *Separate Roads to Feminism: Black, Chicana, and White Feminist Movements in America's Second Wave.* Cambridge: Cambridge University Press, 2003.

Rothschild-Whitt, J. "The Collectivist Organization: An Alternative to Rational-Bureaucratic Models." *American Sociological Review* 44 (1979): 509–527.

Rowbotham, Sheila. *Promise of a Dream: Remembering the Sixties.* London: Allen Lane, 2000.

———. *Woman's Consciousness, Man's World.* Middlesex: Penguin, 1973.

Rowe-Finkbeiner, Kristin. *The F Word: Feminism in Jeopardy.* Seattle: Seal Press, 2004.

Rubin, Jerry. "Excerpts from *Do It.*" *Rat* 26 Jan.–9 Feb. 1970.

R. Z. S. "Up Against the Men's Room Wall." *Time* 31 Aug. 1970.

Sakler, Myra and David. *Failing at Fairness: How America's Schools Cheat Girls.* New York: C. Scribner's Sons, 1994.

Samson, Ronald V. *The Psychology of Power.* New York: Random House, 1968.

Sandell, Jillian. "Adjusting to Oppression: The Rise of Therapeutic Feminism in the United States." *"Bad Girls"/"Good Girls": Women, Sex, and Power in the Nineties.* Eds. Nan Bauer Maglin and Donna Perry. New Brunswick: Rutgers University Press, 1996. 21–35.

Sarachild, Kathie. "Consciousness Raising: A Radical Weapon." *Feminist Revolution.* Ed. Redstockings. New York: Random House, 1975. 144–150.

———. "Guide to Consciousness Raising." nd. Women's Movement General Files. Tamiment Library, New York University.

———. "The Power of History." *Feminist Revolution.* Ed. Redstockings. New York: Random House, 1975. 7–29.

———. "A Program for Feminist Consciousness Raising." 1968. *Radical Feminism: A Documentary Reader.* Ed. Barbara A. Crow. New York: New York University Press, 2000. 273–76.

Sayres, Sohnya et al., eds., *The '60s Without Apology.* Minneapolis: University of Minnesota Press, 1984.

Schultz, Debra. *Risk, Resiliency, and Resistance: Current Research on Adolescent Girls.* New York: National Council for Research on Women, 1992.

Schwartz, Maralee, and Kenneth J. Cooper, "Equal Rights Initiative in Iowa Attacked," *Washington Post* 23 Aug. 1992: A15.

Scott, Ann. "How to Make Trouble: It's Time for Equal Education." *Ms.* (Oct. 1972): 122–125.

Senna, Danzy. "To Be Real." R. Walker, *To Be Real* 5–20.

Shah, Sonia. "Tight Jeans and Chania Chorris." Findlen, 113–119.

"Shakira: 'I'm No Feminist.'" www.contactmusic.com. February 16, 2006. http://www.contactmusic.com/new/xmlfeed.nsf/mndwebpages/shakira%20im%20no%20feminist_16_02_2006.

Shange, Ntozake. *for colored girls who have considered suicide/ when the rainbow is not enough.* Berkeley, CA: Shameless Hussy Press, 1975.

———. *Nappy Edges.* New York: Bantam, 1980.

Shapiro, Lauren. "Sisterhood Was Powerful." *Newsweek* 29 June 1994: 68–70.

Shelley, Martha. "Notes of a Radical Lesbian." Koedt et al., 306–311.

Sherfey, Mary Jane. "A Theory on Female Sexuality." Koedt et al., 220–230.

Shulman, Alix Kates. "A Marriage Agreement." *Up from Under* (Aug. 1970).

———. "Organs and Orgasms." *Woman in Sexist Society: Studies in Power and Powerlessness.* Eds. Vivian Gornick and Barbara Moran. New York: Basic Books, 1971. 198–206.

———. "Sex and Power: Sexual Bases of Radical Feminism." *SIGNS* 5.4 (1980): 590–604.

Siegel, Deborah L. "Reading Between the Waves: Feminist Historiography in a 'Postfeminist' Moment." *Third Wave Agenda: Being Feminist, Doing Feminism.* Eds. Leslie Heywood and Jennifer Drake. Minneapolis: University of Minnesota Press, 1997. 55–82.

———. "The Legacy of the Personal: Generating Theory in Feminism's Third Wave." *Hypatia* 12.3 (Summer 1997): 46–75.

Sinclair, Carla. *Netchick: A Smart Girl's Guide to the Wired World.* New York: Henry Holt, 1996

Small, L. L. "How to Know When You're Stuck and Other Career Tips." *Ms. Magazine* (July 1989): 56.

Smith, Barbara. "'Feisty Characters' and 'Other People's Causes': Memories of White Racism and U.S. Feminism." DuPlessis and Snitow, 477–481.

Smith, Barbara, and Beverly Smith. "Across the Kitchen Table: A Sister-to-Sister Dialogue." *This Bridge Called My Back: Writings by Radical Women of Color.* Ed. Gloria Anzaldúa and Cherríe Moraga. Watertown, NY: Persephone Press, 1981. 113–127.

Snitow, Ann, Christine Stansell, and Sharon Thompson, eds. *Powers of Desire: The Politics of Sexuality.* New York: Monthly Review Press, 1983.

Solanas, Valerie. "Excerpts from the SCUM Manifesto." Morgan, *Sisterhood* 514–519.

Solomon, Akiba. "Boss Lady." *Essence* (July 2006): 69.

Sommers, Christina Hoff. *Who Stole Feminism? How Women Have Betrayed Women.* New York: Simon & Schuster, 1994.

Sprengnether, Madelon. "Generational Differences: Reliving Mother-Daughter Conflicts." In *Changing Subjects: The Making of Feminist Literary Criticism,* eds. Gayle Greene and Coppelia Kahn. New York: Routledge, 1993. 201–210.

Springer, Kimberly. *Living for the Revolution: Black Feminist Organizations, 1968–1980.* Durham, NC: Duke University Press, 2005.

———. "Third Wave Black Feminism?" *SIGNS* 27.4 (Summer 2002): 1059–1082.

Stambler, Stookie. *Women's Liberation: Blueprint for the Future.* New York: Ace Books, 1970

Steinem, Gloria. "The City Politic: After Black Power, Women's Liberation." *New York* 7 Apr. 1969: 8–10.

———. "Foreword," *To Be Real.*

———. "I Was a Playboy Bunny," *Outrageous Acts and Everyday Rebellions* (New York: Holt, Rinehart and Winston, 1983), 33–78.

———. *Moving Beyond Words: Age, Rage, Sex, Power, Money, Muscles: Breaking the Boundaries of Gender.* New York: Simon & Schuster, 1994.

———. *Outrageous Acts and Everyday Rebellions.* New York: Holt, Rinehart and Winston, 1983.

———. *Revolution from Within: A Book of Self-Esteem.* Boston: Little, Brown, and Co., 1992.

———. "Sisterhood." *Outrageous Acts and Everyday Rebellions,* 127–133.

———. "What It Would Be Like If Women Win." *Time* Aug. 1970.

———. "Why Young Women Are More Conservative," *Outrageous Acts,* 238–46.

———. "Words and Change." *Outrageous Acts and Everyday Rebellions.* 169–81.

Stimpson, Catherine. "'Thy Neighbor's Wife, Thy Neighbor's Servants': Women's Liberation and Black Civil Rights." *Woman in Sexist Society: Studies in Power and Powerlessness.* Eds. Vivian Gornick and Barbara Moran. New York: Basic Books, 1971. 453–479.

Susan, Barbara. "About My Consciousness Raising." Tanner, 238–243.

Tanner, Leslie B., ed. *Voices from Women's Liberation.* New York: New American Library, 1970.

Tarrow, Sidney. *Power in Movement: Social Movements and Contentious Politics.* Cambridge: Cambridge University Press, 1998.

Taylor, Jocelyn. "Testimony of a Naked Woman." R. Walker, *To Be Real* 219–238.

Thom, Mary. *Inside Ms.: 25 Years of the Magazine and the Feminist Movement.* New York: Henry Holt and Co., 1997

Tiger, Lisa. "Woman Who Clears the Way." Findlen, 192–204.

Tobias, Sheila. *Faces of Feminism: An Activist's Reflections on the Women's Movement.* New York: Westview Press, 1998.

Toffler, Alvin. *Future Shock.* New York: Random House, 1970.

Trimberger, Ellen Kay. "Women in the Old and New Left: The Evolution of a Politics of Personal Life." *Feminist Studies* 5.3 (1979): 432–450.

Tsaliki, Lisa. "Women and New Technologies." *Routledge Critical Dictionary of Feminism and Postfeminism.* Ed. Sarah Gamble. New York: Routledge, 2000. 80–92.

U.S. House of Representatives Committee on Government Reform/Minority Staff Special Investigations Division. *The Content of Federally Funded Abstinence-Only Education Programs.* Prepared for Representative Henry Waxman. Dec. 2004. http://www.democrats.reform. house.gov/Documents/20041201102153–50247.pdf.

Vaid, Urvashi, Naomi Wolf, Gloria Steinem, and bell hooks. "Let's Get Real about Feminism: The Backlash, the Myths, the Movement." *Ms.* (Sept./Oct. 1993): 34–43.

Valdes, Alisa L. "Ruminations of a Feminist Aerobics Instructor." Findlen, 12–20.

Vance, Carol, ed. *Pleasure and Danger: Exploring Female Sexuality.* Boston: Routledge and Kegan Paul, 1984.

Vinson, Joyce, Rosemary Gaffney, and Lynne Shapiro. "Open Letter: Why Did We Walk Out of the Coalition and Why Are We Staying Out?" 1970. Women's Movement General Files. Tamiment Library, New York University.

Wald, Alan. *The New York Intellectuals: The Rise and Decline of the Anti-Stalinist Left from the 1930s to the 1980s.* Chapel Hill: University of North Carolina Press, 1987.

Wald, Gayle. "Just a Girl? Rock Music, Feminism, and the Cultural Construction of Female Youth." *SIGNS* 23.3 (1998): 585–610.

Walker, Alice. *In Search of Our Mothers' Gardens: Womanist Prose*. San Diego: Harcourt Brace Jovanovich, 1983.

———. *Revolutionary Petunias and Other Poems*. New York: Harcourt Brace Jovanovich, 1973.

Walker, Rebecca. "Becoming the Third Wave." *Ms*. Jan.-Feb. 1995. 39–41.

———. *Black, White, and Jewish: Autobiography of a Shifting Self*. New York: Riverhead Books, 2001.

———. "An Interview with Veronica Webb." R. Walker, *To Be Real* 209–210.

Walker, Rebecca, ed. *To Be Real: Telling the Truth and Changing the Face of Feminism*. New York: Doubleday, 1995.

Wallace, Michele. "To Hell and Back: On the Road with Black Feminism in the 1960s & 1970s." DuPlessis and Snitow, 426–442.

Walter, Natasha. *The New Feminism*. London: Little, Brown, 1998.

Wandersee, Winifred. *On the Move: American Women in the 1970s*. Boston: Twayne Publishers, 1988.

Ward, Jill, and Deborah Biele. "Statement." 1970. Women's Movement General Files. Tamiment Library, New York University.

Ware, Celestine. *Woman Power: The Movement for Women's Liberation*. New York: Tower, 1970.

Watkins, Bonnie, and Nina Tothchild, eds. *In the Company of Women: Voices from the Women's Movement*. Minneapolis: University of Minnesota Press, 1997.

Weisstein, Naomi. "Days of Celebration and Resistance: The Chicago Women's Liberation Rock Band, 1970–1973," *The Feminist Memoir Project*. 350–361.

———. "Psychology Constructs the Female." 1971. Koedt et al., 178–197.

Weisstein, Naomi, and Heather Booth. "Will the Women's Movement Survive?" *SISTER* (1971): 1–2. Women's Movement General Files. Tamiment Library, New York University.

White House Project. *Who's Talking Now: A Follow-Up Analysis of Guest Appearances by Women on the Sunday Morning Talk Shows*. New York: The White House Project, October 2005.

Whittier, Nancy. Feminist *Generations: The Persistence of the Radical Women's Movement*. Philadelphia: Temple University Press, 1995.

Williams, Brooke. "Quicksand Politics." *Meeting Ground* 1 Jan. 1977: 5–11.

Willis, Ellen. "The Conservativism of Ms." *Feminist Revolution*. Ed. Redstockings. 1975. 173–174.

Wilson, John K. *The Myth of Political Correctness: The Conservative Attack on Higher Education*. Durham, NC: Duke University Press, 1995.

Winslow, Barbara. "Primary and Secondary Contradictions in Seattle." DuPlessis and Snitow, 225–248.

Wittig, Monique. *Les Guérillères*. Paris: Éditions de Minuit, 1969.

Wolf, Naomi. *The Beauty Myth: How Images of Beauty Are Used Against Women*. New York: William Morrow, 1991.

———. *Fire With Fire: The New Female Power and How It Will Change the 21st Century*. New York: Random House, 1993.

WomanTrend and Lake Research Partners. "Generation Why?: Lifetime Women's Pulse Poll." Lifetime Networks. March 2006.

"Women Rap About Sex." *Notes from the First Year*. Ed. New York Radical Women. New York: Author, 1968.

"Women Unite for Revolution." 1969. Tanner, 129–132.

Women's Strike for Equality Coalition. Flyer. 26 Aug. 1970. Women's Movement General Files. Tamiment Library, New York University.

Woolf, Virginia. "Professions for Women." *The Virginia Woof Reader.* Ed. Mitchell A. Leaska. New York: Harcourt Brace Jovanovich, 1984. 276–82.

Wurtzel, Elizabeth. *Bitch: In Praise of Difficult Women.* New York: Doubleday, 1999.

Zimmerman, Patricia. "The Female Bodywars: Rethinking Feminist Media Politics." *Socialist Review* 23.2 (1991): 35–56.

INDEX

READING GUIDE QUESTIONS

Discuss the latest portrayal of a "feminist catfight" in the news:

    a.   What were the *real* differences of opinion underlying the so-called fight?
    b.   How do these positions resemble or depart from the various feminist stances revealed in this book?

Sexual freedom is one of the lightning-rod issues animating popular feminist debate today. Do you think that this focus on what Betty Friedan once called "orgasm politics" is (a) a distraction from the "real" work of the women's movement or (b) among the most important issues facing younger women today? Discuss.

Who are today's most prominent feminist spokeswomen, or "stars"? What brand of feminism do they embody? What do they stand for? Do you agree or disagree with their ideas about what women need most right now?

What is the current relationship between your personal life and your politics? Has that relationship changed for you over the years? How? And why?

What does "feminism" mean to you? Is it a lifestyle choice, a style, a culture, or a cause? What do you think the word meant to your mother? What do you think it means to your daughter or your son?

Do younger men today relate to "feminism" differently than do older men? If so, how?

To younger readers: What element of feminist history, as presented in this book, surprised you the most?

To older readers: What element of younger women's battles to define feminism for themselves surprised you the most?

Historian Gerda Lerner has noted that the only constant in feminist history is a perpetual forgetting of our past. Why do you think this is so? Does this forgetting take place in other social change movements as well?

How do you feel about the term "third wave feminism"? Do the differences between generations of feminism warrant the term? What are some additional differences—or similarities—between generations of feminists not discussed in this book?

What are current obstacles to "mainstreaming" feminism as a movement today?

How do class, race, geographic location, religion, and other specific categories of identity factor into women's decision to identify with or reject the "f-word?"

Does sisterhood have a future?

Do you agree with the author that age is an unnecessary divider?

Do you agree with Gloria Steinem that women become more radical with age?

How can younger women relate to their movement mothers and narrow the chasm between their mothers' style of empowerment and their own?

How can older women relate to feminism's daughters and narrow the chasm between their daughters' style of empowerment and their own?

ONLINE RESOURCE GUIDE

WHERE TO GO TO LEARN MORE ABOUT DEBATES IN FEMINISM

BLOGS

Alas, A Blog
http://www.amptoons.com/blog/

Bitchblog
http://www.bitchmagazine.com/blogtest/

Bitch PhD
http://bitchphd.blogspot.com/

Blac(k)ademic
http://www.blackademic.com/

Broadsheet at Salon.com
http://www.salon.com/mwt/broadsheet/index.html

Culture Cat: Rhetoric and Feminism
http://culturecat.net

Culture Kitchen
http://www.culturekitchen.com/

Feminist Blogs
http://feministblogs.org/

Feminist Moms
http://feministmoms.blogspot.com/

Feministing.com
www.feministing.com

Feministe
www.feministe.com

Mamacita
http://www.mamacitaonline.com/

Our Bodies, Ourselves Blog
http://ourbodiesourblog.org/

Pandagon
www.pandagon.com

What's Good for Girls
http://whatsgoodforgirls.blogspot.com/

Women of Color Blog
http://brownfemipower.com/

ARCHIVES AND CHRONOLOGIES

Note: Some of the listed resources are university library collections and do not offer online access to archived materials.

Archival Sites for Women's Studies, WSSLINKS Women and Gender Studies Web site, Women's Studies Section, Association of College and Research Libraries
http://home.gwu.edu/~mfpankin/archwss.htm

Archives for Research on Women and Gender, University of Texas, San Antonio
http://www.lib.utsa.edu/Archives/WomenGender/links.html

Compiled list of Collections Outside the United States, University of Wisconsin System Women's Studies Librarian
http://www.library.wisc.edu/libraries/WomensStudies/progs.htm

Chronologies, The "Second Wave" and Beyond, Alexander Street Press and the Center for the Historical Study of Women and Gender at SUNY Binghamton
http://scholar.alexanderstreet.com/display/WASM/Chronologies#

Documents from the Women's Liberation Movement, University of Alaska Anchorage & Alaska Pacific University
http://lib.uaa.alaska.edu/articles/moreinfo.php?item_id=138&contact_id=8

Documents from the Women's Liberation Movement, Duke University
http://scriptorium.lib.duke.edu/wlm/

The Feminist Chronicles 1953–1993, The Feminist Majority Foundation
http://www.feminist.org/research/chronicles/chronicl.html

GenderWatch
http://il.proquest.com/products_pq/descriptions/genderwatch.shtml

Guide to Resources on Women in the Processed Manuscript Collections of the
   Moorland-Springarn Research Center, Howard University
http://www.founders.howard.edu/moorland-spingarn/Wom.htm

Lesbian Feminist Chronology, Kate Bedford and Ara Wilson, The Ohio State
   University
http://womens-studies.osu.edu/araw/chrono1.htm

Lesbian Herstory Archives
http://www.lesbianherstoryarchives.org/

Pathfinder for Women's History Research, National Archives and Records
   Administration Library
http://www.archives.gov/research/alic/reference/women.html

Radcliffe College Archives, Schlesinger Library
http://www.radcliffe.edu/schles/archives/index.php

Redstockings Women's Liberation Studies Archives for Action Catalogue
http://www.afn.org/~redstock/

The "Second Wave" and Beyond, Alexander Street Press and the Center for the
   Historical Study of Women and Gender at SUNY Binghamton
http://scholar.alexanderstreet.com/display/WASM/Home+Page

Simmons College Archives and Special Collections
http://www.simmons.edu/resources/libraries/archives/about.html

Sophia Smith Collection, Smith College
http://www.smith.edu/libraries/ssc

University of Maryland Historical Manuscripts and Archives Department
http://www.lib.umd.edu/ARCV/arcvmss/arcvmss.html

ViVa: Women's History, International Institute of Social History
http://www.iisg.nl/~womhist/vivahome.php

Women's History Source: A Guide to Manuscripts and Archival Collections,
    Rutgers University
http://www.libraries.rutgers.edu/rul/libs/scua/womens_fa/womenhomepage.shtml

Women's Studies Listserv (WMST-L) File Collection, University of Maryland,
    Baltimore
http://research.umbc.edu/~korenman/wmst/wmsttoc.html

Women's Studies Manuscript Collections, Center for Archival Collections,
    Bowling Green State University
http://www.bgsu.edu/colleges/library/cac/womenbb1.html

ONLINE JOURNALS AND MAGAZINES

Bitch Magazine
http://www.bitchmagazine.com/

Bust Magazine
http://www.bust.com/

ColorLines
http://www.colorlines.com/

The F-Word
http://www.thefword.org.uk/index

Feminista!
http://www.feminista.com/archives/v2n11/

Feminist Africa
http://www.feministafrica.org/

Genders
http://www.genders.org/

Hip Mama
www.hipmama.com

Jenda: A Journal of Culture and African Women's Studies
http://www.jendajournal.com/

Magazines and Newsletters on the Web (women-focused), University of
    Wisconsin System Women's Studies Librarian
http://www.library.wisc.edu/libraries/WomensStudies/mags.htm

Meridians: Feminism, Race, Transnationalism
http://www.smith.edu/meridians/

Ms. Magazine
http://www.msmagazine.com/

Our Truths/Nuestras Verdades
http://www.ourtruths.org/

The Scholar & Feminist Online, Barnard College, Barnard Center for Research on
    Women
http://www.barnard.edu/sfonline/

Tint Magazine
http://www.coloredgurl.com/tintmagazine/

Trivia: Voices of Feminism
http://www.triviavoices.net/index.html

FEMINISM IN THE MEDIA

Center for New Words
http://www.centerfornewwords.org

Feminist.com
http://www.feminist.com/news/index.html

Feminist Majority Foundation, Daily Feminist News
http://www.feminist.org/news/newsbyte/uswire.asp

International Museum of Women - Imagining Ourselves
http://imaginingourselves.imow.org/pb/Home.aspx?lang=

Lesbian News
http://www.lesbiannews.com/

Media Report to Women
http://www.mediareporttowomen.com/

the REAL hot 100
www.therealhot100.org

Truth Out
http://www.truthout.org/women.shtml

United Nations, WomenWatch
http://www.un.org/womenwatch/

Women in Media and News (WIMN)
http://www.wimnonline.org/

Women's eNews
www.womensenews.org

Women's Feature Service
http://www.wfsnews.org/

The Women's Media Center
http://www.womensmediacenter.com/

Younger Women's Task Force, The Younger Women's Movement: News for
    Younger Women
http://ncwo-online.org/YWTF/Media/news.htm

GUIDES TO WOMEN'S ORGANIZATIONS

Feminist Majority Foundation Gateway
http://www.feminist.org/gateway/feministgateway-
    results.asp?category1=organizations

National Council for Research on Women
http://www.ncrw.org/about/centers.htm

National Council of Women's Organizations
http://www.womensorganizations.org/

YOUNG FEMINIST ORGANIZATIONS

Association for Women in Development, Young Women and Leadership Program
http://www.awid.org/ywl/

Center for Young Women's Development
http://www.cywd.org/

Feminist Majority Foundation, FMF Campus Program
http://www.feministcampus.org/default.asp

Fierce!
http://www.fiercenyc.org/

Girls for Gender Equity
http://www.gges.info/

National Council of Women's Organizations, Younger Women's Task Force
www.ywtf.org

National Organization for Women, National NOW Young Women Taskforce
http://www.now.org/issues/young/taskforce/index.html

Next Genderation
www.nextgenderation.net

Sista II Sista
http://www.sistaiisista.org/

Sistas on the Rise
http://www.sistasontherise.org/

The Third Wave Foundation
www.thirdwavefoundation.org

Women's Ordination Conference, Young Feminist Network
http://www.womensordination.org/pages/projects_femnet.html

The Young Women's Project
http://www.youngwomensproject.org/

ADDITIONAL CONTEMPORARY FEMINIST ORGANIZATIONS AND PROJECTS MENTIONED IN BOOK

Chicks Rock the Vote
http://www.rockthevote.org

CODEPINK
http://www.codepink4peace.org

Guerrilla Girls
http://www.guerillagirls.com

Mothers Movement Online
http://www.mothersmovement.org

See Jane
http://www.seejane.org

V-Day
http://www.vday.org

Women for Women International
http://www.womenforwomen.org

Woodhull Institute for Ethical Leadership
http://www.woodhull.org

FEMINIST THEORY 101

Feminist Theory Syllabi Collection, National Women's Studies Association
http://www.nwsa.org/other.php

Women- and Gender-Related Course Syllabi on the Web, University of
    Maryland, Baltimore
http://www.umbc.edu/cwit/syllabi.html

Women's Studies Courses via the Internet, Syllabi, and Other Course Materials,
    University of Wisconsin System Women's Studies Librarian
http://www.library.wisc.edu/libraries/WomensStudies/curriculum.htm

Women's Studies Syllabi Database, University of Maryland, College Park
http://www.mith2.umd.edu/WomensStudies/Syllabi/

LISTSERVS AND WEB GROUPS

Electronic Women's Forums, Feminism and Women's Studies Website
http://feminism.eserver.org/links/forums/e-womens-forums.txt

Women of Color Web
http://www.hsph.harvard.edu/grhf/WoC/discussions/discussions.html

WMST-L, University of Maryland, Baltimore
http://www-unix.umbc.edu/~korenman/wmst/wmst-l_index.html

Women's Studies Email Lists, University of Maryland, Baltimore
http://www-unix.umbc.edu/~korenman/wmst/f_wmst.html